MW01493543

GAMES GREAT LOVERS PLAY

Mastering the Game of Love

L. Michael Hall, Ph.D.

Games Great Lovers Play

This book is one in a series of Neuro-Semantic books— *the Frame Game series.* What is a "frame game?" *Frame* refers to your frame of mind which typically is expressed as a belief, understanding, idea, concept, intention, or decision. *Game* refers to your responses, your emotional, behavioral, and relational set of actions.

Frames and Games correspond to the inner and outer dimension of human experience. *On the outside* what we see are actions— words, gestures, and behaviors. And where do these come from? What creates these? The inside. So, *on the inside* there are your mental models and maps of the world, your understandings, representations, and beliefs.

So, if we take any dimension of life and consider the systematic behaviors as a "game," then the next question is, What are the rules of the Game? How do you know when to play, where, and with whom? And what are the rules that govern the game? What constitutes a "win" or a "loss?"

In Neuro-Semantics, the key principles governing *frame games* are these:
*   When you win the inner game, the outer game is a cinch!
*   Where there is a game, there are multiple frames.
*   Where there is a frame, there will be a game.
*   Whoever sets the frame governs the game.
*   Someone always sets the frame for every set of actions.
*   When you can detect the frame, you can then choose your frames and your games.
*   For frame game mastery, develop your framing skills.

Other Books in this series:
>   *Games for Mastering Fear*
>   *Games Business Experts Play*
>   *Games Fit and Slim People Play*

TITLE PAGE

© 2004, *L Michael Hall, Ph.D.*
   Games Great Lovers Play: Mastering the Game of Love
   2010 Second Edition

TXu1-150-372 Copyright Certificate of Registration, Wash. D.C.

All Rights Reserved
   No part of this may be reproduced, stored in a retrieval system, or
   transmitted in any form or by any means (electronic, mechanical,
   photocopying, recording, etc.) without the prior *written permission*
   of the publisher.

Published by: **NSP: Neuro-Semantic Publications**
                       P.O. Box 8
                       Clifton, CO. 81520-0008 USA
                       (970) 523-7877

Catalog for Neuro-Semantic Publications— go to
www.neurosemantics.com. Click on Products and then Catalog.

Neuro-Semantics® is the trademark name for the International Society of
Neuro-Semantics and all of the Institutes of Neuro-Semantics. For more
than 5000 pages of *free information* (articles, patterns, books, reviews, etc.)
see the following Neuro-Semantic web sites:
                       www.neurosemantics.com
                       www.self-actualizing.org
                       www.meta-coaching.org
                       www.metacoachingfoundation.org

The Frame Games — or Winning the Inner Game series of Books:
If we treat any experience as a "Game," then what are the frames? The rules of the game,
the set up, the players, the benefits, the cost for losing, the skills for playing, etc.?
   Winning the Inner Game (original title: *Frame Games*)
   Games Great Lovers Play
   Games for Mastering Fear
   Games Business Experts Play
   Games Fit and Slim People Play

Games Great Lovers Play

Foreword   4

Introduction
1: Games and Great Lovers   11

The Games
2: *The Dance of Romance*   20

3: *The Dance of Attraction*   32

4: *The Fill-Me Up Dance*   44
    Emotional Bank Account Game

5: *The Self-Disclosure Game* 54

6: *The Dance of Appreciation* 62

7: *Communicating Love Dance* 76

8: *The Dance of Getting in Sync*
    Meta-Programs for Couples 87

9: *The Dance of Conscious Loving*
    Mindfulness in Loving   110

10: *The Dance of Pleasure*   116
    Love as Pleasuring

11: *The Dance of Sexual*
    Pleasuring   123

12: *The Dance of Healthy*
Fighting   Fighting *for* the
Relationship
                                    133

13: *Rules of the Fighting Game*
    Effective Conflicting   142

14: *Dance of A Love that Heals*
                                    154

15: *Dance of Healing Thresholds*
    Healing Wounded Love   164

Theoretical Frameworks   175
16: Connecting   176

The Bonding Game

17: Centering: Becoming Inter-
    Dependent Enough to Bond
                                    186

18: Co-Creating Responsiveness
    The Responsive Game   199

19: Coalescing   219
    The Merging of Worlds Game

Let the Games Begin   227
    Summary of Games

Appendices

A: NLP & Neuro-Semantics   233

B: From Pleasuring to
    De-Pleasuring   235
    The De-Pleasuring Pattern

C: Frame Game Analysis   236
    Frame Game Worksheets

Bibliography   240

Author   242

FOREWORD

Love works like magic. Intuitively, if you have loved or been loved, then you know that *love works magic in your heart and unleashes the highest and best potentials in human nature.* Whether it is the love of a mother for a newborn, the love of a man for a woman, the love of two life-long friends, or the love that we feel for our pets, love does magical and wonderful things within us.

Like what? What does love do to you on the inside? Love warms your heart inviting you to care about others in new ways. Love moves you for the sake of another. Love causes you to melt in appreciation for another's kindnesses. Love evokes awe in you of the mystery and majesty in another. Love transforms you. Love moves you to become more real, more authentic, and more human. Love validates you and allows you to esteem yourself more fully. And because love does these wonderfully magical things within human beings, we ask:

- How do we promote such love in our hearts?
- How can we make love our highest frame of mind as we relate to our special one?
- How can we discover and play the best Love Games?
- How can we win at the Games of Love?

This transformative magic of love stimulates curious fascination, does it not? As a psychologist, I have long known that the state of love offers an incredible power for transformation. If only I could enable clients to fully access this state! I have worked with hundreds of couples to re-ignite this very quality when their relationship or marriage became troubled. As a dynamic for change, love transcends all psychological techniques for turning a relationship around. Yet love is a principle and experience that psychology has only begun to probe:

- How does the magic of love work?
- How does it do such magical things in our hearts and lives?
- How can we tap into its power?
- How can we become more loving as persons?
- How can we learn to play the Games of Love?
- What are the Games that Great Lovers play?

What's in This Book?

Games Great Lovers Play is a book about *how to love—how to play, enjoy, and win at the Games of Love.* If you're interested in that—this book is for you. This book is based on two models: NLP and Neuro-Semantics.

Neuro-Linguistic Programming (NLP)[1], a model about how to run your own brain and how to nurture your best mind-body states. In this book I focus on those mind-body-and-emotional states that support love. As a communication model, NLP focuses on how we communicate within ourselves to create our "sense of reality." Our sense of reality arises from our *map* of reality (our model of the world) and is made up of hundreds if not thousands of *frames*. And as a map, our maps (or frames) allow us to go certain places and controls what we can experience. From the map, we experience the territory as we do. Sometimes this makes for wonderful loving experiences, sometimes it creates living hells. NLP enables us to become *mindful* about both so that we can choose to reframe our maps and create richer and more magical experiences.

Yet our maps about love are just that—*maps*. They are no more real than you and I give them reality. They are just *frames* of understanding, beliefs, values, memories, imaginations, etc. And because they are invented maps, we can alter them so that they will more effectively work for us. *Games Great Lovers Play* is about identifying your love maps and altering them so that you can have a greater and richer and more resourceful experience of loving.

I began applying NLP to relationships in the late 1980s. I packaged what I knew of NLP at that time into a ten-week training, *The Love Workshop*. I designed it to enhance the romance of lovers by focusing on:
- Connecting and creating rapport with each other.
- Recognizing our different mental maps as just maps.
- Working with our belief maps about love and about the process of loving.
- Learning how to evoke the best in our partner.
- Restoring love when there has been hurt and disappointment.

Neuro-Semantics is the second model used here to model the love state. Neuro-Semantics is all about the *meanings* (semantics) that we incorporate in our *bodies* (neurology). It's about how we create and install meanings —*embodied* meanings that govern our feelings, actions, conversation, and sense of reality. Your neuro-semantics, as your states and layers of embedded states, operate as your mind-body maps. And it's these maps that determine how you show up in the world as you navigate through your experiences using your maps.[2]

Is There a Structure to Love's Magic?

The central premise of *Neuro-Semantics* and *Neuro-Linguistics*[3] is that *every experience has a structure.* Experiences do not just happen. There is a structure, process, and form to them. Where there is *structure*, there is order, sequence, and syntax to the framework processes. These are the prerequisite structures that allow certain things to happen. The magic of every experience has an incantation.[4] Those who know how to "cast the spell" can have the experience. Are you ready for some love spells?

This means something very important: *Love, as a state and experience, has a form.* There's a structure to love, to passion, to intimacy, to romance, to bonding ... and sadly, to dis-bonding, to hate, resentment, regret, etc. There's an incantation to becoming and remaining a great lover. To discover that spell and to cast it on ourselves enables us to play *the Love Game.*

During the past three decades, researchers and developers in NLP and Neuro-Semantics have busied themselves looking for, and articulating, the structure of magic in therapeutic language, business excellence, expertise in training, managing, negotiating, and selling, as well as high level skills in education, law, and marketing. We have even gone after the structure of various pathological experiences—schizophrenia, multiple personalities, etc.

Yet one of the most magical and mysterious experiences around today remains. It's not that many have not attempted the exploration. Many have. And many people have identified many of its sparkling facets. Yet no experience continues to remain as inarticulate and indescribable as the love phenomenon that occurs between a man and a woman. We call that phenomenon *love.* We notice how love binds them mind, emotion, body, and soul. We speak about them becoming soul-mates.

- How does this work?
- What explains how it arises and grows?
- How do we narrate the process by which a couple experiences this magic?
- Why does it sometimes stop?
- What drives this experience?
- Why are some people so afraid of it?
- Why do so many take such a cynical attitude toward it?
- How can we understand not only how it works, but its structure?

Accessing the Best Love States

At the heart of the experience of love between a woman and a man lies various emotional states. When you love, or are "in love," you experience such states as the following:

> e*xcitement, desire, appreciation, admiration, compassion, gentleness, generosity, magnanimity, transcendence, loyalty, wonder, exploration, support, empathy, joy, playfulness, and many more.*

Is that all? Does that put a cap on the mystery of love? No. That's just the beginning. Love, and especially romantic love—coupling love —involves much more than that as you will soon discover.

Using the NLP and Neuro-Semantic models, I have sought to unpack the wonder of a loving relationship so that we can model it and replicate it in our own lives. Will this reduce the magic? No. Not at all. It actually leads to a deeper and more profound appreciation. Ultimately, after we expand our understanding of the role of all the frames and games that make up the Game of Love, after we articulate the values and beliefs, the visions and dreams, the meta-levels and the meta-states, there is still *the experience of deeply loving and feeling in sync with another person.*

Here you will read about how we can fall in love and let love and appreciation guide our everyday lives to convey a very special sense of the specialness of connecting and bonding with a like-soul. Here you will read about many of the prerequisites for a fulfilling love life with that special one that you commit yourself to. And yet... when all is said ... beyond all of those words ... lies *the experience itself, the experience of a loving bond with the mind-heart body and soul of another.* May your experience be a rich and rewarding one.

If Love is a Game—What are the rules os that I can play?
* If *Love* was a game, what games are you playing?
* How well are you playing those games?
* Are you winning at the game of love?
* Are the one's you love also winning at the game?
* Do you like the games that you're playing?
* Where did you learn to play those games?
* What are the rules of the games?

These are but a few of the questions that arises when we begin with the metaphor of a "game" and apply it to the way we relate when we are loving and being loved.

> *Games* simply refer to all of the things that we *do*. Our actions, behaviors, relational patterns, the talk, and all of the expressions that make up our transactions with others. These are our outer games. *Frames* refer to our mental understandings, beliefs, values, expectations and comprise the rules of the game. Frames make up the inner games we play in our mind. There are healthy and empowering games and there are unhealthy, toxic, and sick games.

Games, as an idea and a metaphor, gives us the ability to quickly recognize the set of interactions and to evaluate how well they work in allowing us to feel valued, appreciated, and loved. It is in the nature of things in human reality that we can get caught up in games without even recognizing whether the game works or not, whether we want to win at it or not, or whether it is ecological or not. We can get so caught up in a game that we forget what we are trying to accomplish except we seem to be playing out a ritualized set of interactions.

The inner game of our frames govern the outer games of our experiences. If a game is not working, if it is not enhancing life, it if it not really allowing us to feel loved and valued, we can examine the rules, expectations, understandings, and intentions of the game and change them. It's as easy as that. The *ease* comes from the higher level awareness of the game itself and its driving frames. Without that awareness, it is not easy. And as you will soon discover, it is as profound as that.

As you take a moment now to rate yourself in terms of how much you understand, appreciate, and enjoy your interpersonal relationships with friends, loved ones, and associates, how are you doing?

- How skilled are you at navigating the strange and challenging terrain of relationships?
- How easily can you "fall in love" and stay in love?
- How skilled are you at enabling another to feel loved, valued, and honored?
- How loving can you be when there's conflict, disagreement, or just grumpy states?

Using *Lovers* for more Intimacy in your Life

Games Great Lovers Play focuses exclusively on the intimacy between a man and a woman. While the principles and skills can be applied to other relationships such is not my focus here. Here we will explore the central skills for effectively dealing with our most intimate loved one and on how to effectively *stay in love for the rest of our lives*. Here we will focus on our experiences of intimacy as a lover in the coupling relationship. The principles, secrets, models, and techniques work for anyone who cares about, and wants to experience, healthier and more satisfying relationships.

What's the key to make *The Love Games* real for you and your relationships? *Experience* the patterns and processes. Don't just read about it. Don't you want to *experience* a richer giving and receiving of love? Then *do* something about the Love Games. Experiencing and implementing are at the heart of making the relational skills yours. By putting the principles into action you will develop new competencies and re-map your relational skills as you relate more lovingly.

What does it take to become a more loving person with your loved one? What skills are involved?
- Inducing yourself into your best mind-body states.
- Accessing and transforming your strategy for love.
- Listening to and entering your loved one's inner world.
- Anchoring and amplifying positive feeling states.
- Effectively communicating your love and affection.

Games Great Lovers Play describe healthy relationships. At times I will contrast healthy games with sick and morbid games. The healthy games allow us to love each other deeply, feel the warm feelings of care for each other, and add enthusiasm and excitement to our relating. These are the games that enable us to keep our passions alive and strengthen the bonding we already have.

If you are reading this and suffer from a troubled relationship where the bonding itself is in question, you have to first deal with "the wounds" in that bonding (chapters 14-15) before you can begin to play *the Love Games*. Where there are ongoing wounds to the bonding itself (i.e., judgment, contempt, apathy, discounting, mind-reading, etc.), these games must stop. Immediately and completely. No matter how right or righteous you are in your side of things, *you* must stop. The chapter on *healing wounded love* addresses this. Read it first, then go to the chapter on having a *healthy fight* (chapters 12 and 13).

When a person reaches or has gone over threshold, we must treat that person and the relationship as "deeply wounded," and in need of emergency help. At this point we must respond as we would to a wounded human being in a highway accident. We would immediately get that person to the hospital and treat him or her with lots of gentleness and patience.

So with a love-wounded person. Before working on the relationship, we must treat the person with a gentle care and compassion. The person will *not* be in a position to "work on the relationship." Respect that. Give the person time and space. Get professional help so that each person first becomes much more resourceful. Forgive. Forgiveness will be a part of the healing of the psychic wound.

Let the Games Begin!

Throughout the chapters, I have offered numerous *patterns* or *processes* for you to do. Treat them like *love experiments*—like a lab of hands-on experiments to develop your skills in loving, caring, and relating. Some are designed to work on the inner game of your frames, others are designed to work on your outer games of communicating, receiving feedback, nourishing, etc.

Stop and *do the experiments.* To merely read *about* it will only fill up your head with more knowledge *about* caring relationships without training and equipping you to know it *in your body.* And now, with all of that in mind—*Let the Game of the Love Games Begin!*

Endnotes:

1. See *Appendix A* for a description of NLP and Neuro-Semantics.

2. Neuro-Semantics is made up of three models: Meta-States, Frame Games, and the Matrix. The book *Frame Games* (2000) simplified Meta-States using two metaphors, Games and Frames to translate the psychology of reflexivity and the "logical levels" of our layered consciousness. Three applications of *Frame Games* precede this work:

> *Games Slim People Play* (2001)
> *Games For Mastering Fear* (2001)
> *Games Business Experts Play* (2002)

We have also applied meta-states and frame games to numerous other areas:

> Wealth Building: Games for Financial Independence.
> Accelerated Learning: Games that Accelerate Learning.
> Sales: Games Great Sales People Play.
> Writing: Games for Writing Mastery.

3. See Appendix A for a description of both NLP and Neuro-Semantics.

4. I am here using "magic" and "spells" metaphorically. It plays off of the original NLP books, "The Structure of Magic" which are books about language, and the structure of information coding—the "magic" that explains how experts can do what seems "magical."

Chapter 1

GAMES
AND GREAT LOVERS

This book is about *games*. It's about *the Games of Love* that we play in our minds, our hearts, our talk, and then in our actions and interactions. It's also about the games that defeat and sabotage us. It's about the games that fill life with wonder and ecstasy. It's about the games that we have inherited and may have no awareness of, and those that we mindfully create to take us to new places. It's about the games that we learned from our parents and culture. It's about the games that we will leave for our children and lovers. It's about the games that we can invent and play that will enable us to take charge of our lives and bless the lives of others.

It is also about how the experts in matters of the heart, that is, the *Games that Great Lovers Play*,[1] and how we can find and replicate their frames of mind. It's about the games that detail the secrets of being a great lover. It's about how to set new frames of mind and how to refuse the old frames.

What is a Game?
The term *game* is a metaphor for thinking and talking about both our inner and outer games. Our external behaviors are our actions and communication patterns—the outer game. The inner game is more subtle. It's the mental and emotional micro-behaviors that go on inside our heads. These processes govern how we relate. They define how we relate to our loved one and how we relate to ourselves. They determine our everyday experiences.

"Are they bad?" They can be. We can play hurtful and ugly games. We can play *the Blame Game* and make life miserable for our loved ones. Or, we can play *the Solution Game* and turn our relating into a positive exploration. We can play games of selfishness or we can play games of caring compassion. When you know about games, the choice is up to you.

Whether a game is toxic or empowering depends on our *frames* of mind and the meanings that we create. That's why I call them *frame games* and have written several books on this theme. Yet whatever we call a game, the most important matter concerns whether our games work for us or against us.

Thinking in terms of the "game" metaphor enables us use it as a template for analyzing the quality of our actions and interactions with each other. As a template, we can now explore the following:
The Name and *the Description* of the Game:
•   What is the game, how does it work?
•   Does the game enhance or limit?
The Rules of the Game:
•   How is the game set up, structured, who plays the game, when, etc.?
The Cues of the Game:
•   What are the questions that elicit the game, the terms that reveal a game?
•   What triggers recruit us to playing the game?
The Payoff of the Game:
•   What are the benefits, values, and outcomes of the game?

In speaking about behaviors as *the outer game,* I am not speaking about actual games, but about the set of actions and transactions that we engage in with ourselves and others as *a game.* There a Game is:
•   A set of actions and transactions.
•   Performance to obtain an outcome and payoff.
•   Activities designed for efficiency and productivity.

We typically do not do this consciously. While we can, consciousness is *not* required. We can and do carry on without much awareness about what we're actually doing. Amazing, but true. We can get into habitual ways of acting, thinking, talking, and feeling and really *not* notice the "game" in play, how it affects others, or even how it affects us... at least not in the short-run. If we step back, take a breath, and think about it using *a larger vision,* we can then "catch the game in play."

The Games of Jane and Joe
Jane was 31 when I met her. She was a young mother of one child of two-

years old, with another on the way. She had been married to Joe for five years. Joe was 36 and very success in the stock market. Well, until all of the troubles began in 2001. He had been heavily invested in the technology sector and had suffered losses to the tune of $60,000 US dollars. But worse than that loss was his attitude about it and what that did to his relationship with Jane.

In business, Joe played the Competitive Game, the *It's a Dog-eat-Dog World\ Game,* the *Don't Trust Them, They'll Stab You in the Back Game,* and the *There's not Enough to Go Around Scarcity Game.* Of course, playing these games and "not winning" at them (which the loss of sixty thousand meant to him) did not put him in the best moods when he came home. To say that he was stressed-out, angry, and defenseless is putting it mildly.

When all of this happened, Joe began playing a new Game with Jane. He didn't do so consciously. If he had been conscious of what he was doing, he definitely would not have gone that route. But he didn't know. It began when he acted out the *My House is my Castle Game* which meant for him that he began acting like an enraged tyrant. All day long he would hold in his stresses, angers, and frustrations and then he would come home. The problem with this was that when Jane tried to "help" with suggestions, Joe would explode. For him, it felt like "the last straw."

Then as King of his Castle, he would tear into Jane with anger, sarcasm, and insult. It was displaced anger. But Jane didn't know that. That was not how she interpreted it. At the emotional level it felt like betrayal to her, unjust and uncalled for betrayal of their relationship. Then, when she felt that, she felt like a victim. Then together they began playing *the Game of Escalation* by blaming, accusing, counter-attacking and playing *If only you Understood Game.*

Joe's games served as his way to cope with stress, negative emotions, and a sense of loss. Yet in the context of relating to Jane, they became the games of hurt and distance. Jane experienced Joe as angry and distancing. She felt pushed away and punished by him. She handled this in a resourceful way at first, giving him space and patiently giving him room to be angry. But after a few weeks with his attitude not improving, she tried another tactic that only made it worse, advice giving. That's when Joe directed his anger directly at her. That's when *the Game of Attack and Counter-Attack* really escalated.

Then in the presence of Attack and Counter-Attack both felt unsupported and unloved. They began questioning the other's commitment. They began playing the Blame Game more earnestly, *I'd be Happy if You weren't Doing this to me!*

The fact that they didn't even know *what* they were doing, *why* they were doing it, or what they really wanted speaks about how our frame games can operate outside of our conscious awareness. And that, of course, makes the games all that more powerful.

Game Awareness

To get a clear view of the games we play in love and relationships, the games we play as lovers, step back for a moment from your everyday experiences and for just a moment, view your relating through the eyes of *a game*. As you do, now explore these questions:

*   Viewing my activities, actions, and interactions with others, my roles, persona, etc., *what games* do I play?
*   What games does my loved one or intimates play? Name some of the games.
*   What games do I *intend* to play? What games would I *like* to play? What games do I actually play?
*   Which games do I consider fun and enjoyable?
*   Which games brings out my best?
*   Which games do I find sick, stupid, and worthless?
*   Which games do I play unwillingly?
*   Which games do I get suckered into playing even when I know better?

Then There are the Frames

By *frame,* we refer to the most basic process of human consciousness, namely, *frame-of-reference.* Your frame first identifies *what* you are referring to. Without knowing that, we really can't communicate. This explains why we so frequently ask each other, "What are you talking *about?*" We ask this when we're not understanding someone.

To talk or think, we have some *reference* in mind. Yet we never just have one level of reference. As soon as something happens, we develop conceptual frames of reference. As we have thoughts-and-feelings about one event, these higher frames govern how we experience it. This is the inner game.

Joe's experience was a loss. A big loss. Joe's thoughts-and-emotions about that loss was even more crucial. What did he think or feel about it? He hated it. He interpreted it as a sign of his own stupidity and inadequacy. He felt powerless to correct it. These were his frames. Nor did it stop there. He had more thoughts-and-feelings about that idea.

Each of these thoughts-and-feelings about the previous thoughts-and-feelings creates frames about frames, layers of frames and it is these references govern the games we play. Our mind has levels upon levels of frames of references. We develop these from actual events. We refer to these and we then transform these referent experiences into the *mental structure* of our mind to make sense of things.

Figure 1:

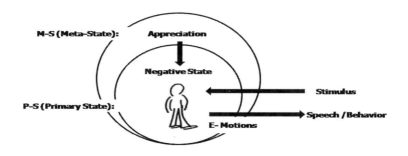

That's what we do with the external references that we call "experiences." We use our life experiences to establish a reference structure for making sense of things. We create meaning and a map of the world. We take our experiences and draw conclusions. We make generalizations from the events about the events, about the people involved, about ourselves, etc. It's like we mine the events for the *meanings* that we think lie inside the event as we would mine gold, silver, lead, copper from the earth. Yet it doesn't happen like this. Yet this is precisely where we all go wrong.

Wrong? Why wrong?

>   Because **meaning** does not exist in events and experiences. We
>   create meaning—we invent it in our minds, and we then impose it

on the brute facts of everyday life.

As you will shortly discover, it cannot exist there. "Meaning" is predominantly a thing of the mind . . . a function of our entire nervous system and brain. We *create* meaning. We *invent* it. It only occurs in the "mind" of some meaning-maker. In communicating with another, we often seek to *find* and *discover* another person's "meaning." Yet that's fairly difficult to do. To do so means listening apart from all of our mental filters, intensive listening, reflecting back what we think we've heard, correcting our impressions, etc.

Figure 1:2

> **Meaning**
> **about**

↓

"Experience"
Represented
in the mind

—> Experience in the
World

Because you internalize your experiences and use them as *reference points*, you build up a system of "meanings" and then see the world in terms of those frames or meanings. Eventually you develop layers of nested frames within frames. Then you take your *frame of mind*, and with lots of repetition it habituates so that your way of thinking eventually becomes your cognitive *framework*. This entire *framework* of nested frames govern what and how you understand, think, perceive, reason, believe, etc. All of this describes the Inner Game. The framework forms and structures what we call "personality."

Eventually you develop an entire reference system that you carry with you everywhere you go and use it to play Love Games. Depending on the meanings that you've made, your *frame of mind* prepares you for specific games.

Frames describe the content and structure of your thoughts which make up your inner game. They set you up for the games that you are permitted to play, know how to play, and want to play. Within the term *frame* includes all of the higher level cognitive structures. This includes what we commonly refer to as: beliefs, values, understandings, paradigms, mental models, expectations, assumptions, decisions, identifications, etc.

Figure 1:3

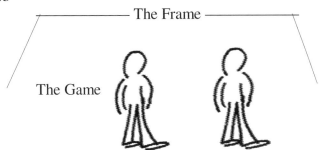

Game Awareness

Putting *games* and *frames* together gives us *frame games*. I use this to describe both the internal and external facets of our experiences, and the full range of mental and behavioral games that govern and to a great extent define the life that we live. In work, like in personal life, health, fitness, wealth building, learning, etc., we all play various frame games. Our *frames* establish the games, both the good ones and the destructive ones. Our *games* imply and flow from the governing frames. The governing frames create the games we willingly play.

With this introduction, let's now look at some of the not-so desirable *frame games* that go on with lovers:

- What games are currently playing you with your loved one?
- Do you consciously choose to play these games?
- Do these games support you and your loved one to move in the direction you want?
- What game or games would you prefer to be playing?
- What cues and triggers hook you into the games?
- What frames drive these games?
- What do you believe about these games?
- What historical or conceptual references do you use to generate the frame to play the game?

Unhealthy and Destructive Games

There are numerous games that undermine the very quality of life and loving.

These are the games that, when unchecked, make life itself seem meaningless and futile. Here's a check-list of some unhealthy games that many couples play. Check those that you find yourself involved in.

__ *The Helpless Game:* I Can't Really Change Anything.

__ *Peevishness Game:* Every little thing about you irritates and frustrates me.

__ *Unfairness Game:*   Why Try? Life is Unfair and Nothing Ever Changes

__ *Over-Responsible Game:* I'm responsible for everything.

__ *Stress Game:*   There's too much to do, I can't juggle everything. I don't have time to be very loving.

__ *The Blame Game:*   You're wrong and need to recognize it!

Summary

- We don't have to say, "Let the Games Begin!" because they have already begun. There are already plenty of Games going on in our lives with the one or ones that we love. We play games in how we get along, talk, relax, make love, play, etc.

- Behind (or above) every game there is a frame.   *Frames drive games.* To play a game, we have to learn the rules, the structure, the payoffs, etc.

- *Frame Games* gives us a new way to think about the sets of interactions on the behavioral, communicational, and psychological levels for analyzing, understanding, and effectively working with the games that aren't enhancing. They also show us those games that are enhancing.

- As there are a lot of sick, toxic, and morbid games that can make us unsane, so there are a lot of enhancing, empowering, and fun games that make for an increased sense of sanity and enable us to become highly productive.

- If you want to become *a great lover* and develop the expertise in making your loved one feel wonderful, you need to know how to stop playing any and all destructive games, and how to play the ones that bring out your best. Are you ready for that? Have you made that commitment?

End Notes:

1. The "great lovers" that I refer to in this work are those couples who know how to give and receive love and affection, acceptance and appreciation, who honor and respect each other, who maintain state control under stress and negative emotions, etc. They have a high level of Emotional Intelligence (EI or EQ) as delineated by Daniel Goleman. I have relied heavily on the research data of John Gottman for the criteria of those who succeed in making loving relationships work.

Chapter 2

THE DANCE OF

ATTENTIVE LISTENING

Since the quality of your listening
determines the quality of your relating,
the Intensely Listening Game
is where the Games Great Lovers Play begins.

- What is the first game that great lovers play?
- What is the game that starts the passion and romance?
- What initiates the connecting and bonding that can lead on to a sustained game of love and affection?
- How do you fully enter the conversation of love so that you offer your minds, your hearts, your bodies, and your entire selves?

Those who know how to greatly love invest lots of energy into it. They invest themselves. In *the Games of Love* there's passion, desire, hope, love, compassion, wonder, appreciation, enjoyment, affection, and ecstasy . . . just to mention a few of the energy states. These are among the most positive emotions that we experience when we bond with someone in the giving and receiving of love and affection. We often speak of these as *romantic feelings*. There's something about the bonding experience and these feelings that touch us very deeply, that call to the heights of our imaginations and dreams.

You access and express all of these emotions when you engage in the first dance of romance—*deep and attentive listening*. For this reason we now turn to the process of truly listening to our loved one.

What's involved in that? How do we play this game? What games prevent us from being present and showing up?

Extending Your Ego-Boundaries

When you truly love someone or something, *you extend yourself* to the person and for that person. You do so as an expression of your love. This happens naturally and easily when the object of your love is cute, adorable, lovely, and beautiful. *Opening* yourself up to the object in that situation of your desire is easy, natural, and exciting. This is the first game of bonding.

It could be a newborn baby, a new litter of kittens, a new job, a new home, a new idea, a new friend, or a new potential mate. If the object of your love is *adorable* to you in some way or on some level—you easily open up to it. You extend your ego-boundaries to extend a welcome, "You are welcomed into my world." You also typically *identify with* your love so that you have the sense that the idea, friend, job, or person has entered into your inner world. This makes your world bigger.

The ecstasy of love involves many things yet it begins with this touch of transcendence. When you find a new adorable object, experience, or person that you open yourself up to, the very extending of your ego-boundaries gives you the sense that you have just *transcended* yourself and your life, and that life itself, has just opened up and transcended old limitations and definitions. We call this experience—"falling in love."

Falling in love is exciting, thrilling, and intoxicating precisely because *you become more* in the experience. You are invited into re-defining yourself and your life. You sense that you have stepped outside of yourself and into something bigger. Sometimes this can create so much of an altered state that you feel as if you are in a hypnotic trance. You may feel disoriented, unsure about what to think or feel, and even outside-of-your-body for awhile.

In this way opening your ego-boundaries initiates a feeling and experience of transcendence. As you extend your ego boundaries, you transcend yourself. You transcend your self-definitions and understandings and in extending yourself, you become more. It is this sense of expansion that gives you the rush of excitement and ecstasy and passion. Your aloneness is transcended as you share your consciousness with another and as you co-create a special world which you then share together.

Yet within this experience there are numerous sub-elements which come together to create this overall sense of romance. As a gestalt experience and state,[1] *romance* is made up of some more common states: appreciation, desire, hope, imagination, connection, rapport, etc. And because these make up the heart of romance, let's turn our attention to them. At the heart of all of these lies something so simple, something so basic, something so obvious that it is so easy to overlook, listening— *listening and attending.*

The "Listening to Understand" Game

You, like me and all of us, were born to bond. Bonding is what we all naturally do with each other, with our pets, and even with inanimate objects. In fact, we become human through bonding . . . and, as adults, the bonding doesn't end. As we grow up and become independent, we move to a place where we can bond with a special one in a healthy inter-dependent way. This necessitates some additional skills, skills of independence, skills that allow the bonding to continue, namely, *the Game of Rapport:*
*   How do we make contact?
*   How do we establish friendly relations with another?
*   How do we communicate in a way that promotes understanding?

The short answer is by *entering into* your lover's world. By matching or pacing your loved one's way of thinking-and-feeling, you come to understand him or her. The metaphor of *pacing* suggests that you move alongside and go at the other's pace, slow, moderate, or fast depending on the person's speed. It means that you take your lead from them and match responses. *Pacing* describes the process by which you skillfully *match* some portion of the other's ongoing experience. It could be the person's physiology, breathing, posture, thoughts, feelings, values, meanings, or just about anything. When you do this, it creates a sense of connectedness which leads to the sense of being in rapport.
*   How do we enter into each other's world and share that reality?
*   How do we deeply connect with another person?
*   How do we welcome the differences?

First comes *the Listening Game.* If the qualitiy of our relating and connecting is directly related to the quality of our listening—then are you pleased with how you and your loved one listen to each other? Do you feel heard and understood? Does your partner? How much quality time do you spend *being present and just listening?*

Listening means entering each other's world empathically with a passionate desire to understand, to truly understand your loved one, it means being present, it means being fiercely focused in the here and now, and it means not going elsewhere. To play this *Intense Focusing and Listening Game*, adopt the eyes of appreciation, wonder, amazement, and respect for the world out of which the other person comes. Also add zest as you play this game by making it safe for your loved one to open up and disclose his or her internal world.

If the conversation *is* the relationship, and if you relate to your loved one ... *one conversation at a time*—then every conversation enriches or impoverishes the quality of your loving. Listening is the process of engagement by which you come into the conversation. This makes critical *how* you listen. Do you do so half awake or fully alert? Do you do so engaged and committed or as routine and habit? It makes all the difference in the world.

The "Seeking First to Understand" Game
In communication *we seek first to understand.* If we don't begin by seeking to understand, we will answer questions not asked and solve problems that the other doesn't care about solving.

Yet how often do you listen thoroughly enough to engage in this kind of dialogue? How often you just jump in talking with another person, thinking that you are communicating, when you really have not engaged in a dialogue for the purpose of understanding? This is especially challenging for anyone highly skilled at offering advice. Yet to jump to advice-giving is to fail to truly listen. A better game is to seek first to listen for understanding.

Yet how many of us have any formal training in listening, in empathic listening? This subject is not often taught. What listening models are there that allow you to deeply understand another person's frame of reference? Apart from content, what do you listen for? What *can* you listen for? And as you listen, what attitude governs your listening?[1]

Isn't it obvious that to interact effectively with anyone, and especially your loved one, you must first *understand* the person? This is especially true if you want to influence. When you try to influence without listening you descend to merely manipulating. Reverse the roles. Would you give anyone permission to influence you who doesn't take the time or effort to understand you first? Of course not! Whenever you sense that someone is manipulating you, or just using a technique on you, trust evaporates. You don't trust them. You don't feel safe to open up to them. Here are some questions about your skills in the dance of attentive listening:

- To what extent am I influenced by my partner's uniqueness?
- Do I appreciate and value his or her differences?
- How is my partner different and how do I frame the differences?
- How open am I to listening to my partner and seeking to truly understand on his or her own terms?
- How aware am I that listening fills the emotional needs of my loved one?

Inadequate Listening Games

How often do you engage in *pseudo-listening?* Pseudo-listening looks like you are listening(!), yet the response that we might call "listening" is hardly listening at all. You are not really listening. You have not actually *shown up* but are only going through the motions of listening. Inside you are not really hearing, registering, or being with the other person. For most of us ineffective listening habits are deeply scripted. We probably learned to listen this way at school and with parents when we gave them half-an-ear. The answer is that you first need to become aware of these pseudo-listening styles and how they undermine your ability to be a great lover.

What are the key barriers to good listening? The most neutral one is a fact that we all have to live with and recognize—the speed of our mind travels far faster than anyone's tongue. Speaking occurs between 100 to 150 words a minute. How fast can you read? 700 words? When I took Evelyn Woods Reading Dynamics, they scored me at just over 3,000 a minute? The fastest speed readers are able to read and comprehend at 10,000 words a minute! Now that makes for a very high speed-differential. The difference in the speed of tongue, ear, and mind give lots of space for going somewhere else.

The biggest offenders include the following: judgment, evaluation, problem solving, analysis, distraction, ignoring, and assuming. When you respond in these ways, why should the other person open up? If your lover exposes his or her soft underbelly, and you elephant stomp on it with advice, criticism, preaching, judgment, superiority, insult, and mind-reading, is it any surprise to find your loved one defensive or closed?

All pseudo-listening is actually ego-centered listening. You are not actually listening *to* your loved one at all. Instead you are listening (if you can even call it that) through your own autobiography and so listening for ways to be right, to satisfy your wants and concerns, and to solve your problems. It's hardly "listening," is it? And none of us want to be listened to in that way, do we? Do you? I certainly do not.

Listening autobiographically, we are not getting sufficiently out of ourselves to listen. When we do that, we are meeting our loved one at our map of the world and so will be hearing things entirely *on our terms*, not our lover's. If you listen autobiographically you listen to evaluate (agree/disagree), to probe (asking questions like a district attorney), to advise (problem-solve, tell, preach), or to interpret (analyze, explain their motives, mind-read). These responses limit you from understanding others and prevent you from being able to truly step inside and see the world from the other's perspective.

The Defensive Listening Game

Do you ever listen to your loved one defensively? In this kind of so-called "listening" you listen with the intent to reply, to explain, and to defend yourself. When you listen defensively, you seek to catch words, ideas, and phrases that you can attack. You listen for the weakness of the other's position—for weak spots in words and ideas. It is pseudo-listening to the extent that you are filtering things through your own belief frames. You are using and reading your own autobiography into what the other says. You are looking for weaknesses and points of disagreement. Is it any wonder that such listening inevitably leads to a failure to understand and creates much misunderstanding?

The Leisure Listening Game

Listening in a leisurely way comes from a lazy and non-focused state. In lazy listening you only attend to what pleases or delights you, what you find delightful, fun, or interesting. Leisure listening lacks the energy to be truly attentive to your loved one and to invest your heart and soul. It may look like listening on the outside, but it is not.

The Analytical Listening Game

In analytical listening, you do not listen to understand as to gather facts. It's an external kind of listening. The listening may be intense, yet in it you are seeking to not so much listen for the person's inner world, as for surface facts and details. Listening in this way works well for lectures, college classes, and gathering technical information. It does not work well for intimate relationships precisely because it misses the most critical subject—your lover's heart.

The Game of Attentive Listening

Authentic listening demands a deep shift in your own thinking, feeling, and behaving. Very few of us really know how to do it. And no wonder, how many of us have had any training in it? No wonder few fully appreciate or experience its power and magic. Very few of us have had this kind of listening effectively modeled for us. We haven't seen it in action. How do we do it? What are the steps to enter into this game?

1) Set your aim to attend without having any agenda except exploring.

Begin by truly attending with no agenda other than to understand. Seek to understand the perceptual and emotional reality of the other. Attentively follow the other's line of reasoning, inquiring about his meanings, exploring things not understood, listening with your eyes, giving "go ahead" messages (encouragers), and paraphrasing back to assure understanding. In dropping your agendas you step into a state of simply witnessing and being with your loved one.

2) Aim to see the world from your lover's point of view

In empathic listening, intentionally listen to understand and so you can step inside the other's way of perceiving and see things the way he or she does. Here your intention is to be highly focused on understanding your partner's perceptions, understandings, beliefs, emotions, values, and experiences. Why do this? Because the person is importance to you and to enable your partner to feel safe, that's why!

3) Be present in the moment to the other.

Step into this present moment—into the now. Open all of your senses so that you can truly and fully see, hear, and feel the other. Being in sensory awareness itself is a very special state, an altered state for most people, and one that gets you out of your head with all of your past and future representations. It invites you to live in this moment and to experience it fully for what it is.

4) Step inside the other's world

By such listening, you step inside the frames of your partner. You come to see the world from your loved one's viewpoint and this enables you to understand your loved one's internal world, how it is organized and how it makes sense to him or her. In empathic listening, your aim is not to agree, confirm, and validate the other's point of view, not at first. Make it your aim only to more fully understand. To do this, listen for feelings, meanings, intentions, wants, etc.

Why Play the Game of Focused Listening?

What will you and your loved one *win* when you play this game? You probably already recognize many of the values in attentive listening. First and foremost, it provides you more *accurate data* about your lover and his or her world. Since you are dealing with the reality inside your lover's head and heart, only by listening can you obtain this information. If you listen auto-biographically, you will project your maps and will hear things in terms of your own reality, not your partner's. That feeds misunderstanding and guarantees low quality information.

Actually, you offer an unique gift when you attentively listen. You give your partner psychological air—room to breath and think. This kind of listening is also deeply therapeutic and healing.

In addition to this kind of listening giving you accurate information to work with, it enables you to get to the heart of matters quicker, to emotionally bond with your lover to increase your mutual influence with each other, to deepen understanding to save lots of time in the long run that you otherwise would take to undo, redo, correct, etc. when you haven't listened and misunderstandings have arisen.

How to Play the Listening Game
1) Begin by framing listening as highly important.
To become skilled and professional at intense listening, you have to value listening enough to give yourself to its practice. That's *the* question, isn't it? The skill of showing up and being present with someone in truly listening to them takes time to develop to become skilled in it.

2) Set your goal to become an excellent listener.
Have you made attentive listening a personal goal? Have you ever set a goal that you will spend an entire day focusing on listening attentively? As you proactively decide to develop your ability in attentive listening, it will turn this kind of listening into a habit. It will become your default frame of mind, something that you just do as you move through the world, you just always seek first to understand.

3) Center yourself as you listen.
Use the centering exercise (chapter 17) to create a base from which to listen. This will prevent you from getting sucked into another's story, from personalizing, and from needing to fix the one speaking. The more centered we feel, the richer our sense of personal security and the more you get your ego out of way. Listening is risky to the extent that it involves opening yourself up to another and caring about another.

4) Cue yourself to put aside your own autobiography.
Because it is so easy to fall back into listening in terms of your own history and experiences, you have to continually cue yourself to stay awake and to be present. Interrupt the old patterns by recognizing that you're focusing more on you than the other. Do you hear a lot of self-chatter in the back of your mind? Interrupt that self-talk and call yourself back to a listening mode. At that point inwardly quiet yourself so you can just listen.

5) Invest energy as you listen
How active or passive do you find listening as an activity? How engaged are you in terms of all of your mind, emotion, body, actions, etc.? While it's tempting to think of it as passive, the kind of fierce, intense, and focused listening is very active. It involves being in the moment, staying with the speaker, seeking to understand, and giving encouragements to continue.

You listen best when you ask questions and give the other person your undivided time and focus. You can get into the habit of actively reflecting meanings and feelings to check accuracy. You listen energetically by actively reflecting back what you have heard in a tentative way and ask for feedback. This works magic. This lets the person know that you are listening attentively and gently empowers the other to open up.

6) Make speaking completely safe for the other.
Would you open up and share if you thought the other would ridicule or use it against you? Of course not. Great lovers know how to *make it safe* for their loved one to speak freely. They do so by avoiding all judgments, criticisms, labeling, put-downs, advice giving, and anything else that comes across as negative. Nothing shuts down communication like judgment. Any negative response like criticism, a put-down, or even advice will shut the doors. Conversely, safety, trust, and openness makes communication feel safe and easy. It opens the door and validates the other person.

7) Approach with a genuine win/win attitude.
In all areas of life, attitude is everything. While this is true in business and sports, it is even more true in intimate relationships. You first need a win/win attitude whereby you validate the other, make the communication a shared experience, seek to cooperate, and build a mutual exchange. Patiently listening to your loved one allows your partner to get to the core issues and invites self-discovery of his or her own solutions.

8) Match or pace the other's reality.
Use matching and mirroring to connect. How? Use words that agree with, and are congruent with, your partner's internal experience. In doing this,

you will make it possible for your lover to open up to you, trust you, and turn the transaction into a transformational opportunity.

9) Demonstrate your understanding.
How can you demonstrate understanding? Do this by accurately describing the person's ideas, concerns, and understandings. Often, you can put back in words what the other is trying to say in a way that's more accurate and descriptive. This adds value to the other. It lets the other truly know that you do understand and understand in depth. To do this, say, "Let me see if I really understand what your concerns and objectives are..."

Exploring Your Current Skills in this Game
Identify your current listening patterns. Which of the following do you sometimes use with your loved ones?
      __ Defensive Listening (thinking how to respond).
      __ Lazy, Leisurely Listening (distractively)
      __ Analytical Listening (technical listening)
      __ Problem Solving Listening (thinking "how to fix it")
      __ Autobiographical Listening (thinking with your filters)
      __ Judgmental Listening (thinking evaluatively)
      __ Attentive Listening (attending their words, meanings)
      __ Empathic Listening (attending their feelings, reality)

Are there any barriers that prevents you from practicing empathic listening? Common barriers include the following:
      __ Preoccupation with my own ideas, emotions, and issues.
      __ Wanting to tell and give advise.
      __ Impatience: wanting to hurry up and get to the bottom-line.
      __ Judgmental mind-set: thinking in right/wrong, black-and-white.
      __ Fear of what I might hear.
      __ Inability to deal with another's negative emotions.
      __ Inability to deal with my own negative emotions.
      __ Other:

To practice attentive listening, invite someone close to you know about the Listening Game and how you want to develop it as a habit.
      "I would really like to develop my empathic listening skills. Would you help me by letting me practice listening, reflecting, and pacing with you?"

Listening and Ego-Boundaries

The first game that great lovers play is a game so simple that it is really easy to miss. It is *the Game of Genuinely Attending and Listening*. Of course, there's a hitch in this. And the hitch is that we have to *open our ego-boundaries* to truly listen.

This is the challenging part. This explains why we find it more natural to listen defensively, lazily, analytically, judgmentally, and ego-centrically. Yet in these pseudo-listening modes, we fail to open ourselves up to the other person. We stay safely behind our ego-boundaries and do not venture forth to truly meet the other person.

In authentically listening you will open your ego-boundaries to the other. In this way you enter into his or her world and let that internal world affect you. That's the rub: *you let the other's internal world affect you.* It takes a lot of resourcefulness to allow this. It takes a lot of centering self-esteem and self-knowledge to be able to truly *be* with the other and to give the other your presence, compassion and understanding.

The word *understanding* is fascinating in this connection. In understanding someone, you *stand under* that other person as a support to him or her. This is what gives the person the courage to share her internal world. Your lover can trust that you will be there to *stand under* him or her in support. If you don't, they will feel that you do not truly understand. If you do, they feel bonded to you and that you truly understand them. This is the magic of the understanding that arises from listening—from attentive listening. And it's the first dance that great lovers play.

Summary

- May the magic and wonder of *just listening* become fully felt in your mind and body as one of the very best *Games that Great Lovers Play*. As it does, it will change *listening* from a mere mundane activity of life to one of the key ingredients of romance, one of the profound ways we can touch each other.

- Listening with your whole mind, heart, body, eyes, and ears is not simple or easy. Lots of things can get in your way. Yet with practice and commitment, you can become highly skilled attentive listeners. Use active listening to love and care about your loved one. Dance with them the dance of romance by authentically entering into your lover's world to support and to stand under him or her.

- By attentive listening you not only love and romance your loved one, you extend yourself, get out of your little narrow worlds and open yourself up for the adventure of experiencing your loved ones. So, how much attentive listening will you do today ... for the rest of your life?

End Notes:

1. *Gestalt* is German and refers to something that is "more than the sum of the parts." In *Meta-States* we distinguish three kinds of states: primary states, meta-states, and gestalt states. Typically, gestalt states are multiple layer meta-states, states with many elements and features from which then emerges some quality that's more than the sum of the parts.

1. If you are interested in learning how to listen and support, we train these skills in the Meta-Coaching. See www.meta-coaching.org for more about this.

Chapter 3

THE DANCE OF
LOVE'S ATTRACTION

- What is love?
- What is the strategy for *falling* in love?
- What is the strategy for *staying* in love with that person?
- How do I know when I am loved?
- How do I know if I am a loving person?
- What does it take to be a great lover and to sustain those skills and states?

What is the relationships between *love* and *attraction?* When you love someone or something, you feel attracted to that person or thing, do you not? And as you feel drawn to wanting and desiring the object of your love, passion arises and you begin to chase or pursue your love. This facet of love shows up in a lot of our words and language about love: passion, pursuit, fall in love, conquered by love, etc. About this kind and quality of love we feel that it is mysterious, wonderful, ecstatic, exciting, intoxicating, etc.

The Game of Appreciation
A key game that great lovers play is   *The Game of Appreciation and Adoration.* They pursue the object of their love and they never stop the pursuit. It is not just a phase during dating and courting, it is part of the ongoing experiencing of loving and relating.

It is common for most of us to experience the love for our special one as exciting and intoxicating during the first days or months of the relationship

and then to experience the excitement and romance diminishing, maybe disappearing entirely, as things settle down.
- Yet does it have to be this way?
- Is the loss of passion built into a long-term relationships?
- Is it possible to keep the excitement alive over time?
- If it is, how do we do that? What's the secret?

Inducing and Seducing Another into the Feelings of Love

The Games that Great Lovers Play begins with the foundation of becoming personally independent and responsive. Being responsive to yourself and your loved one allows you to use your personal resources as you relate. Then, with your full resources available you connect, open your ego-boundaries, and genuinely attend your loved one. These powers allow you to love and to be loved, to feel loved by another and to induce such feelings of love into another.

Of course, you do *not* "make" the other feel loved as if you did this to them apart from your loved one's thinking and feeling. It is rather that you discover what really counts in your lover's mind-body-emotion system and respond to that. You extend yourself to give your lover what he or she wants which counts for being valued, respected, and loved. In this, the giving and receiving of love is a very simple, organic, and natural process. The chief rule for playing this game is this:

> *Find out what your lover values and treasures, then extend yourself in a responsive way to give what is important.*

The challenge in this is to *not* use your own map of the world and frames about the things that count to your loved one. The challenge is to hear and respond to your lover *on his or her terms*. It is to continually ask:
- What counts for my loved one?
- What does my lover want that conveys love and respect?
- What conveys to him or her the sense of being special and important in my eyes?

Each and every one of us operates from the map of the world that we have constructed from our experiences, learnings, and encounters with others. Our individual models of the world are made up of multiple belief frames, value frames, and understanding frames . This is our Matrix. To understand and truly love we invest the time and effort to discover these. Ultimately, we can only love by understanding what counts for the other and then seek to give that to our loved one.

Discovering Your Love Language
- What lets you know that you are loved?
- What stimuli, in terms of behaviors, communications, gestures, etc., trigger you to "fall in love" in the first place?
- What are the bonding factors that allow you to feel close and connected with your loved one?
- What behaviors cause you to just melt?
- What elicits feelings of passion in you?

Test yourself by writing the sentence stem, *"I know I am loved when . . ."* at the top of a page. Then complete that sentence by writing out five to ten items in response. Write them in empirical terms. This means to write things that you can see, hear, and feel (sensory-based terms) that a video-camera could pick up and record.

What behaviors in another tend to trigger feelings of being loved in you?

A certain way s/he touches	Kisses and caresses
The way she says my name	Saying seductive things
Giving me a hug every time we meet	Getting a backrub in the evening
Looking into each other's eyes	Listening to me when I'm upset
Arguing with me in a respectful way	Getting an unexpected gift
Laughing at my jokes	Calling during the day to say hi
Taking trips together	Taking a course together
Flirting in special ways	Exercising together
Showing affection in public	Taking long baths together
Going to church together	Meditating together

Sharing music together: singing, playing, musicals   Dancing
Sending messages during the day via email, phone, etc.
Inventing and using a special language between each other
Joins in when I'm working when I need some help
Playing along with me when I'm joking and being corny
Going for drives and enjoying the scenery
Talking to me about plans and taking my opinion into account
Leaving me alone when I'm working and respecting my space

What behaviors work for you as your equivalent of feeling "loved?" This question explores your internal mappings and will find out what in your mind-body-emotion system induces you into the feeling state of love. What *behavior* equals *love* for you? What actions do you interpret and feel as "loving behaviors?"

A few behaviors are universal enough that most people count them as "loving" behaviors, and yet there are always exceptions. The key is to find the specific behaviors and actions that activate the love magic for you and for your loved one.

When someone performs one of these magical behaviors, you experience that person so attractive. You feel bonded by that action. It works like a magnet. If you attribute to a behavior the quality of "Intelligence," and that's something you value, then that behavior communicates, "This person is intelligent and attractive." If it means "charming" to you, you will experience the person as charming.

Because you give such meanings to behaviors, you empower behaviors to communicate and induce abstract ideas and values—kindness, beauty, sensuality, gentleness, sense of humor, warmth, caring, etc. It is in this way that behaviors become loaded semantically. As you load them with significant meanings, *the actions mean a lot to you* . These behavioral equivalences of love convey the higher meaning of love, importance, specialness, etc. and so work as an anchor or trigger for "love."

The Love Strategy Game
A *strategy* refers to how you create your mind-body-emotion states as you use your brains and bodies. A strategy is a set of steps that create the experience. Similar is a formula for baking a cake. There's certain ingredients that go into the mix and there are a certain sequence or order to follow. Follow the instructions as given and you can replicate the chocolate cake or omelette or whatever.

Because brains go places, there's an ordered structure to where your brain goes, what it represents, and how the neuro-linguistic system of your mind-body responds to create your states. The *Swish Pattern* is a strategy for sending your brain in the direction of seeing yourself as more centered and independent. That's a mind-body-emotion process, or strategy, for taking charge of your map of "self." (See chapter 17)

There's also a strategy for becoming more resourceful, for getting motivated, for being resilient, for building wealth, for selling, for persuading, and for a thousand other things. There's a strategy or formula for every experience because there's an internal structure.

This holds true for love as well. There is structure to loving and being loved. This means you can identify and install enhancing strategies for loving, communicating, working through differences, opening up, healing old hurts, and so on. Because every internal experience has a structure, you can find and develop strategies for opening up your ego-boundaries, becoming more trustworthy, proactive, for affirming another person, attending to them, bonding, etc.

We even have strategies for depression and learned helplessness. Actually, such experiences are pretty easy to create. Make a picture of some outcome that you didn't want, then run a sound track in your movie with a low whiny tonality, "This is terrible... nothing ever goes my way, why don't I ever get any breaks?" Continue this internal self-talk in a tone of self-pity as you zoom in on the picture making it bigger and closer so that it feels overwhelming, and you feel helpless to do anything about it. In no time you will induce a state of victimhood.

Within every strategy there are thinking-and-feeling steps which create your inner responses and this continues until you fully experience the state. Discovering a strategy can be challenging due to how quickly you think. As your brain-body streamline a formula for how to do something, awareness of *how you do it* drops away, and you just do it. The behavior becomes intuitive and unconscious. It becomes so habitual that it operates outside of consciousness. That's why you really don't know how you do it, we just do. It's like riding a bike or tying a shoe string.

The same thing happens with love strategies. Most of us have not given conscious thought to what "counts" as "love" for us. In the process of growing up we learned from what we experienced, were taught, and the accidents of events. Today, it is intuitive. It is intuitive (in-knowing) to your experiences and the frames and meanings you developed in being loved and cared for. "Intuitive" does not guarantee that it will be useful, productive, or healthy, just efficiently automatic. The entire phenomenon has now become so streamlined that it works incredibly fast and outside of your awareness.

This means that your brain has become so used to this direction that you really don't know how you do it. It just seems "the way it is" and almost silly to articulate it. And because your lover also lives in a Matrix, a different one, he or she will not have the same love strategy. To discover the structure to this experience, you will have to slow down the process and/or speed up your noticing.

Eliciting Your Love Strategy for the Game
Since your *love strategy* consists of the internal processes that you go through to create the sense of being in love or of expressing love, then

becoming consciously mindful of this process gives you access to a very powerful resource. It provides your partner a way of understanding where your brain goes in response to certain stimuli and so informs them about how to truly love you.

1) Access the behavior.

Have you ever felt loved? What was that like?

When did that happen?

How do you know that it was love?

Allow yourself to go back in your mind to a time and place where you felt loved. Experience it fully. Allow yourself to step into that movie and be there again. As you think back to a time and a place in which you felt totally loved, allow your unconscious mind to pick out a good memory from a specific time. It only matters that you begin to recover those feelings of being totally loved . . .

2) Explore your love strategy.

What are you experiencing that brings on this feeling?

What do you need to see, hear, or feel to know that you are totally loved?

Is it something you see?

Something that you hear?

Is it a certain way that you are touched?

What lets you know?

What has to be there for you to feel loved?

As you go back to that time, and experience it now... you can feel those feelings even more intensely than ever before, now . . . because we want you to recognize what it is that allows you to feel those deep feelings of love.

Visual system check:

Is it absolutely necessary for your partner to show you that your partner loves you by taking you places?

By buying you things?

By looking at you in a certain way?

What is absolutely necessary for your partner to show you so that you know he or she totally loves you?

Auditory system check:

In order to feel these love feelings, is it absolutely necessary for your partner to tell you that he or she loves you in a certain way?

Is it the kind of voice?

The kind of tone used?

Certain words or kinds of words used?

Kinesthetic system check:

> In order to feel totally loved, is it absolutely necessary for your partner to touch you in a certain way?
> Where does the touch need to be?
> What kind of a touch?
> How would you want this touch given, etc.?

When you know what it is that is *absolutely necessary* for you to experience for the love feelings, notice the cinematic features that make up and drive your internal movie. If you are not quite sure, then check by eliminating stimuli.

> If you saw the things that are important to you, but were not touched, would you feel totally loved?
> If you heard the words or tones of voice, but didn't see what you want to see, would you feel totally loved?

Once you have accessed the love state, then use your physiology and let your whole mind-body-emotion system show on the outside what you sense and feel on the inside. What does it look like when you fully go into this state?

The One-Step Dance in the Love Game

This process will enable you to discover your own strategy for feeling loved as well as your partner's. Once you get the structure of it, then you can evoke this state by simply *triggering* the exact stimuli that evoke this feeling in your loved one. This is what makes the love strategy so valuable. Knowing your own love strategy gives you more awareness, control, and choice in life. It empowers you to take charge of your states, especially your love state. It enables you to be more skilled in facilitating the state of feeling loved in others. The *triggering* enables us to "anchor" it so that we have it at ready access.

Love strategies typically differ from other strategies in their *speed*. Instead of a three-step procedure or a seven-step strategy, it is more typical that you develop a one-step strategy to feeling loved. One touch, one place for the touch, one thing to say, one way of talking, one way of looking at the person, etc. and with that one trigger, and you go into the love state. It triggers you to feel totally loved. Isn't that fabulous?

Does this mean that everyone needs just one thing to feel loved? No, not at all. Most of us like having triggers in all three systems—what we see, hear, and feel. That always makes things much better. I want to be touched in just the right way, and told that I'm loved in just the right tonality, and shown that they love me in ways that count for me. Yet just as one sense often dominates our lives so that most of us have a highly favored sensory system (visual, auditory, or kinesthetic), most of us also have a highly favored way of communicating and experiencing love. When you find it you have at our disposal the key that unlocks your heart's combination. This gives your partner *the very key to your heart*.

All of this becomes really useful when you enter into an intimate relationship. You now have the ability to teach each other how to really love you so that it authentically evokes the kind of feelings of love that you want to elicit in the other. While it is nice when this occurred naturally and spontaneously, you don't have to wait. Why wait for it to just happen? Now you can run your own brain and discover how your partner's mind-body-emotion system operates. You can generate the enhancing states that make your relationship much more passionate.

The Anchoring Game
In anchoring, you *trigger* or *evoke* a response. In this way you can link or associate one experience with another. You can get an experience like being totally loved linked to or associated with another stimuli. When you have a trigger or an anchor for a state, you have a mechanism that works as the operant conditioning Pavlov established with his dogs.

Do you remember Pavlov and his dogs and his bells? He would get his dogs into a salivating state by putting some meat powder before them. The meat would activate (or evoke) their saliva glands and they would be salivating for the food. At that point, he would ring a bell. This would *anchor*, or link, the bell to the salivating response. Eventually, the bell itself would set off or trigger a very unnatural response, namely, their glands would salivate. It wasn't that the dogs wanted to eat the bell, it was that the bell cued them to think about and access the eating state.

Anchoring works as a form of conditioning or learning and is based on how things get connected. Anchoring explains how a look, tone, word, expression, behavior, etc. can set off a state. In anchoring you connect mind-body-emotion states to a trigger. The anchor creates an associative meaning. Bell equals eating state. In this way, the association of any trigger with a state can set up what we call an "anchor."

How do you do this? One way to do this is to wait until your loved one gets into a strong emotional state of desire, passion, joy, excitement, etc. Then, at the very height of that state, when it is strong or intense, set an anchor by associating some trigger. It could be a touch on the elbow, it could be saying the word "love" with a special tonality ("Don't you just *love* that?"), it could be by looking at the other in a special way, etc. Any stimulus can become an anchor. Nor does the anchoring process have to be conscious to work. It works just as well when the stimuli is outside the person's awareness.

You can intentionally elicit and anchor states. Because of this you can use *anchors* with your loved one to trigger, and re-trigger, love states and other resourceful states to enrich and delight your relationship.

Anchors naturally get set in relationships. We only have to be feeling good and in a great state, hear a song, concur that the song is "our song," and so it becomes. The song then becomes an anchor for that event and those good feelings. We can anchor a state with a single word or phrase. We can say, "That year in Chicago." Or, "Remember that vacation in the mountains when we stayed in the cabin?" It also works the other way as well. We can tragically anchor negative and hurtful states using this same mechanisms of association. "It's just like last Thanksgiving at your Uncle Charley's house!" "Don't use that tone with me!"

The Love Strategy Pattern
1) *Think of a time when you felt totally loved.*
      When did you feel totally loved? Where were you?
      How did you know that you were being treated very specially?
2) *Find the essential ingredients.*
      What allowed you to know that you were totally loved?
      What has to absolutely be there?
      What sensory based factor or factors have to be there?
      Is it something you see, hear, or feel?
3) *Identify the internal cinema and its features.*
      What would I see if I peeked into the theater of your mind?
      Describe the movie that plays in your mind.
      What are the editorial features of that movie?
      How close or far, bright or dim, etc.?
      Would you like to amplify these? What else would put my pizzazz into it?
4) *Anchor the love state and validate.*
      So when you are *feeling this* fully and complete (add trigger as you say *feeling this*), you like this? Really?
      You'd like to *have access to this* anytime you would like?

You feel resourceful as a person when you feel loved like this?

The Heart of the Appreciation Game

With all of this in mind, what lies at the heart of love? *Valuation*! Isn't this the heart of love? At the core of what we call *falling in love*, and of experiencing this phenomenon of love is valuing. How do I know that? Because *love* as a verb is almost synonymous with valuing, appreciating, cherishing, and caring. Appreciation arises from attributing a high value to some external expression.

Check it out for yourself. What do you love? What do you value? Don't these terms point to the same persons, experiences, ideas, etc.? *Love is valuing.* When you don't value something, when you dis-value it, treat it as unimportant, can you love it? Of course not. What you value, you love; you extend yourself for. You devote time, energy, money, and effort for that object or person.

Go through your list of love behaviors, are not these the items that you really value? Getting your shoulders rubbed, kissing, holding hands, having someone to talk to, etc.?

It is in seeing things with *the eyes of appreciation* then that expresses the essence of what it means to "be in love." In the state of love, you notice, recognize, and express *appreciation* for the value of these qualities, traits and behaviors in others, do you not? Everybody has behaviors which represent value. To those behaviors they attribute high valued meanings.

Frames for the Love Game

Understanding the behaviors that you equate to the state of love helps you to get a much better grasp on what you mean by love. Yet that's not the end of the story. Many people have limiting beliefs about love, beliefs that sabotage them from ever reaching or experiencing it or ever maintaining it. Let's explore this facet:

*   What do you believe about love?
*   What do you believe about deserving or not deserving love?
*   What do you believe about needing or not needing love?
*   What do you believe about tenderness or gentleness?
*   What do you believe about the nature of love? Will it last or does it just come and go? Can we manage it or is it beyond our ability to manage? A mysterious force that you feel?
*   What do you believe about the relationship of thinking to feeling love?

Use these questions to identify your beliefs about love. Write out your responses. Once you have your list, step back from it and quality control your list. Are your beliefs enhancing or limiting your life?

- Do my beliefs about love make this a compelling and attractive state, value, or quality in my life?
- Which of my beliefs are most empowering and enhancing?
- Which beliefs are actually limiting and sabotaging?
- Do I have any beliefs about love that put it outside of my ability to experience?
- Do I have any beliefs that undermine keeping a loving relationship?

When You are in the Game and Ready to Play
- What is it like when you love something?
- What does love feel like?
- What does love do to us in terms of focus, energy, health, and vitality?

While we all experience love in different ways, generally we all also experience the emotional state of love as a positive state in which we open up and extend ourselves to the ones we love. In the state of love, we extend our thoughts and concerns to care about another. We come out of ourselves in a relaxed and open way. This invites other emotions in—compassion, thoughtfulness, consideration, kindness, patience, forgiveness, etc.

What is the state of love like for you? To find out, access a series of times and places in which you felt "love." As you do, go back to those experiences so that you fully see what you saw then, hear what you heard, say to yourself what you were saying to yourself, and feel what you felt. Do this with friends, lovers, mentors, children, and pets. As you do, continue to notice the quality of mind-and-emotion and body that the love state elicits in you.

Now compare your experience with the following description of love. This one comes from a Bible verse. As a classic expression of what love is like, it offers an elegant description of the resourceful states that love creates. This is the Phillips paraphrase of I Corinthians 13.

> "This love of which I speak is slow to lose patience—
> it looks for a way of being constructive.
> It is not possessive:
> it is neither anxious to impress
> nor does it cherish inflated ideas of its own importance.
> Love has good manners

and does not pursue selfish advantage.
It is not touchy.
It does not keep account of evil
or gloat over the wickedness of other people.
On the contrary, it is glad with all good men when truth prevails.
Love knows no limit to its endurance,
no end to its trust,
no fading of its hope;
it can outlast anything.
It is, in fact, the one thing that still stands when all else has fallen."

Summary

*   *Love* is a state, a resourceful state, and a strategy. *Love* is supported by beliefs and frames of mind that value it. And *love* is the valuing process that sees the object of our love with the eyes of appreciation.

*   To feel love is to feel valued, appreciated, adored, supported, and understood. To give love is to give value, appreciation, adoration, support, and understanding. This allows you to more fully understand what it means to say that "love makes the world go around." It certain makes you go around and forward with more resourcefulness and health!

*   There is structure to the giving and receiving of love. We call that structure a *strategy*. And knowing your strategy for feeling loved and the strategy of the special one you love puts this experience within our control rather than being a victim of its whims.

Chapter 4

THE EMOTIONAL
BANK ACCOUNT GAME

- Do you feel *full and complete* in your lover's love?
- Do you fill up your partner with rich expressions of your love?
- Do your expressions of love count to your partner?
- Would you like to be a great lover in stimulating your partner to feel *full of love*?

Since there is a strategy to evoking our loved one to *feel loved*, and since it involves finding out what counts for him or her (what our lover values as important) this gives us a process and a strategy for keeping the exchange economy of the relationship energetic.

The what? *The economy of exchange.* The "love economy" of things that count to each. That's why we relate to each other and enter relationships, *we want to experience the rich fullness of the give and take of love.* When a relationship works, the give and take is mutual, valued, enriching, and brings out the best in everybody. When out of balance, the relationship will not work well or may stop working altogether. When that happens, the give and take exchange will not be reciprocal. We will be giving, but not receiving what counts for us.

- How well is the economy of exchange working?
- How balanced and mutually enriching is that exchange system?
- How full do you feel satisfied in getting what counts for you?
- How full does your partner feel?
- Are you getting the things that *really* count for you?

- Is there something that you would like to receive or like to give?
- Does your partner seem full and happy?

The Emotional Bank Account Game

The nature of relationships as give-and-take interactions allows us to think of them in terms of our *commerce* with another, our *accounting* of how much *investment* we have made and are making, of *depositing* and *withdrawing* from our emotional bank account, etc.

As a metaphor, an emotional bank account enables you to think and talk about things that are otherwise vague and intangible. Now you can speak about *depositing* relational wealth in each other's emotional bank account and making *withdrawals* of wealth from that same account.

- What comprises a *deposit* into your emotional bank account?
- What begins your love strategy? What counts in it?
- What enriches you?
- What triggers you to feel more loving, more resourceful, more of who you are?

Relational d*eposits* typically consist of behaviors that induce a sense of trust, safety, care, kindness, courtesy, honesty, commitment keeping, etc. Withdrawals come from bad habits of showing disrespect, discourtesy, cutting off, overreacting, ignoring, being arbitrary, betraying trusts, threatening, etc. These are the things that cause us to quickly overdraw our account.

If a large reserve of trusting behaviors is not sustained through continuing deposits, the relationship will deteriorate. Healthy relationships require constant deposit. Our "accounts" with those we relate to require constant investment to keep a positive balance. If we have made huge withdrawals we may undo all the good we have done. Impatiently snapping, dumping on another, lying, betraying trust—these are ways that bankrupt relationships.

Relational Wealth in Your Emotional Bank Account

Relationships, as give-and-take interactions, work by what you invest in your loved one and by what you *withdraw*. While you have an emotional bank account with everybody you are in relationship with, this is especially true for your lover.

- How skilled am I in making emotional deposits with my lover?
- What emotional investments do I deposit with my partner?
- What emotional investments really count for me?
- What withdrawals do I make from my partner?

- How is it a withdrawal?
- What behaviors really make a withdrawal from me?

Deposits	Withdrawals
Little acts of courtesy/kindness	Discourtesy, Unthoughtfulness
Cooperative/ Open	Argumentative/ Closed
Honesty: truthful	Dishonest: lies, cover-ups
Integrity	Disloyal
Listening without judgment	Judgmental, critical
Positive in intent	Negative in perspective
Seeking to understand	Too busy/ occupied to listen
Hearing out negative emotions	Defensive in face of negatives
Recognizing other's values	Unaware of what's important
Accepting in attitude	Rejecting, critical
Tender/ gentle	Rough, rude
Affectionate	Cold, untouchable
Expresses endearment, affirmation	No kind words
Apologizes sincerely when wrong	Can't be wrong; can't admit it
Makes it safe/ secure to communicate	Pushes buttons; intimidates, threatens
Respectful of basic dignity	Disrespectful
Patiently listens	Cuts off/ won't take turns
Responds kindly/ gently	Over-reacts
Pays attention/ interest	Ignores
Thinks things through	Arbitrary in decisions
Predictable, solid	Unpredictable
Enhancing/ empowering language	Talks in rude, crude, nasty ways
Asks, inquires	Orders, tells, preaches
Holds voice down	Yells, shouts
Believes in the best in people	Runs people down

Want to play *the Emotional Bank Account Game?* Then explore with each other the things that count as deposits and withdrawals. While this is quite subjective, there are things that hold true for most people. For instance, deposits include attending to little things, doing little kindnesses and courtesies, keeping commitments and promises, and surprising the other with some small delight from time to time.

Making promises and keeping them are critical for maintaining a loving relationship. This is fundamental because it deals with trust, integrity, the kind of people we are, and a sense of safety and security. No wonder love is undermined whenever you make promises that you don't intend to keep or don't keep. To say things without acting on them or making good on them erodes trust and corrodes the very fabric of relating. Conversely, when you keep the promises that you make, the small ones and the large ones, you build a bridge of trust that enables you to span the gaps of understanding. Unclear expectations have a way of undermining communication and trust and so sabotage love and safety.

Actually anything you do which demonstrates personal integrity makes a deposit. Integrity means that you are willing to do whatever it takes to make external reality conform to your words. You *do* what you can to make your words and promises come true.

What if you make a mistake or fail to come through on a promise? The most responsive thing is to *quickly* acknowledge and apologize. Apologizing for a withdrawal takes a lot of character strength, yet demonstrates a willingness to be held accountable. It's much easier to forgive mistakes of the mind and judgment than to forgive the mistakes of the heart. Ill will, bad motives, prideful covering-up, etc. are the things that wound the spirit and undermine our trustworthiness. It breaks the bonds of trust so that the other has reason to *not* trust you. Eliciting trust requires that you are trustworthy.

By building trust, you can now frame the problems that arise in a relationship as opportunities to make deposits in your emotional bank account. By rising above the content of an issue, see the other's problems as opportunities which invite you to be helpful and supporting.

> "Here is a great opportunity for me to invest in this relationship and to prove that I can give as well as receive!"

Self-Exploration:
- Do I have a large reserve of trust and emotional deposits in our emotional bank account?
- What withdrawals get me into trouble or bankruptcy with my lover?
- How consistent am I in providing ongoing deposits?
- Do I truly know that healthy relationships require constant deposits?
- Do I want a quick fix to avoid dealing with problems or negative emotions?
- Am I willing to take the time to build and repair my relationships?

Speaking Up for Love's Mutuality

Did I mention that there is a difference between *love* and *relating*? *Love,* as an emotion and an attitude of mind, is something completely within your power to give and to give unconditionally if you so choose. You can *love* without conditions simply when *you* recognize the person's value as a human being, regardless of his or her actions. The prototype relationship for this is the parent-child relationship. As parents we love our children *simply because* they are our children. During infancy and childhood we love them with an undying love regardless of the messes they make or how they misbehave. Our love is unconditional.

But the degree and kind of *relationship* we have with that child, or anyone else for that matter, is always *conditional.* Relationship is conditional. It is first conditioned upon what each person is willing to give and to receive. It's conditioned upon whether both persons *want* to be in relationship. One person *cannot* create and maintain a relationship alone. It takes two. A single individual can care, love, communicate, give, etc., yet that is not a relationship. That is giving and giving and giving. Without receiving, without the mutuality of giving and receiving, the "relating" that makes up relationship is missing.

Relationships differ from love in this regard. Relationships are conditional. Loving is your response and so it can be unconditional. You can unconditionally choose to love regardless of the response you receive. You can approach and offer your love without expectation of any response. This is the ideal image of the Judeo-Christian God, as a benevolent intelligence who loves without conditions. He loves because it is his nature to love as one verse puts it, "God is love." Of the five words for love in Greek, and *agape* is the love of benevolent good will that seeks first and foremost for the best of the other. Of course, only God can love this way consistently, you and I can only strive for such.

This kind of benevolent good-will love is intentional, attitudinal, and behavioral. *Benevolent good will* describes a victory over self. This kind of love doesn't occur easily or naturally. It emerges as you commission the values and beliefs of love which chooses to act for the good of the other. This expands your capacity for love and loving.

Because relationships are based upon conditions, you cannot have an *unconditional relationship.* You can *offer* to relate, yet the other may not take you up on that offer. With all your good will, friendship, compassion, etc., if they are not returned, there is no relating, no relationship.

Giving love and offering friendship is one thing, entering relationship is another. It is in the giving and receiving of responses (i.e., respect, warm feelings, listening, etc.) that we relate to each other. This is what allows us to become responsible *to* each other. In this relating we can specify the responses given and received. We can name the things we do for love's sake. So while love may not be dependent upon how another behaves, relationship is dependent upon the other's response.

Reject someone's good will and what relationship is there? It takes two to relate. You cannot force relationship upon someone who will have none of it. *The giving and receiving conditions* of an intimate relationship is expressed in the traditional wedding vows:

> "I will honor and esteem you, I will cherish you, I will forsake all others and be yours and yours alone. For better or worse, for richer or poorer."

The intimacy a couple attains depends on how well each invests time and energy in making good on these vows. When you break the vows in small or big ways, you violate the conditions of the relating. This undermines the relationship. To be close you need to view such violations seriously and develop your capacity for graciously confronting such. Knowing the relationship is conditioned on nurturing and cherishing each other, and on patterns of respect, recognize also that inter-dependency means *mutual accountability*. To request no conditions, to let anything and everything go, to let another get by with neglect, abuse, or any unloving behavior does not indicate authentic love. It is the lack of it.

Inter-dependency and loving intimacy involve living with a mindfulness of consequences. You make yourself mutually accountable to another for what you have promised. In this, love must be strong and tough enough so that you help each other live up to your promises. This highlights the importance of integrity, doing what you say, as a skill of love. Integrity is the strength of character that allows you to not only *feel* love, but to *act* loving in the way you behave.

Sentimentality doesn't work. As a pseudo-love, sentimentality is weak and excusing. The care-taking that "loves too much" rescues others from the consequences of their behaviors and actions and, in the long run, destroys relationship. Your motive may be caring, yet these actions are not. "Saving" people from facing and coping with this reality cripples them. Such love is not fierce or robust enough for the work of love.

It is one thing when someone can't take care of his or herself and asks for help. But when you are on a "project" of rescuing, saving, or care-taking, an entirely different dynamic is under way. If you ask to be "loved" unconditionally and mean that you do not want to be held accountable for what you do, you are asking for something that will destroy the relationship. Given the nature of interdependency, you are not behaving sanely.

Tim and Suzie's Emotional Bank Account

When I met Tim and Suzie, her emotional bank account was at a "2" and his was a "7." One month prior to seeing them, Tim's bank account was at a "9." He thought things were great. He was getting everything he wanted from the relationship. He didn't have any problems. These numbers began plummeting during the past month. Suzie had reached a threshold and began withdrawing, first sex and then conversation. Only then did Tim get the impression that something was wrong.

For years, Suzie had been telling him that she was unhappy and wanted more intimate conversations, more time alone together, and more affection. Most of the time he never really "heard" this. From time to time he seemed to hear it a bit and would act more responsive for a few days, but he slipped back into being over-involved.

In gauging their satisfactions and dissatisfactions, I quickly learned who was ready to "work" and who was not, who was tired of trying to make things better and who had tolerated non-responsiveness far too long. As both wrote their *want lists,* I had to keep prodding Suzie about what she really wanted because the mere fact of saying so made her feel vulnerable. It frightened her. She said she was afraid of opening up and hoping something would change this time.

I attempted to help Tim realize how close to threshold she was, and that his integrity was absolutely crucial for sustaining love. "What you say you will do, you have to come through, or it will create an even deeper wound." They made their lists and came for a session in which we exchanged them. As I took her list and handed it to him, I said,

> "Tim, here is a list that gives you the key to Suzie's heart. If you want her to melt in your arms, these are the things that count. You don't have to do them, that's your choice. But if you love her and want to keep her, these are the things that make her feel valued and respected and admired and cared for."

Tim dutifully began doing things on the list, things that Suzie wanted, but within two days he became distracted with things at work. It wasn't that he stopped doing them immediately, it was rather that he did them perfunctorily, as if just fulfilling an obligation. He put no passion or heart in them. First things were first, and for him that meant his business, not his relationship. Suzie sensed this and, for her, that was the final straw. "Enough!" she said inside herself and filed the divorce papers which she had filled out several months earlier.

The limitation of the emotional bank account metaphor is that it is not just making deposits, but *wanting* to. Your attitude and spirit is a great deal of what you give and offer or "deposit"with the other. You feel loved and valued when the other gets excited at your excitement. When it is by obligation and rote performance, the spirit is missing and this can undermine the bonding.

Loving Enough for there to be Accountability
*   Does your love include accountability?
*   Do you make yourself available and accountable to your lover?
*   Or do you want a free reign to do anything?
*   Are you willing to give that same free-reign to your loved one?
*   Do you see and experience *accountability* as part of a healthy and wonder-filled love?

Accountability empowers you to use your powers of thought, emotion, speech, and behavior in ways that enhance your lives. Accountability arises from a positive and empowering attitude toward feedback. Through recognizing the significance of feedback as the fast track to mastery and excellence, you see "being held accountable" as a crucial secret of success. Accountability is positive—it's wanting to know what is working and what is not. When you discover what is not working, that is a success—you know what to no longer do. Recognizing what does not work enables you to make adjustments and focus on what does work.

Accountability keeps you on target and focused. It keeps you real and authentic. It keeps you reality-based. With accountability, it's harder to be seduced by deceptions and delusions or to get out of touch with the very real consequences of your actions.

Accountability and Mutuality
Relationships are conditioned upon the quality of your give-and-take exchanges. What describes a truly loving relationship? Holding yourself accountable to how you're meeting each other's needs. It is *the Game of Accountability* that makes the relationship sustainable.

That may be a bit abstract, so let me rephrase it in everyday language. It is always in my best interest to ensure that I'm doing my part in delighting, pleasing, pleasuring, and helping my lover to fully experience wonderful feelings. My long-term interest and well-being is supported when I'm held accountable for my part in the relating. For all that counts in her emotional bank account, I will do what I can so that my partner *feels full*.

This can be challenging. It challenges our tendency to project our auto-biographies and to suppose that what our loved one really wants and needs is what *we* think he or she wants or needs. This is where a person can create the illusion of having a happy relationship when there is non! The key is that *what counts to your loved one is what he or she says and feels counts.* When you use your own strategy to understand your partner, you are not getting outside of yourself to meet that other person. You are seeking to meet him or her at *your* model of the world!

What counts? *What your loved one says counts.* Period. That's why we spend time talking and listening. The metaphor I'm using here is that of an *emotional bank account*, with *deposits* (the things that count) and *withdrawals* (the things that do not count, and the things that violate values; the things that wound love). While many in the field of couple therapy use this metaphor, there are limitations to it. Yet the metaphor does provide a language for talking about the exchange of the intangible things that we want from the one we love.

- What counts in your emotional bank account?
- What counts as a deposit?
- How much of a deposit is it?
- What counts as a withdrawal?
- How much of a withdrawal is that behavior?

What builds up a person's emotional bank account with you is not what you believe is a deposit, but *what the other says counts.* If your lover doesn't *interpret* your effort to be loving or considerate as a "deposit," but as a withdrawal, then it will work as a withdrawal, not a deposit.

Lastly, since you (and all of us) are forever growing, developing, and changing, it's essential to update your Emotional Bank Account list every two or three years to see where you are.

Summary

- Because relationships are give-and-take ventures, they are *conditional*. That's why you can *love* far more than you can *relate*. That's why we often say, "I love him, but I can't stand being around him." Love can motivate you to be caring and considerate, yet the actual process of relating involves giving and receiving.

- The metaphor of an "Emotional Bank Account" gives some new ways to talk about the exchanges that we invest in each other and how to think about how well a relationship is working.

- Identify the things that count in your emotional bank account and the things that make withdrawals. Evaluate them. See where you are. Then engage in a dialogue with your partner to see if you can balance the relationship so that it works equally well for both. If it doesn't, it will only be a matter of time until someone becomes emotionally bankrupt.

Chapter 5

THE SELF-DISCLOSURE
GAME OF LOVE

"To love is to be vulnerable.
Love anything and your heart will certainly be wrung and broken.
If you want to make sure of keeping it intact,
you must give your heart to no one, not even an animal.
Wrap it carefully round with hobbies and little luxuries;
avoid all entanglements;
lock it up safe in a casket or coffin of your selfishness.
Your heart will not be broken, but it will change."
C. S. Lewis

- Can we love with words?
- Can we love more effectively by expanding our communication skills?
- Can we love through disclosing and making ourselves vulnerable in the eyes of our loved one?

With words we bless and curse, we bond and dis-bond, we connect and sever connections. Words powerfully effect us as they influence the nature and quality of our relationships. What we say, and how we say things, can last with another person as an encouragement or as a source of mental torture for years. We can also love with our words. It's one of the gifts of relationship and one of the secrets that great lovers know.

Great lovers excel at communicating their hearts and hopes, their support and reassurance. Great lovers have superb skills at communicating thoughts, feelings, hopes, desires, appreciation, and love. They magnificently communicate their understanding of each other as they reflect their thoughts and feelings. They consistently communicate their patience, thoughtfulness, and consideration for the other. In communicating, they listen attentively, clarify mis-understandings, and show care via their conversations. Great lovers know how to be intimate with words and language, to bond and share affection, and to use language to allow other forms of intimacy to arise. In this rich and loving communication, it is not the elegance of the communication that matters as much as its authenticity—the sharing of each person's heart and reality.

Assertive Intimacy

How does the phrase *assertive intimacy* strike you? Does it sound contradictory? Can you be *intimate* when you are *asserting* what you think, feel, and want?

Assertive intimacy is actually the only kind of *authentic* intimacy. This intimacy means that you are being open, direct, and forthright with your loved one. You intimately present or assert what you actually think, feel, and want—kindly, considerately, tactfully, and gracefully. You present what you think and feel without playing the games of passivity or aggression.

It takes a lot of healthy independence to pull off this kind of forthright communication. To say what you *really* think and believe in kind and gentle ways that make your ideas clear and gracious—that's true art. Doing this makes your conversations robust, vigorous, and strong—they make them "fierce." You become fiercely real with each other—fiercely intimate. This allows you to get to the heart of things and to speak your truths to others in love. To do this, pace each other's reality which allows you to work with and through each other to build a synergistic relationship bringing out the best in your partner.

Language is funny and weird and powerful—all at the same time. It can map new realities and it can create pseudo-distinctions that limit. In using the language that I'm using here to describe communication you could easily get the impression that *communicating* is a different thing from *relationship*. It is not. Both terms actually refer to the same experience. When you verbally and non-verbally *communicate* something—you are, at the same time, *relating* to that person.

Every communication is a bid for relationship. Isn't that what you're doing when you initiate a conversation? Are you not making a bid for a relationship? Both terms refer to the process of interacting, sending messages, and evoking meanings. If there's no communication, there's no relating. If there's no relating, there's no communication. Communication *is* the relationship. We relate by communicating. We build our relationship with our lover—one conversation at a time.

Playing the Communication Game
We have all heard it a million times—relationship problems are due to "poor communication." Conversely, relationships thrive when there is healthy and forthright communication. If ineffective communication is one of the major saboteurs for a loving relationship, then—

- What do we need to communicate to be truly great lovers?
- How do we need to communicate? And when?

When you put our thoughts, perspectives, values, beliefs, understandings, emotions, and wants into *words*, you enter into an uniquely human arena. You enter into the world of language (linguistics) and semantics (meanings). It is this which makes us neuro-linguistic creatures—beings who *speak reality* into being. "In the beginning was the word..." As you *say* things and *describe* things and *tell stories*, you bring worlds of meaning and emotion into being. This introduces semantic realities. Since "meaning" doesn't exist "out there" in the world apart from a meaning-maker, it takes a human mind-body-emotion system to create meaning. It is meaning that you communicate.

No wonder you can do so much with words. To the person not familiar to your symbol systems, words seem like just puffs of air, sounds emitted from your throat but meaningless—without significance. Yet for the insider, you can do a wide range of things with words. You can—

Gather Information	Learn new ideas
Understand another's perspective	Seek further clarification
Bond with another person	Express endearments
Reinforce behavior	Extinguish behavior
Influence and persuade	Sell ideas
Unload emotional stress	Experience a catharsis
Transform our mind and emotions	Update our mental maps
Hypnotize	De-Hypnotize
Mystify and confuse	

Since words can carry such a diversity of meanings, you can accomplish many things by communicating. This makes communication complex and challenging. More often than you might suspect, you don't know the other person is actually doing with words.

- What is the design of the words?
- How is your loved one using a particular expression?
- Why is he or she saying these things in this way?
- What are his or her intentions and motivations?
- What effect?

To be effective at communicating you need to develop an awareness of the words you use and how your words elicit the meanings they do in another. You also need to appreciate that communication is an exchange in a system involving feed forward and feedback loops. This refers to how you take information in, draw conclusions from it, and then feed back our emotion, speech, and behavior.

The Self-Disclosure Game

Loving is all about self-disclosure, is it not? Can you relate and bond with another person if you don't make yourself known? No, you can't. It is in making yourself known and visible to your loved one that you bond. Disclosure is a prerequisite for connecting. People who fall in love with people they don't know, actually only fall in love with   *an image* and a persona. They don't fall in love with that person. How can they? They don't know that person.

We make ourselves known in order to relate and connect. Through making ourselves know we fall in love and in the process we discover *what we love* in our partner—the qualities we adore. If we want to be a great lover, we take responsibility to make ourselves seen, known, and understood. This presupposes that we relate know ourselves.

- How well do you understand yourself?
- What do you understand about your thoughts, feelings, values, hopes, dreams, preferences, etc.?
- How skill are you at making yourself known and understood?
- How skilled are you at presenting your thoughts, feelings, values, perspectives, wants, etc. in a winsome way?

Part of the excitement of meeting someone new is that you present yourself in a new and fresh way. In doing this you usually discover more about yourself. As you interact and relate to another, who you become in that person's presence is also instructive about who you are and who you are becoming. Because you are ever-developing, the process of self-understanding is a never-ending one. As you continue to develop, you learn to balance courage and consideration in your self-presentation.

- *Consideration* is needed when you seek first to listen and understand and to enter into another's world. You show consideration by respectful listening and taking interest.
- *Courage* is needed when you need to communicate your understandings in terms of your values, beliefs, perceptions, feelings, etc. In the face of the fear of disapproval, criticism, and judgment, it takes courage to speak up.

The dance between courage and consideration involves moving in and out of these states of mind-and-emotion. There's an art in making the dance beautiful and gracious. Too much courage and you will probably come on far too strong. Your words will feel aggressive. You will come across as too caught up in yourself. Too much consideration, you go in the other direction. You come off as too soft and kind so that there's little presentation of yourself. Your words will feel too tentative, unsure, and non-committed. It's the dance back and forth that allows you to inquire and express, to explore and expose, to know and to be known.

Disclosure Depths
- How much do you disclose about yourself?
- How quickly do you disclose the depths of your stories?
- How deep do you go with someone you're getting acquainted with?

Figure 5:1
Communication Depths

	Roles	
External		*See-Hear-Feel*
	Activities	*World*
	Behavior	

	Thoughts	
Internal		*The Inner*
	Emotions	*Matrix of*
	Values	*Mental-Emotional*
		Frames
	Heart	
	Hurts	
	(the "dark" side)	
	Vulnerabilities	

Everyday ... with friends and at work, we disclose ourselves. We disclose ourselves to associates at work and to our loved ones at home. Yet typically we do not bare our souls. We usually only disclose surface things: what we do, what we think about the local sporting teams, what we think about this or that new program, what we're going to have for lunch, etc. It's after work with friends that we are more apt to disclose more of ourselves: how we feel about work or a relationship, or our struggle with a co-worker. It depends on the depth and quality of relationship. Yet even there we usually don't disclose it all.

We all have a longing to disclose, to be known, to make ourselves visible to the eyes of another human being. We also find disclosure scary. What if he laughs at me? What if she rejects me? What if another comes to despise or hate me? It's these dangers that we fear and which explains why it takes a lot of safety and trust—that we are safe in the hands of someone, before we open up. Often we don't even feel safe enough with ourselves to open up since we are quick to judge ourselves.

In disclosing more than the surface concerns, we turn to our friends and loved ones. Yet there's a skill in disclosing and in making it safe for us to disclose. We have to provide confidentiality, trust, and acceptance. This has to be earned. In terms of communication or disclosure depths, we can think about going from surface things down deeper and deeper into our inner world. Generally, it takes a strong relationship characterized by lots of trust and confidentiality to share our very heart or our vulnerabilities. At this level, the person is our confidant.

- How deep do you go with your lover?
- What stops you from disclosing your very heart?
- Is there sufficient trust and confidentiality?
- Have you proved yourself trustworthy for the confidences of your loved one?
- Do you know how to make it safe for your partner?
- Do I create the context in which my lover feels free to share thoughts, feelings, fantasies, etc.?

When you are alienated from yourself, self-disclosure is impossible. You cannot disclose what you don't know. You have to know yourself to disclose yourself. Brandon says that in romantic love "it is precisely the self that we make visible and share with one another."

> "If we are forbidden to know, if we are afraid to know, if we ourselves have never encountered who we are—then we are crippled and incapacitated for genuine intimacy." (144)

"Romantic love entails a desire to see and to be seen, to appreciate and to be appreciated, to know and to be known, to explore and to be explored, to give visibility and to receive it." (155)

Truly *seeing* each other is essential when you love and love passionately. Contrast this with what happens when people stop loving. They also stop looking. We see this in couples who have fallen out of love. They have grown tired of each other and hardly ever look at each other. As they do not actively *see* each other, they lose awareness of each other.

Becoming Visible through Self-Disclosure

As you negotiate the fearful barriers of being vulnerable and open to each other, there are numerous pleasures and delights. Among these is the pleasure of being "seen," of your loved one *seeing* you, and accurately reflecting back. To some extent you can see yourself. Yet that's the problem, you can't do so directly. Is there a mirror in which you can see yourself—see into your soul? Yes there is. It is the mirror of another's mind. You see yourself reflected in your lover's eyes.

To understand this pleasure of being loved and being seen, contrast it to when you are not seen. Nathaniel Brandon describes the effect of finding another's consciousness that seems so alien to our own. It's disconcerting. The "me" I see in another's eyes as they mirror me back is wild and distorted. I don't recognize myself reflected in that person's eyes. It's like those distorted reflections in an amusement park's Chamber of Horrors.

There is the consciousness that enables me to see myself clearly and with love. When I make myself visible to his or her eyes, I feel both seen and valued. "The experience of significant visibility requires a consciousness congruent with our own," writes Brandon in *The Psychology of Romantic Love*. This again explains why we connect around commonalities and bond with those who are like us.

Love, after all, *is a response of valuing.* When we respond to another by valuing, appreciating, adoring, and accepting, we give much pleasure to making our vulnerabilities visible. This initiates a feeling of affinity as we see and experience our self through the other. The areas wherein we are alike give us a sense of *being at home.* Brandon calls it the "shock of recognition." We feel fascinated with the other, attracted, passionate, and yet at the same time, oddly familiar.

Love, and especially romantic love, entails a profound sense of a sharing the same sense of life. This doesn't mean total agreement, but experiencing a similar and familiar emotional "sense of life." We describe this as finding a *soul-mate*. The other's attitudes about life, self, and the world fits so snugly with our own. This "sense of life" may reflect a healthy self-esteem, value in life, optimism, and that the universe is open. Or it may reflect self-doubt, anxiety in living in an unintelligible and hostile environment. Either way, the other seems to share our "sense of life."

This sense of life is not merely agreeing upon certain issues whether political, religious, or even philosophical. Nor is it created through merely conforming to the other's ideals. It is a deep affinity about life and self which the intimate exposure of vulnerability and openness reveals and which then draws us into the space and heart of the other.

Summary
- Great lovers know that loving involves self-disclosure, and so play the Self-Disclosure Game so that each feels seen and known and sees and knows the other.

- The intimacy and vulnerability of self-disclosure invites you into a depth of connection that has a very special satisfaction.

Chapter 6

THE APPRECIATION GAME OF LOVE

There are many bonding Games—many ways and means by which you can connect with your lover. There are also many prerequisites for healthy connecting and loving: personal independence, being sufficiently grounded and centered in your own visions and values, personal growth and resourcefulness, building rapport, getting your ego out of the way, attentive listening, learning to find and use the other person's love strategy, etc.

I mentioned earlier that the heart of loving is *valuing* and that the heart of valuing is appreciation. This makes *appreciation* central to being a great lover, doesn't it? And isn't the role of appreciation evident to being a great lover?

- How can you be a great lover without appreciating your partner?
- How can love grow where there is contempt, discounting, judgment, and other negative appraisals?
- How can you love well if you don't appreciate yourself or the very process of loving?

Yet focusing on appreciation as the heart of loving, do you now feel the challenge of true love? After all there are numerous things that we all find hard or challenging to appreciate—differences, idiosyncracies, irritating habits, as well as the things that hurt love. How can we*appreciate* the other person in the face of these things?

The Appreciation Game's Magical State

It takes a very special state, a magical state, to play this Love Game. It takes the state that we call *appreciation.*

If you're ready to access this state, do this. Think of something that you appreciate. ... Good. Now another thing. Take your time with this. Stop and take a moment to identify something that you adore, that you consider delightful and wonderful and then go inside and see it, hear it, and feel it. Turn on the movie and be there. Go inside it. A glorious sunset. A conversation with a good friend. A holiday in a special place. Soaking in a hot tub. Having a glass of wine. Playing with a bunch of puppies. Walking in an old Redwood forest.

Anything that evokes within you a sense of appreciation will do. You can use small and simple things, or you can think about something magnificent and glorious. It's *the feeling* that counts. Just notice the person, thing, or experience that you appreciate and the state that it elicits in you.

- What does appreciation feel like inside you?
- How does the state of appreciation affect your breathing, muscle tone, countenance, and walk?
- What does it feel like on the inside when you just melt in appreciation?
- What is it like when you look with the eyes of appreciation at something?

Appreciation is powerful. It is magical. Abraham Maslow put appreciation at the very top of the hierarchy of the qualities and characteristics of self-actualizing people. He described it as moving through the world with "the fresh eyes of continual appreciation."

To play the *Appreciation Game,* you have to operate from the appreciative state wherein you can *see* value and acknowledge that value in others. Appreciation has the power to enable you to go more gently in the world as you *count* all of the things that matter. In the state of appreciation you deem them as important. This counter-acts the negative states of judging and discounting everything that doesn't measure up to your demanding standards. It enables you to nurture the things that *are* so that they can become even more. It gives you a penetrating glance into the heart of value and to recognize value everywhere. It opens up your eyes to new possibilities.

No wonder *appreciation* is relational magic when it comes to caring and loving someone. Appreciation creates a focus of valuing and supporting from the beginning and avoids the hurt and anxiety that discounting creates. In appreciation you live in a search for value. Appreciation puts you on a journey for possibilities.

Begin the Game with Appreciation of Excitements
The foundation of *passion* with your loved one arises from, and is grounded in, your personal *passion for life itself.* I like what Michelle Duval, an Executive and Life Coach, says. She says that we "fall and stay in love with the other's passions." What makes us passionate about each other is *our passion for life itself.* Passionate people are attractive because they are exciting people. No wonder sharing and appreciating each other's excitements makes us great lovers. Much of the excitement in a relationship arises from the excitement which each individual brings.

It is a passion for life that makes us creative, exciting, and alive. These are the very qualities that attract us to each other. These are the qualities of creativity that make us fresh and spontaneous. Anything that dampens this passion dampens your passion of love. The loss of passion from your loved one occurs when a person becomes empty, tired, bored, stressed-out, burned-out, and numb. What this means is that *relationship passion* is not separate from your general passion about life. Lose your passion for life and your romantic passion will suffer.

And because great lovers know this, they make themselves a friend to each other's excitements. They may not share or participate in the excitements themselves, but they support each other's passions. They know that the more alive and excited their loved one is about life, about developing, contributing, succeeding, etc., the more alive and passionate they will be in the relationship. No wonder they want their partner to be full of eagerness, expectancy, and enchantment. They play *the Game of Being a Friend to the Other's Excitements.* In this, sometimes the fear of intimacy is really a fear of excitement, a fear of giving oneself fully to a goal and going for it.

For Advanced Players, Appreciating Differences
The test of appreciation really shows up when we apply it to those areas where we differ from one another. *Appreciating differences* becomes the challenge when we live closely with someone—anyone.
•   What do you feel when you hear the word differences?
•   Do you have any semantic reactions to the idea of "differences?"

At the emotional level, many of us—if not most of us—really don't like differences. In relationships we feel that differences create conflict and separation, and we fear differences as threatening connection. Yet we also know that there are differences that excite us, seduce us, invite us to explore another's world. In *the Game of Becoming a Great Lover* we began by seeking first to understand our loved one. In this *seeking to understand* process, we discover in greater detail how we differ. What then? What do we do when we find differences in perspective, values, visions, etc.?

Actually, both in our similarities and differences we have many ways to connect and bond. Precisely because we live in different psychological universes (or matrices), driven by different mental maps in how we perceive, value, believe, frame things, etc. that we have fodder for both stability and excitement.

> *Our similarities create the foundation for our relationships and our differences create the excitement.*

There is a catch. For this to work *you have to welcome the differences.* You have to appreciate, value, and validate the differences. This means refusing to judge, complain, insult, or make the differences "bad." This is the new inner game that we're called to, is it not? How new or different is this frame of mind for you? How much of a shift will you have to make to see and treat differences as neither good nor bad, but something that just is? First we accept it, then expect it, and eventually we can even learn to appreciate the differences. After that we come to enjoy and embrace the differences.

Playing the *"But That Doesn't Count!"* Game

Dale and Melody wanted to get away for the weekend and do something special. It was winter time in the mountains of Colorado and they both loved getting out in the high country with their snowmobiles. They also loved going to new places, so they drove 175 miles north for the four-day get-away. But it didn't go well. They ended up snapping at each other and being irritable. So I inquired, "How did it go?"

"Okay, I guess." Melody said with resignation in her voice.
So, what went wrong?
Nothing, really.
I can see that it was really thrilling! What did you expect would happen during those four days that did not happen?
I thought it would be a romantic time together.

Since Melody was the only one responding, I continued with her. "What was not romantic about it?"

Well, for one thing we didn't even make love once.

"And why not?" I prodded.

I tried once, but he was a cold dishrag.

Okay, dishrag, how come you were so wimpy about making love with her?

Well, she was always griping about anything I did that was romantic.

And she knows what that does to me.

So you did some romantic things during those four days?

Yeah.

Like what?

I took the snowmobiles out and got them all fueled up and ready to go while she waited in the warm motel. I tried to engage her in a conversation and I opened the door for her...

That's when she cut him off.

That's not romantic. He always does that.

Let me see if I understand this. He says he opens the door and does other things with the intent to do something special for you, something romantic, but you don't see or experience it as romantic. Some ladies would consider having the door open for them an act of romantic thoughtfulness. Do you not recognize that or is there something else going on?

It's not romantic because he always does it. It's just a habit.

So a behavior doesn't count if he offers it to you consistently? Does that work for you also, that the romantic things lose their value if you do them too frequently?

As the conversation continued, I discovered and highlighted all the things that they were doing with the intent of doing something special for the other. Yet both were *discounting* the romantic behaviors. They didn't count them as significant. As that discounting had continued, both felt unappreciated and were feeling less and less willing to extend themselves. They were playing the *"But that Doesn't Count!" Game.*

The Magic of Being Understood

We seek first to understand because if we assume that we already know our loved one, we make the big mistake. It's a mistake that blinds us to our loved one and to any new development in him or her. If we do that long enough, we will arrive at a place where we will not know our loved one. The truth is, we have a hard enough time understanding ourselves. To assume that because we understand ourselves or another at a given point in time—we fully understand and will always understand only deceives ourselves and hurts our loved one.

"What is there to understand about another person?" Jim said.

The answer is: Everything. Why is that? Because we do not live in the same mental and emotional worlds. We differ from everybody else in many ways.

  So while our similarities tie us together for the foundation of our connection, we also are very different. We differ in how we think, feel, create meaning, experience love, and value things. These differences can make the connection exciting.

We all live in different worlds governed by different maps. It's like we all grew up on different planets. Actually the metaphor is not all that far from the truth. We do live inside of different Matrices. At the higher levels of our mind we all have developed understandings, perspectives, values, beliefs, referent experiences, how we cope, our drives, motivations, etc. These frames that make up the matrix of our mind initiate our differences. This dimension of meaning describes our sense of self, the world, our goals and dreams, how we process information, and the worlds we live in. We may not even be very aware of this psychological world (the Matrix) that we have created. And even if we have, we may not understand it or appreciate it.

To connect and bond with a lover the first item on our agenda is to spend time exploring to understand. Stephen Covey (1987) expressed it in a memorable form in his succinct statement, "Seek first to understand, then to be understood."

Is not *understanding* an expression of love and one of the things that we all seek, is it not? We want to be understood. There's a certain pleasure in being understood and this pleasure continues even when the other may not agree. Being understood means to be seen and acknowledged for who we are. It's one of the truly magical gifts that we can give to our lover. It's one of the bonding pleasures of a couple in love and it is much of the excitement in first getting to know someone.

Conversely, consider what it feels like when you are not known or understood. What does it feel like when you do not feel seen or known for who you are? Isn't that experience unpleasant and distressful? And in the context of one whom we love, most of us find it horribly painful. Frequently we seek out the presence of a friend, loved one, or counselor just so that what goes on in our heart and mind can be seen and understood by another human being.

Recognizing Our Different Matrices

Great lovers know that they enrich the relationship and make it more fulfilling by seeking to understand and respecting each other's similarities and differences. Knowing that these are the very factors that create the initial attraction, they seek to use them for continual attraction. What you have in common unites you. Similar values give a sense of familiarity, trust, and safety so you feel "at home" with the other. The differences make the connection exciting by expanding and extending your own sense of reality giving us new things that enrich your live.

The Appreciating Differences Game
- How do you think and feel about your lover when you realize that he or she thinks and frames differently from you?
- What happens in you when you find a specific area where your partner believes and values different things from you?

If you differ in these things, *you can expect your expectations to differ.* You can expect your expectations to get shocked, surprised, and thrown off.

As you allow yourself to think about differences for a moment, sit back and welcome any and every thought that may rattle around in your head. Let them intrude into your awareness. Thoughts are only thoughts, and you can let them come and go as you please. You can do that, can you not? And if you find thoughts that you dislike, that don't serve you, that don't reflect your highest values, you can wave goodbye to them as you let them pass on down the stream of consciousness.

Now write at least six statements that complete this sentence. *"When I think about differences..."* Complete it with whatever thoughts begin to intrude into your mind.
- So, what did you discover from that?
- What ideas rattling around upstairs came downstairs?
- Do you like those ideas?
- Do they serve you well?
- If you gave yourself to those thoughts, what state would they induce?
- How open, accepting, validating, and appreciative are those thoughts regarding differences?

Use them as a gauge. To the extent that you view differences as negative, harmful, unacceptable, bad, wrong, problematic, conflicting, etc., to that extent you will not experience a good adjustment to reality. At least you will not adjust effectively to *the reality of the differences in others.* You can count on that. People will think, emote, talk and behave in ways different from you.

The Similarity/ Differences Quadrants
The following chart (Figure 6:1) highlights the kinds of differences and similarities that we create from the similar things which we like and those which we dislike. Into this template identify a loved one and fill in the traits and qualities for each quadrant.

Quadrant I: *Liked Similarities.*
> List the things that you find attractive, compelling, and desirable about your partner. These will be the things that characterize both of you which you like.

Quadrant III: Disliked Similarities.
> List the similar traits and qualities of your thoughts, emotions, and behaviors that you dislike or even hate. List the things that both you and your lover share that you dislike (for example, you both yell when in conflict). These are the things you consider your "dark" or shadow side.

Quadrant II: Liked Differences.
> List the differences in your lover that you find attractive, desirable, and compelling. These differences usually provide some of the most intense, wonderful, "mysterious," and seductive kind of attractions. They represent those attractions that we want to "marry" into our personality. When we marry our lover's differences, we expand our consciousness and complement our personality.

Quadrant IV: Disliked Differences.
> List the differences in the other that you really dislike, even hate. Here we confess to the "dark" side of the other person. These become the things that the other person does says, thinks, or feels that "push our buttons" and "rattle our cage." Ironically, many times (if not most of the time), these comprise the differences of Quadrant II taken to an extreme. That is, they are the other person's strengths, uniqueness, powers and gifts *over-done*.

Figure 6:1

	Similarities	**Differences**
Those I find Attractive	Similarities Liked	Differences Appreciated
Those I find As Aversive	Similarities Disliked	Differences Disliked

Exploration of your Quadrants

• How did you do with that process?
• What insights did you gain through it?

Your answers in Quadrant II inform you about *the differences that attracted and continue to attract* you about the other. These differences probably tell about the "holes" in your personality. The reason you feel attracted as you do may lie in what the other offers, something that *complements* your own personality. If you will now align yourself with that attractive difference, you can become a learner and model that trait to enrich yourself. You could "marry" that trait.

These complementary differences enable you to feel both *seen and valued* by your loved one. As you make things known and visible to each other in this quadrant, this stimulates self-discovery and an expanded awareness or enlarging of yourself. It stimulates your fascination with the strangeness of your lover, making your encounter all the more engaging.

The similarities of Quadrant III tell about *areas wherein you want some personality development and growth*—some of the unfinished or unaccepted areas of your self. They may describe areas for greater self-development indicating the lack of resources in certain circumstances, or even areas of mis-identification.

The aversive differences in Quadrant IV describes the areas that you must address if you will ever develop a "good," satisfying, bonding, and enhancing relationship. The more differences you list here, the more these create feelings of aversion, withdrawal, and dis-bonding for you. These endanger your relationship. Differences here speak about how you have not adjusted yourself to the other person's reality.

Of course, the secret of a successful adjustment involves first learning to accept the differences within Quadrant IV.
          No! No! Anything but that!

Yes, *that*. This doesn't mean you have to like it, approve of it, or endorse it, but just that you recognize it for what it is, and accept that *at this moment in time* this trait, quality, or way of functioning does indeed exist as one of the differences between you.

The *"There's Always a Positive Intention"* Game
The second step involves stretching your awareness in such a way that you begin to look for *the positive intent* behind the aversive difference. Yes, you read that right. Look for the "positive intent" behind and within the disgusting differences. As an empowering way to deal with things, the premise in all solution-focused models is this: *"Behind every behavior is a positive intention."*

This premise allows you to frame behaviors as serving some value to the person. You can then align with the person and discover what the person is trying to do that's of value and significance by the behavior. This offers a new and wonderful way of perceiving the world, looking for and creating positive intentions.

Unbelievable? Then think about some of your disgusting behaviors. Think about when you become critical, insulting, impolite, rejecting, or whatever.
•   What did you hope to accomplish that would be positive for yourself by those actions?
•   And by doing that, what did you hope to accomplish that would be positive?

Here's an important process that helps us to become more appreciative in the face of unpleasant behaviors:

> *Our intentions often differ from the results that our actions produce.*

Though we operate from good intentions, our history is littered with the results of inter-relational wars because others did not see, recognize or acknowledge our positive values and intentions.

This offers a great resource for our most intimate relationships. By learning to adopt this way of looking at differences, especially aversions, empowers us to identify the other's positive intentions. Doing this allows us to see and hear higher (or deeper). Instead of feeling put off by obnoxious behaviors and going into a reactive, defensive state yourself, you will find yourself capable of "listening with a third ear" to the depths or frames from which the behavior came. We will develop the ability to recognize *the goodness* of the person.

That last statement crucially summarizes this art. Yet I can put this in yet another way: *Separate the person from the behavior.* Or, I can say it in another way: *Stop over-identifying a person with his or her behavior.* People are so much more than their behaviors. You also are so much more than your behavior. To define yourself by your behavior alone misperceives you, doesn't it? It under-estimates and under-values your worth, potential, uniqueness, and genius.

This explains why I carefully used the phrase "dark" side and put it in quotes. The "dark" side is "dark" because it appears "dark" to us. "Darkness" represents our evaluation and judgment of it. "Darkness" describes our judgment, our standards, our thinking—not what actually exists *out there* in the behavior, emoting, speaking and thinking of the other person.

"Darkness" exists in our mind about that behavior *because we do not see the light* (that is, the positive) *within or behind it.* "Darkness" serves as a reminder of our limited way of thinking. We "curse the darkness rather than light a candle." We call it darkness rather than figure out what positive intent drives that behavior.

Every *vice* (i.e., wickedness or bad trait) has within it, behind it , and above it a value. All we have to do is find it. To do that simply take all of the aversions in Quadrant IV and put them on *a value continuum.* That is, draw a line for a continuum that represents some value. Then put the "vice" at either end to represent it as *a value under-done or as a value over-done.*

Now name the continuum after some value—some positive trait, quality, thought, emotion, behavior, etc.

Figure 6:2

Under-done   Over-done

_____

"Evil"   *A Value Continuum*   "Evil"

If you put "laziness" in Quadrant IV, and laziness pushes your buttons, and you respond to it by going into a reactive state that fills you with aversion and disgust, then put it at either extreme of the continuum. Now explore,

On what value continuum would I perceive laziness as an under-done value? An over-done value?

Try it. Come up with some answers. One over-done value could be relaxation. After all, the lazy person has really achieved a high level skill of relaxing, has he not? "My, oh my, can he relax! And for so long!" This frames laziness as an over-done value. And laziness becomes an under-done value on the "achievement" continuum.

How does this process help? *It informs us as to what direction we need to move, on what scales, to obtain a balance.* The person who behaves in a lazy manner can now see that he needs to avoid *over-doing* his relaxation thinking and behaving. Seeing this, he can now move to a more balanced position. He can see that he needs to move his under-achieving behaviors to the right on the scale so he can accomplish more with his life. With *under-done* traits and qualities we ask:

•   What does this person not have enough of yet?
•   What quality, trait, behavior, etc. do they need more of?

With over-done traits and qualities, we ask:
•   What does this person have too much of?
•   What strength, gift, or resource have they become too skilled in?

Some of our antagonistic differences arise from not understanding, from framing them in negative ways, i.e., from negative meta-stating with impatience, intolerance, fear, etc. Yet once valued and appreciated they can sometimes offer the most stimulating and exciting emotions to the relationship for being more alive and for growing.

Sometimes the art lies in transforming the differences from being antagonistic to being complementary.

- How can you frame the differences so that they become mutually enriching?
- How can you tap into the potentials in each other and allow the intimacy to become more alive?

How? Do this by *owning* your own responses, even your intolerance, then explore such. Frequently your intolerance arises from things you have disowned in yourself. The person who rejects anger in others may also disown it in self. The person who disowns sensitivity may also disown it in self.

- What human quality, emotion, and impulse do you disown?
- What would happen in terms of your conflict over differences if you simply owned it?

Through the acceptance of complementary differences you can turn conflicts into the source for stimulation, enhanced self-discovery, and intimacy. This takes the threat out of "differences" and puts you on a journey of growth. You may find a new stage of development struggling to emerge.

Valuing and Appreciating
The Disgusting Differences of Others

With these processes, you have the resources to align yourself with differences. Take your list in Quadrant IV and put each one of those items on a value continuum. Keep exploring the following questions to expand your consciousness.

- What can I appreciate about this trait?
- What can I find as positive about this difference?
- What part of this quality do I need to "marry" into myself?
- To what extent do I need to "marry" this difference into myself?
- How can I live with this difference more comfortably?

Summary

- *There's magic in appreciation.* Appreciation as an attitude, a frame of mind, and a resourceful state that enriches your loving and bonding.

- Appreciating is easy and natural with things that you love and desire. The challenge is when you are face to face with behaviors and responses that you don't like. Yet appreciation for self, for relating, for the other person can turn things around so that you can move through the disliked thing and find better ways to relate.

- Loving through appreciation—this is one Game that all Great Lovers Play. And now you also can play that game if you so choose!

Chapter 7

THE DANCE OF COMMUNICATING LOVE

- What is the relationship between love, the Games of Love, and communication?
- What kind of communicating deepens and enriches the loving?
- Can you love another and be assertive?
- Can forthright and assertive communicating deepen and sustain a loving relationship?
- Does clarity and precision of communication enrich the magic of love between lovers?

*C*ommunication— what a telling word! Within it we see the twin ideas of *union* and *communion*. It speaks about how two people *commune* their ideas, thoughts, memories, frames, and meanings back and forth in exchange until a state of *union* (or co-union) emerges that keeps them connected. True communication operates as a co-creative phenomenon wherein two people co-create a new shared reality together. And there's more.

*The communicating **is** the relationship.* To relate is to communicate. After all, it is in the communicating that we are relating. And if the communication *is* the relationship, then *the quality* of the relationship completely depends on *the quality* of the communicating. All of this introduces a critical variable in the Games of Love—how we communicate for bonding.

The Game of Rapport

We often talk about *rapport* without identifying what we're talking about or how in the world we create it. It's hard to play *the Game of Rapport* without knowing how this magical state arises. What specific behaviors create the sense of connection that we call "rapport?"

In identifying the structure of rapport, NLP has identified two kinds of behaviors. What are these? We create rapport by matching another person's responses verbally and behaviorally. When we match in this way, we call it *pacing*. What do we pace? Verbally we can pace or match a person's words, values, beliefs, world-view, and non-verbal we can match a person's physiology and gestures (i.e., breathing, standing, posture, movements, etc.).

How does *matching* create the magic of rapport? At the simplest level when you match another person's speech and behavior, you convey a sense of familiarity and validation. It's as if you enter the person's world and reproduce a bit of it, this creates a feeling of safety. We seem known and familiar. Most of this "sense" is not recognized consciously, most of it is outside conscious awareness. When we feel rapport, we register it only as a *sense* of connection.

Matching or pacing someone's outputs verbally and non-verbally in this way enables you to "get on another's wavelength." In doing that, you convey the sense of understanding and appreciating the person with whom you speak.

This basic rapport-building process is based on matching various aspects of the other's world. By matching you adjust aspects of your own external behavior to approximate similar aspects in the other. The on-going process of pacing means that *you take on* the other's movements, neurology, words, and ideas. Because these factors of experience are typically outside conscious awareness, pacing unconsciously communicates:

> "I know your world, I can sense and feel and think in terms of your world of experience ... Therefore I'm like you."

The Verbal Pacing Game

Verbal pacing begins when you use your sensory awareness to come into the moment, attentively listen, and enter into your lover's world. Doing this puts you in a position where you begin to pace. Pacing is difficult to the extent that it challenges you to come out from behind yourself and into a sensory awareness to be present in the moment. It is difficult only to the extent that you haven't develop the skills of stepping out of your ego perspective to take on the perspective of another.

To verbally pace, *make verbal descriptions* that agree with, match, and are congruent with your lover's internal world. That's the primary rule for how to play this game. Listen—really listen, listen with a third ear to seek to understand your loved one on his or her terms rather than on your own.

Doing this demonstrates that you are tuning in. And that, in turn, conveys the sense of having been heard and recognized. In so   *stepping out* of yourself and *into* your lover's world, you "empathize" or see the world as if from inside your loved one's perspective. Empathy puts you into the other's frames to momentarily experience the world from the other's perspective. This takes imagination and the ability to attend to the other's world.

In doing this you move to a higher level of communication effectiveness. How does this work? It works because you enter into your lover's reality, take the words you have heard, and imagine how the words are true for him or her. In entering your loved one's reality you do not lose your own. Not at all. It does not mean that. It means you are imagining and appreciating the other's reality in its own right. By verbally pacing you join your lover's Matrix of reality in a more profound way.

All of this requires recognizing the other's Matrix. To that end ask yourself the following questions to develop this skill:
- What does this word, phrase, metaphor, or style of expression imply?
- What is my lover's orientation to reality?
- What is it like on the inside of her world?
- What could be the sources of his understanding or emotion?
- What frames of meanings are at work within?

There's another way to think about pacing that I like. In pacing you engage in *map listening*. You listen to your lover's map of frames that make up his or her Matrix. This enables you to use the other's language patterns and to linguistically match his or her internal state by making statements that agree with, and are congruent with, his or her experience.

You can even *break pace* to engage the other to invite greater rapport. How? By over-stating or under-stating something with an openness for feedback. Do that with anyone and stand back to watch what happens. What will happen? Typically, the person will become active in seeking to make him or herself known with more accuracy. Why does this happen? I believe this happens because we all want to be understood. Don't you? Isn't it our basic nature and disposition? Being mis-represented can be so discomforting that when it happens we just have to straighten it out. So over-stating or under-stating our guesses actually can create an opportunity to receive more accurate information.

Verbal pacing functions as a *feedback mechanism.* When you pace your words and non-verbals and then feed back to the other person regarding what you have received, it completes the communication circuit. This process, by the way, lies at the heart of hypnosis and hypnotic communication.

The skill of pacing is extremely powerful when done with appreciation and respect. In so doing you amplify the other's experience, engage it, elicit it, and validate it. Obviously this kind of pacing is easier to understand than to pull off. Why? Because to pull it off you have to get out of yourself and enter your lover's world. That's why you have to restrain yourself from problem-solving, advice-giving, and judgments.

Begin by *verbally pacing* the other's words, metaphors, vocabulary, and thought patterns. Feed back the sensory system words (visual, auditory, or kinesthetic) you hear. When you match the sensory mode this will induce the feeling that you are on the same wavelength. To pace with non-verbals, feed back the non-verbal features such as the other's breathing, voice tempo, tone, etc.

Pacing beliefs, values, and meanings gains rapport, enlists support, and builds a basis for communicating. Begin by assuming the other's words are meaningful. Then imagine how they can be meaningful. Pacing reduces repetition in conversation since once a person feels heard, he doesn't have to keep repeating. Pacing does take some time since connecting with another takes patience, calmness, and respect.

The Game of Clear and Strategic Speaking
Inasmuch as communication involves the sharing or communing of meanings, we really never know what we have communicated. That's because we never know what the other person hears. The *hearing* of the other person depends on so many things within that person: history, processing style, intelligence, emotional intelligence, state, resources, etc.

How can you find out *what* you have communicated? You do so by noting and exploring the response you get. In *the responses* you get you can discover what has been communicated to the other person. Doing this allows you to discover the meanings created and transferred. The NLP communication guideline asserts:

> *The meaning of our communication is the response we get regardless of our intention.*

The meaning we have in our mind and seek to communicate is not automatically transferred to the mind and heart of another simply because we utter words. The meaning of our communication *to the other person* lies in the response that it elicits in that person. And that response arises from the person's interpretations and understandings of our words and gestures. That's why, regardless of our intent or meaning, the *communed meaning* lies inside the response we get. No wonder we need sensory awareness to find out what we have communicated to the other person.

To avoid mis-communication and the mis-matching of *message sent* and *message received* develop an awareness of the responses you get. How is the other responding? Is the other getting it? How do I know? It is only through noticing the responses that you can flexibly use the other's responses. This is the pathway to becoming professional in your communications.

Begin with the awareness that every communication from another is always and completely appropriate. Assuming this allows you to focus on discovering its appropriateness. This does not mean that the communications is right, good, or useful. It only means that it is appropriate to that person's Matrix.

All communication is interpreted through perceptual filters. Your internal processing filters the words and gestures you encounter. You hear and interpret things in terms of your frames. You hear them through the perceptual grid of your matrices. While this is inevitable, it does not have to cripple your communications. You can take these perceptual grids into account. You can become much more aware of your own internal processing, you can learn to distinguish descriptive and evaluative language, and you can learn to move into a more sensory-aware, "uptime" kind of state.

Communication Distinctions
In communicating with your loved ones, distinguish between your strategies, skills, and particular linguistic patterns.

Strategy refers to what you are attempting to accomplish, your intention, purpose, and desired outcome in communicating. Strategy enables you to

move to a meta-position as you identify your intentions and objectives. This level of intent concerns the spirit of your communication and enables you to think about present and the desired states of the relating.
- What am I attempting to accomplish?
- What is my intention and my intention of that intention?

Skill refers to the particular words, behaviors, skills, language, tones, gestures, etc. which enable you to accomplish your goal. The specific behaviors and performances by which you provide stimuli to another to evoke a response.

Language patterns refers to the specific words you use and how you say them (your pauses, tones, etc.) within which you can package messages and meanings. The specific linguistics that effectively transfer your meanings to another's mind. At this level you are engaged in the creation of semantic reality with another and operate within various semantic environments.

Strategic Communication
To think strategically, ask:
- Where am I now with this person?
- Where is he or she with me?
- Where do we want to be with each other?
- What communication styles are being used?
- Which ones would be more effective to moving us to our desired state?

As we think and speaking strategically, do I need to:
- Create a safe atmosphere for communication?
- Engage the other person?
- Disclose my thoughts, emotions, values, and wants?
- Defuse negative emotional build-up in the other?
- Persevere in getting my message across?
- Make it safe for the other to come out and disclose?
- Back down from the ledge I've gotten myself out on?
- Slow the conversation down and target an issue?
- Confront some particular item that needs to be resolved?
- Go around the resistance and use more indirection?
- Get more on the table and negotiate a better arrangement?

In strategic speaking you think in terms of your current present state and your desired outcome. Only then can you effectively develop a preferred

future that is well-formed. You can inquire about which of the strategies would provide the best resources and bridges to that outcome.
*   What set of operations will move us from one to the other?
*   What resources will we need to bridge us from present to desired state?

The Game of Bonding with Loving Words
When it comes to loving and staying in love, sometimes you simply have not let your partner know *how to love you,* or *how to bond with you.* Perhaps you lack the forthrightness and assertive directness to let your loved one know. For that matter, you may lack the internal awareness ourselves and you may not know yourself.

One myth that undermines forthright communication of our wants and needs is the limiting belief that our loved one "should just know" that we care. This assumption seeks to build the relationship on each person's mind-reading ability rather than the ability to communicate clearly and precisely. Yet *mind-reading* pays no dividends in intimate relationships. It is much better to discover how to talk to each other.

It is precisely because we come from our own mental maps and frames that it is necessary to inform our loved one about how we want to be loved and what the other wants from us. Often this is difficult. Perhaps we did not see such intimate behavior modeled for us. Perhaps we don't have internal permission to be expressive and vulnerable (i.e., self-disclosing about our wants, desires, etc.). Perhaps we are driven with fears and apprehensions about rejection, openness, or vulnerability.

Ultimately, we have to speak to our loved one and disclose both what we want and elicit what our partner wants. So rather then wait around for our lover to mind-read our wants, or pick up on our hints, it's best to communicate.   Is this easy for you?

The following pattern offers a way to build this resource of being straight, disclosing, and communing our meanings into our very personality. To build up resources to empower ourselves for this, we need only to evoke a state that gives us the capacity to speak up with directness, clarity, and honesty. This will help us to connect with our partner more effectively.

This is not as simple as merely saying words. "Meaning" does not lie in words, but in *the meaning-making* (framing) of the person who uses the words to convey his or her meanings. Oftentimes people argue and fuss about words and become so word-oriented that they forget it is*the person* who creates the meaning and that the meaning does not depend upon the words used.

It helps if you shift your emphasis to become more person-oriented in communicating. To do this enables you to not fly off the handle about words, to be word-phobic, but to keep exploring *the person's* meanings until you have come to deeply understand what that person is trying to accomplish. The end result of communicating is a state that's characterized by understanding, trust, rapport, care, awareness, sensitivity, gentleness, etc.

Accessing the Resource of Being Direct

Think back to a time and place in your life where you were able to express yourself easily, comfortably, forthrightly and authentically. Let your unconscious mind pick an instance when you did this with something small and simple. Pick something that's not loaded with a lot of emotion, but something that's simple and easy. Because your neurology undoubtedly knows how to simply go up to a person and say, "I would like a hamburger. Would you get me a Big Mac?"

The art of asking for something that you want is actually an unique and wonderful opportunity to be straight by leveling. How difficult would it be for those in the fast food places to have to drag it out of you? If you came up to the counter and just hinted by licking your lips, by darting your eye to the menu board at the Big Mac listing, by looking famished. "Can I help you? Would you like something?"
       "Oh no, not really. I was just thinking."

Well, would you like a milk shake?
       "No, it's alright. I don't want anything (looking hungry and licking his lips)."

I don't know how easy it is for you to say to your loved one,
       "Honey, what I would really enjoy tonight would be to go out to a movie with you and then to snuggle. What would really be nice this evening would be a backrub, etc."

Asking in a straightforward way is not the same as making a complaint, "You never bring me flowers anymore." Nor is it the same as making an accusation, "All you ever want is sex, why can't you just hold me?!" This is what we often do. Instead of being straight, we wait until we're disappointed, upset, frustrated, angry, or at a threshold, and then we let the other have it. That's not the best way to sustain love.

Directness simply means asking. It means leveling. Asking kindly, gently, even romantically. It means making yourself vulnerable, disclosing what you find valuable in your loved one, and making some aspect of yourself transparent. It means inviting your lover to do the same.

Relationships *work* when you get your basic passions and wants met. Relationships cease to work when you do not have your basic desires met. When your wants are not met, you become empty which, in turn, leads to feelings of desperation, disconnectedness, and loneliness—experiences that do not bring out your best or make you more resourceful.

The mutuality of asking and receiving, loving and being loved, of connecting and contacting, of initiating and accepting—these are the things that makes us feel a sense of connection, in sync, and able to enrich each other's life. Then our sense of commitment to be there with and for the other creates a wonderful feeling of pleasure. When we give to our lover and receive from him or her, and when we make it our business to satisfy each other's emotional passions, our bonding strengthens. It becomes richer. When we operate out of fullness, it's much easier to feel and act resourcefully.

> So as your unconscious mind floats back to a time of just saying what you want, begin to see what you saw then, hear what you heard, say the kind of things in your mind that you said, and feel what you felt ... Good, just go with that memory. And you can be there even more completely and honestly... Because this only allows you to access all those feelings that allows you to speak forthrightly and clearly... And as you go fully into this state, anchor it so that you have a cue for associating back into this state.

> Now since there are times in your relationship with your partner that you want to say something that's really important to you that would enhance you and enrich your relationship, you can begin to scan through your everyday life to identify those kinds of situations... and think about an occasion ... And as you think about expressing what you want, the passions of your soul, you can *feel* that state of directness ... as you fire your anchor ... That's right... and know that you can easily and comfortably *just tell them* what you need, knowing that as you inform the one who loves you about what really counts in loving you, and you know that it makes you richer, fuller, and out of that fullness you too can also respond to your lover's needs...

Now you can allow yourself to begin to think of something that you really would like to whisper into your partner's ear that you would like when you are expressing affection to each other... Perhaps it is just a touch, a word, a look, or a tone of voice. And as you think of this thing that would just make the contact between you nicer, you can whisper this little something into his or her ear as you *feel* this love anchor and feel it increasing, can you not?

Accessing A straightforward directness for Communication

1) Access a state of forthrightness, clarity, and being gently direct.
>With a partner if possible, access the forthright state.
>What does it feel like when you're in this state?
>How do you breathe, hold yourself, focus, etc.?
>How much of this state do you have?

2) Amplify and anchor the state.
>When you amplify the forthright state, set a trigger or anchor for it with a touch or word or gesture.

3) Apply forthrightness.
>Think about something that you want and need to say to someone.
>What is it that you need to say? Formulate your thinking.
>Apply your forthright state to that context by imagining it vividly and associating the state to that particular passion.

4) Access and apply your Love State.
>What would you like to say to your lover that would support and nurture him or her?
>Formulate your thoughts and apply the forthright state to that experience.

5) Texture the state.
>What other resources would you like to texture this state with?
>Calmness, respect, love, compassion, firmness, boundaries, etc.?

6) Future pace.
>Now think about something you could whisper into your lover's ear that you would like to say that would be sweet, charming, seductive, delightful, surprising and romantic.
>Intensify the state of your passionate statement that would enhance your romance and relationship and now whisper that something into your loved one's ear.

The Intimacy of Communicating Sweet Nothings

Great lovers not only communicate with clarity and directness, but they also know and practice *The Game of Communicating Sweet Nothings*. This non-purposeful communicating has no objective except just to be with your loved one and have fun. Intimate bonding needs this kind of communicating. It needs the time and space for quietly sharing the things that you experience and that bubble up from the depths of your soul. When your schedule drives you and pressures you to fill every minute, you begin living only on the surface of your mind—living superficially. This undermines bonding. Brandon notes:

> "There is no aphrodisiac so powerful and reliable as authentic communication that flows from the core of our beings."

Communicating sweet nothings enable you to learn the art of nurturing. To nurture your lover is to accept and respect, it is to caress and stroke without making demands, it is to hold and to protect, to allow tears, to offer comfort, to be there for the other. Nurturing is being emotionally available to your lover.

Summary

- There's something delightfully seductive and charming about being innocently direct and forthright in your love and loving of your partner. Forthrightness in your communications along with clarity, precision, and congruence makes for power and effectiveness.

- Refuse to make your lover guess whether you care, still value and adore him or her. Tell your lover. Say it often and in a multitude of ways. Let your lover also know where he or she stands with you and your support and loyalty.

Chapter 8

THE DANCE OF

GETTING IN SYNC

Have you noticed that great lovers seem to have *a magical ability to connect* with each other? They seem to just know how to create the kind of rapport that allows them to enter into a state of synchronization with each other. Is there a secret to this? If getting *n sync* refers to an internal sense of synchronization, how do great lovers do this?

As noted in the previous chapters, we create rapport by matching the other person. Great lovers do this to create a rich and satisfying communication. Yet there must be more. While pacing your lover's states, experience, ways of thinking, valuing, etc. enable you to get *in sync* with each other, there's something else. There is something else that connects with the higher levels of your lover's mind, namely, your lover's *meta-mind*.

Have you ever felt so synchronized with your loved one (or anyone for that matter) that it seemed that you were reading from the same script? Perhaps you were finishing each other's thoughts and surprised by how accurately you were reading each other, how together your very thoughts and emotions were. Perhaps you were responding with touch to each other and each touch was so exquisite, and so right, that it delighted you as much as it surprised you.

Being in sync makes loving relating like a dance. You then move with each other with an ease and grace so that thoughts, emotions, and behaviors flow.

What do we call this? We call it rapport, connection, being in sync, and yet it is more.

- What's the secret for this kind of rich connection with a lover?
- How does a person get into sync and stay in sync?
- Is there a way to manage this synchronization process?
- How does such synchronization come about?
- Is there a structure to it?
- How can we replicate it?
- What are the ingredients and components?
- How do we play this *"In Sync" Game?*

The Synchronization of Energy

At a fundamental level of biology, there's a variable that affects the mysterious sense that we often feel when we are "in sync" with someone. I'm referring to our natural biological rhythms and energy patterns. These internal biological clocks, metabolic patterns, and even muscular patterns of fast or slow responses contribute to how each of us experience ourselves and how we respond to others. These biological rhythms then show up in our speech patterns, body movements, and emotional response styles. They are evident in how quickly or slowly we walk, talk, move, and respond. Arising as they do, from the givens of our nervous system and genetic inheritance, they undoubtedly come more from our biology than our psychology.

That some people are more energetic than others, more physically or intellectually or emotionally active and vibrant than others—we all know. And, when we meet someone with a very different rhythm to our own, we often feel a strange sense of being "out of sync" with that person. Something feels out of kilter. Our rhythms do not fit. Emotionally we may feel irritated by the disconnect. We may feel impatient if they are slower than us or pressured if they are faster. At first we may seek to accommodate the other or we may seek to get the other to accommodate us.

When we differ in rhythm and energy from our loved one, it is more typical than not to argue and fight about this energy incompatibility. We want our partner to respond at the rate and speed that feels most comfortable to us and when he or she does not, we may feel out of sync, unloved, frustrated, or a wide range of other emotions.

- Is this feeling of being out of sync inevitable?
- Can we do anything about this sense of our rhythms not being aligned or congruent with each other?

While these patterns may arise from our biology, *what* we think about them and *how* we interpret them also undoubtedly plays a critical role in how we handle our energies. The first step is to recognize it for what it is. This will stop you from turning it into a right/wrong frame or experiencing it as something that has to inevitably create difference, conflict, or judgment. "It's just that we have different bio-rhythmic patterns, it doesn't mean that we are out-of-sync about values, lifestyle, or our passion."

What you experience as your biological energies and rhythms in your body is also affected by your thoughts, beliefs, expectations, and attitudes. In this, your *attitude* is more important than the primary state of your energy. More important are these questions:
*   Are you caring and patient with your lover when his or her energy patterns differ from yours?
*   Do you seek to understand and accept this?
*   Are you able to separate your loved from his or her behavior?
*   Are you willing to learn how to make adjustments in your different energy patterns?

The rhythm of your bio-rhythms does establish much of the feel of your relationship, and its music. Each of us have an energetic rhythm to the way we move through life with its own affective style. When we find someone with a similar rhythm, it feels like magic. We experience a familiarity that makes the connecting so easy and natural. This often is part of the mystery of being "in love."

The Meta-Program Games
Meta-Programs refer to perceptual filters—the lenses through which we look at things. These higher level programs of *how* we are thinking govern our style of paying attention to things and processing information. As a result, they reflect our higher frames of mind. They also create them. The more we use them, the more they create our model of the world or Matrix.

As the meta filters or frames of our Matrix, our meta-programs make up our meta-mind. These higher levels of mind deal with the *structure* of how we think, reason, encode information, and feel about things rather than the *content* of what we think and feel. Meta-programs are like the software of the brain and so our patterned way of thinking, emoting, choosing, and responding.[1]

This is what makes them so stable and predictable. It's what enables us to develop a predictable and patterned style of operating in the world. So we say that we are creatures of habit. Or, we could say that we have simply learned a style for perceiving and filtering things. Both would be accurate descriptions of *meta-programs.*

The fabulous thing about knowing meta-programs as a model is that it enables you to more fully know, understand, and accept yourself and your loved one. Using the Meta-Programs, you can recognize the perceptual filters of your loved one and use them to enter his or her inner world of perceptual frames. Doing that empowers you to mindfully pace so that you create a greater sense of being *in sync* with your loved one. You can then use the meta-programs as another Love Game. You can use them to play the inner *Game of Seeking to Understand and Creating Deeper Rapport.*

Using meta-programs for playing Love Games depends on developing your skills in identifying such patterns and becoming flexible enough to meet your loved one at his or her model of the world. Simply recognizing your lover's meta-programs also deepens your understanding and appreciation. It enriches your ability to meet your loved one at his or her model of the world and that, in turn, reduces resistance, conflict, and unnecessary misunderstandings.

Overview of the Meta-Programs

Meta-programs operate at, and create, a higher level channel of awareness, an awareness of the mental *software* being used to perceive things. This allows us to think about how we and our loved one thinks, sorts, feels, chooses, and communicates apart from any given content. Our words make up the *content* of our conversation and yet simultaneously we operate at multiple levels.

If each of us come out of our own reality, out of our Matrix, and if we can develop a higher level of understanding of each other as we come to recognize and appreciate each other's frames, then we can begin to pace each other at a higher level—at the level of our structural frames. Doing this allows us to enter into the higher levels of each other's reality. This is the value of knowing and using meta-programs.

Connecting with each other at these higher levels means that you recognize and match the patterned way you are experiencing the world. It means moving above content to recognize structure. In *Figuring Out People,* I divided the Meta-Programs Model into four categories:

> *Mental:*   How you think and process information.
> *Emotional:*   How you emote.

>   *Conation:*   How you make choices.
>   *Semantic:*   How you give meaning and value to things.

These response styles make up the domain of meta-programs which govern how we connect or even miss each other. These patterns are not genetically hard-wired into us, but are quite alterable inasmuch as we learned them.

•   Which meta-programs enable us to play the   *Games that Great Lovers Play*?

•   Which meta-programs transform our thinking patters so that we frame things in more loving ways.

•   Are there meta-programs absolutely essential for love and bonding?

•   Are some particularly challenging to love?

At the *content* level of thinking-emoting-and-choosing, we play a cinema on the theater of our mind. We see-hear-and-feel some representation about something that is *on* our mind. That's what we mean by *content.* It is sensory based. It is encoded in see-hear-feel (or empirical) terms.

Figure 8:1
Meta-Levels

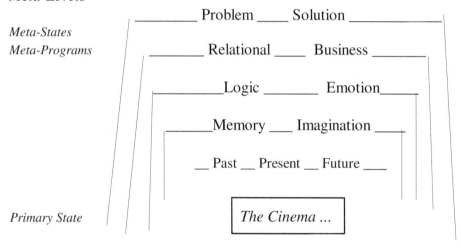

Above and beyond the Cinema we have multiple frames. For example, there are your frames about "time." Are you playing an old Movie from the past or a Movie yet to be experienced in some hoped-for future? You could be processing using a problem frame or a solution frame, a relational frame or a business frame, a logic frame or an emotion frame. You could be seeing a quick overview of the Movie or you could be playing it in minute detail.

The film could be playing in a step-by-step sequence or it could be more random, flashing on a wide range of options. These are but a few of our meta-programs choices.

If being *in sync* is a profound rapport, it is not a shallow rapport lasting only for a few moments. It is a rapport that involves a significantly deep sense of connection. It is one thing to gain rapport through attentive listening and pacing in a conversation, it is quite another to keep and maintain rapport with your loved one that lasts over time and that connects with the highest levels of your mind.

This is the kind of rapport or synchronization you can create by using meta-programs. Meta-Programs provides a way to effectively track with each person at the highest levels of your Matrix. It enables you to see how your lover actually perceives the world and to flexibly respond in appropriate and loving ways.

When you operate from meta-programs that differ from your loved one, your *modus operandi* puts you in different worlds of response and style. If the patterns are complementary, this enriches the relating. If they are not, they can undermine your connection and put you out-of-synchronization. These differences can then put your love to the test.

- Can you extend yourself to and for your loved one?
- How can you take different perceptual styles into account?
- Can you pace your lover to prevent the lack of synchronization from separating you?
- Can you learn to use differing meta-programs to stay in sync?

The following meta-programs are especially challenging for staying connected and in sync with each other. Yet awareness of them and an intention to not let them disconnect you can enable you to put them to good use. As you read them, remember that these are simply response styles and that *you are more than these styles*. Realizing this will free you from over-identifying yourself or your loved one with them. Then it will be easier to not take them personal. They are simply *ways of perceiving* —mental frames for viewing things.

Figure 8:2

Yourself   *Your Loved One*

_____   _____   *The Emotional Coping Game*
Is your style passive, aggressive, or assertive?

_____   _____   *The Compliance / Defiance Game*
How do you experience your self—as strong willed or compliant?

_____   _____   *The Global / Specific Game*
Is your style to watch for global patterns and to dive in for the details?

_____   _____   *The Sameness / Difference Game*
Is your style to sort *for* relationships or *against*?
Do you like best to Match or Mismatch?

_____   _____   *The Favored Representation Game*
What kind of a movie do you prefer to run in your mind: Visual, Auditory, or Kinesthetic?

_____   _____   *The Experiencer / Observer Game*
How do you prefer to see your movie: Inside it or Outside (associated or dissociated)?

_____   _____   *The Motivational Direction Game*
Is your style to move toward or away from?

_____   _____   *The Adaptation Style Game*
Is your preferred style to follow procedures or to go for options?

_____   _____   *The Information Source Game*
Is your style to gather information from your senses or intuitions?

_____   _____   *The Polarization / Holistic Game*
Is your style to think in black-and-white terms or both-and categories?

_____   _____   *The Adaptation / Control Game*
Is your style to judge or to perceive, to control or to adapt?

_____   _____   *The Response Style Game*
Is it your style to be active, reflective, or inactive?

_____   _____   *The Authority Source Game*

Is your style to evaluate internally from yourself or externally from others?

_____ _____ *The Attention Sort Game*
Is your style to pay more attention to yourself or to your lover?

_____ _____ *The Modus Operandi Game*
Is your style to operate from the mode of necessity, possibility, or desire?

_____ _____ *The Convincer Game*
Is your style to quickly believe things or do you need lots of evidence?

_____ _____ *The Primary Interest Game*
What are you mostly interested in: People, Places, Things, Activities, or Information?

_____ _____ *The Going After Goals Game*
Is your style to reject, be perfectionistic, or optimize goals?

_____ _____ *The Time Zones Game*
Where do you mostly live your life—in the past, the present or the future?

_____ _____ *The Time-Lover or Lost in Time Game*
What's your relationship to time?
Do you love it or do you keep forgetting about it?

_____ _____ *Emotional Recharging Game*
What's your style for renewing your batteries—with people (extrovert), by yourself (introvert), or it doesn't matter (ambivert)?

_____ _____ *The Valuing Game*
What do you value? What's important to you?

_____

_____

_____

_____

_____

The Emotional Coping Game
Is your style Passive, Aggressive, or Assertive?
• How do you first operate in the face of stress?
• Do you first react by getting away from it or going at it?
• Do you first respond passively or aggressively?

We differ in how we respond to threat, danger, and overload. Your response pattern when *in stress* from various threatening dangers reflects your basic style for operating in the world and either creates a sense of being in sync or out of it with your loved one.

The aggressing and moving away from responses create the passive / aggressive responses. Those who respond with the aggressive "go at" style enjoy challenges. They like confronting, being direct, and getting things done. Those who respond with a more passive style prefer to "go away from" conflict and stress. They focus on peace and harmony, pleasantness, in getting along and avoiding conflict, and agreement as their highest outcomes.

It is only when you learn to manage these fight/flight responses in yourself that you are able to choose which one will serve you best. This describes *the assertive* response pattern. This one empowers you to choose when to respond passively or aggressively, and whether that's even a good choice. While you respond, you maintain presence of mind which allows you to think and talk out the stresses. What supporting belief, value, or understanding can keep you connected in spite of differing in this meta-program?
• How much *in sync* are you and your loved one about this?
• Is there a conflict or unresourceful pattern regarding this meta-program?
• What do you need to do to honor each person's meta-program *and* find a way to be loving and in sync?

The Compliance / Defiance Game
How do you experience your Self—As Strong Willed or Compliant?
We differ in how we comply or defy orders and rules.
• How do you and your lover respond to orders?
• Does this put you at odds or are you in sync in the way you respond?
• Do you like your response style?
• Do you like your lover's response style?

The strong-willed *defy*. They "can't be told" what to do. When they are told, they feel as if their very "sense of self" is being violated. When *told,* there's an automatic resistance within them. The *compliant* comply. By temperament they are pliable, receptive, open, and sensitive. The first bristles at being told, ordered, demanded, forced, the second just complies.

Strong-willed by temperament people, when in relationships, will frequently feel "controlled, bossed around, and deprived of freedom." Any orders, demands, or obligations seem on their insides to deprive them of the very thing that they use for self-definition, their sense of will or choice.
- How much *in sync* are you and your lover about this?
- Is there a conflict or unresourceful pattern regarding this meta-program?
- What do you need to do to honor each person's meta-program *and* find a way to be loving and in sync?

The Global / Specific Game
Is Your Style to Watch for Global Patterns and to Dive in to the Details?
We differ in regard to the size of information we prefer. Those who prefer small chunks like the specifics and so go for details; they may also prefer data arranged in sequences since they induce upward. They are inductive thinkers. It is their style of reasoning. Those who prefer big chunks want the big picture, the gestalt of the global view. They make sense of the things by the overall frame, the forest first, then the trees. They are deductive thinkers and so move down the scale.

Moving from specific to abstract makes one intuitive and scientific. Chunking down to specifics makes one a philosopher. Which comes first: the big picture or the details?
- How do you and your lover operate in your preference for the size of information?
- How much *in sync* are you and your lover about this?
- Is there a conflict or unresourceful pattern regarding this meta-program?
- What do you need to do to honor each person's meta-program *and* find a way to be loving and in sync?

The Sameness / Difference Game
Is Your Style to Sort for Relationships or Against?
Do you like best to Match or Mismatch?
We differ in how we sort for information and compare data. Some of us sort for how things are alike or the same. We match the new with what we know.

Others sort for what differs, they prefer to *mismatch*. Those who match first and then look for the exception first notice similarities, then differences. Conversely, those who mis-match with exception first notice differences, then similarities.

Find out by simply asking your lover about the relationship between two or more things. How does your job today relate to your last job? What about your current car with your last car?

- Are you in sync with your lover in your style of matching or mis-matching?
- Do you find yourself out of sync due to differing in this pattern?
- Are you willing to recognize your loved one's pattern and to pace it in order to get and stay in sync?
- Is there a conflict or unresourceful pattern regarding this meta-program?
- What do you need to do to honor each person's meta-program *and* find a way to be loving and in sync?

If you find that your lover mismatches, simply pace that style and package your communications accordingly. "Yes, you're right. Taking that approach could have lots of negative side effects, and we don't want that. Yet right now we can't even think of a better alterative."

The Favored Representation Game
What Kind of a Movie Do You Prefer to play in your Mind: Visual, Auditory, or Kinesthetic?
People differ in noticing and representing the sensory data of everyday life. We may favor the visual representation system or the auditory, or the kinesthetic, or the language system. To tell, just listen for the words of your lover and how he or she focuses most on sights (visual), sounds (auditory), sensations (kinesthetic) or words. The predicates in language (the verbs, adverbs, adjectives) are linguistic markers that we use in mapping things.

- What is your and your lover's favorite system?
- What system does your loved one use for feeling loved?
- How does your lover know that you love him or her? What sensory system does your partner primarily use, kinesthetic, visual, or auditory? What combination of these representation system provides the best sequence for your loved one? Do you know what really counts?
- How much *in sync* are you and your lover about this?
- Is there a conflict or unresourceful pattern regarding this meta-program?

- What do you need to do to honor each person's meta-program *and* find a way to be loving and in sync?

The Experiencer / Observer Game
How do you Prefer to See your Movie: Inside it or Outside?
People differ in their emotional response patterns. Some feel strongly and passionately whatever they feel; others seem to live without their emotions, like Mr. Spock from the Starship Enterprise. You can represent your mental movies as if you are *inside* them or *outside* of them. When inside you take the actor's point of view and feel them. When outside, you take the editor's or director's point of view and feel as if external to the action of the movie and just witnessing or observing it.

Associated and dissociated are relative terms. Whenever we *dissociate* from one movie or state of mind-and-emotion, we *associate* into another. We step out of fear and into courage. We step out of joy and into depression. In the stepping out we gain psychological distance from the emotional impact of a movie. We take a spectator's point of view so that we can see and hear and experience the self in the memory.
When we step into the movie, we are one of the characters, usually the lead player. In the *associated* mode, we experience no distance from the movie precisely because we are in it. The movie is immediate, here-and-now, and we are seeing, hearing, and feeling it as we would be when inside the movie. We can now re-experience a memory or an imagination and try the experience on.

- Are you in sync with your lover in how you experience things from feeling them or from observing them?
- Are you and your lover able to fully associate into the experience of making love, being together, enjoying each other's company?

Regarding love making, sharing affection, listening, and most of the ways that we play *the Game of Love,* it is critical that you do not attempt to do so *outside* the movie. These are times to fully step into the movie. By all means, avoid dissociating when you are making love. That will not work if you want to feel close or give your lover a great time. In relating, we especially need our emotions and need to use them effectively in connecting, loving, and being present to the other. We need to know when to step into our representations and feel them, and when to step out to just observe.

- How much *in sync* are you and your lover about this?
- Is there a conflict or unresourceful pattern regarding this meta-program?
- What do you need to do to honor each person's meta-program *and*

find a way to be loving and in sync?

Observing from outside is mostly a male orientation. Many men have not developed the emotional intelligence involved in empathizing or sympathizing that lets them know how to step inside another's description or experience to know how it *feels from inside.* To do so mostly involve permission to do so and then some practice.

The Motivational Direction Game
Is Your Style to Move Toward or Away From?
People differ regarding goals they value as important as those they dis-value as aversive. You may immediately *move toward* what you value, want to achieve, and your goals. This lets your desired outcomes *pull* you into your future. You may *move away from* the things you dis-value and do not want. You avoid what you find aversive.

Find out by simply asking about your lover's objectives, values, and goals. What do you want from a relationship, job, etc.? The person who moves *toward* values and things will speak about goals and wants. The person who moves *away from* will speak about what they want to get away from, avoid, and no longer experience.
*   Are you in sync with your lover about your motivation style?
*   Do you and your lover operate in very different ways in terms of what you move toward and away from?
*   Are able are you to understand and pace your loved one's style?
*   Is there a conflict or unresourceful pattern regarding this meta-program?
*   What do you need to do to honor each person's meta-program *and* find a way to be loving and in sync?

The Adaptation Style Game
Is your Preferred Style to follow Procedures or to opt for Options?
People differ in how they go about doing things. Do you adapt yourself by following the right way to do things or by seeking lots of choices? You may prefer clear-cut and defined *procedures.* If so, you like finding and following the rules. You would then want step-by-step procedures so that you can do things right, and having closure.

You may prefer *options* and so want alternatives and choices. You would then not want to follow rules and procedures, you would rather invent them. You would prefer to improve things and to creatively innovate new things.

Find out by asking a *why* question: "Why did you choose your car?" (or job, town, etc.). Then listen for how the person responds. Those who like options will speak about making a choice and about expanding their options. Those who prefer step-by-step, procedures will tell a story or many stories that will give lots of facts. It is as if they are answering the why question as if asked a how to question.

- Are you and your lover in sync in preferring options and/or procedures?
- If not, how willing are you to understand and pace your lover's preference and style?

Especially be aware of this meta-program if you want to effectively work and act together. This is especially true when you plan, go on a trip, do chores, etc. Couples who radically differ in this can find the other person's style irritating and insulting until they discover what's occurring and then de-moralize this filtering program.

- How much *in sync* are you and your lover about this?
- Is there a conflict or unresourceful pattern regarding this meta-program?
- What do you need to do to honor each person's meta-program *and* find a way to be loving and in sync?

The Information Source Game
Is Your Style to Gather Information from your Senses or Intuitions?
People differ in how they gather information. You may prefer to use your *senses* to gather information through empirical senses. If so, you focus on the sensory input from seeing, hearing, feeling, smelling, and tasting. Liking to deal with concrete experiences, you prefer a more empirical and pragmatic approach. Or you may prefer to gather information by figuring things out from within your thinking and experiencing, by intuiting. You prefer to look for relationships between things, for possibilities, and for meanings. You prefer to approach things abstractly using a more rational and philosophical style.

- Are you and your lover in sync in gathering information? To what degree?
- Do you know your preferred style and that of your loved one?
- Do you know how to pace your lover's style?
- Is there a conflict or unresourceful pattern regarding this meta-program?
- What do you need to do to honor each person's meta-program *and* find a way to be loving and in sync?
- How can you sequence your communications so that empirical and

intuitive knowledge can synergize?

The Polarization / Holistic Game
Is your style to think in Black-and-white terms or Both-And Categories?

People differ in how they classify things and handle categories. You may discern broad categories and think in terms of the polar ends. Doing so makes you more of a black-or-white thinker. Or you may use a more sophisticated discernment as you sort for every nuance of grey. Black-and-white thinkers are able to make clear and definite distinctions, quick decisions, and decisive judgments. This makes them more definite and firm, and can lead to intolerance, being dogmatic, and seduced by perfectionism. *Both-And* thinkers think more systemically and will discriminate at finer levels which makes them more indecisive as they keep qualifying most of everything they say. They talk about gray areas and use lots of qualifiers.

- Are you and your lover in sync in these thinking patterns?
- Do you know your preferred style and that of your loved one?
- Do you know how to pace your lover's style?
- Is there a conflict or unresourceful pattern regarding this meta-program?
- What do you need to do to honor each person's meta-program *and* find a way to be loving and in sync?

The Adaptation / Control Game
Is your Style to Judge or to Perceive, to Control or to Adapt?

People differ in how they adapt to life. Do you adapt yourself to the world or do you seek to get the world to adapt to you? If you want life and events to adapt to you, you will make *judgments* about how things should be and set out to make things happen. This is the style of living life by a plan and doing things in an orderly fashion. It involves wanting closure, having definite boundaries, and clear cut categories and rules.

If, however, you want adapt yurself to life and events, you will move through life *perceiving* more than adapting. You simply perceive, observe, note, accept, and flow through life taking whatever happens for whatever it is. This style involves fewer judgments and more spontaneity. It focuses more on accepting than changing things.

- Are you and your lover in sync in adapting?
- Do you know your preferred style and that of your loved one?
- Do you know how to pace your lover's style?
- Is there a conflict or unresourceful pattern regarding this meta-

program?
- What do you need to do to honor each person's meta-program *and* find a way to be loving and in sync?

The Response Style Game
Is it your Style to be Active, Reflective, or Inactive?
People differ in their activities, especially in responding to new situations. You may be very *active* and immediately want to do something to make something happen. If your style is to act first and think later, you may be more in the class of entrepreneurs, go-getters, and among the movers and shakers. Or you may prefer to *reflectively* study to ponder things and so take a more passive and contemplative orientation. You may feel afraid of being rash. You could also have a mixture of these styles. Or you may be *inactive* and prefer to neither study nor act, but ignore and do nothing.
- Are you and your lover in sync in response style?
- Do you know your preferred style and that of your loved one?
- Do you know how to pace your lover's style?
- Is there a conflict or unresourceful pattern regarding this meta-program?
- What do you need to do to honor each person's meta-program *and* find a way to be loving and in sync?

The Authority Source Game
Is your style to Evaluate Internally from Yourself or Externally from Others?
People differ in their locus of control and in evaluating of people, situations, experiences, and ideas. When you move to the *self-referent* mode, you think and operate from an internal locus of control and things on basis of what *you* think. You motivate yourself, make your own decisions, choose and validate for yourself, and gather information from others when you make a decision. When you operate in the external or *other-referent* mode, you evaluate things on basis of what others think, feel, and want. You look to others for guidance, information, motivation, and decisions.

Find out by asking, "How do you know?" questions. "How do you know that you are right? That you've done a good job? That you chose the right bank (right car)?" People with an other-referent orientation will talk about getting information from outside sources while those with an internal locus of control will say, "I just know. It feels right."
- Are you and your lover in sync in your referencing style?
- Do you know your preferred style and that of your loved one?
- Do you know how to pace your lover's style?

- Is there a conflict or unresourceful pattern regarding this meta-program?
- What do you need to do to honor each person's meta-program *and* find a way to be loving and in sync?

The Attention Sort Game
Is your style to pay more attention to yourself or to your lover?
People differ in what they pay attention to. Do you adapt yourself to the world or do you seek to get the world to adapt to you? You may prefer to first pay attention to yourself—what you want, think, feel, choose, or do. Self Sorters tend to know their own mind and heart; they tend to be able to more easily center themselves within their circle of response. And when over-done, they may have less awareness of others than is important for healthy relationships. This is the Self Attention Sort.

Conversely, you may prefer first to pay attention to others—what they want, think, feel, choose, or do. This leads you to be very understanding, sensitive *to* others, empathetic, helpful, intuitive about the feelings and states of others. When over-done, it may lead to not knowing yourself, and dogmatically declaring that you know best what others need and so lead into care-taking and co-dependency.

Find out by asking a *what* a person is paying attention to. "What are you aware of when you are at the party or engaged in a conversation?" Listen for what the person talks about attending, is it more about self or other?
- Are you and your lover in sync in operating from your attention on self or other?
- If not, how willing are you to understand and pace your lover's preference and style?

Especially be aware of this meta-program for feelings of being loved and valued. To not be attended in a context where that's important and significant is to feel unloved. It can lead the other to question whether they are noticed at all. It may lead to charges and accusations of the other being selfish and egocentric.
- How much *in sync* are you and your lover about this?
- Is there a conflict or unresourceful pattern regarding this meta-program?
- What do you need to do to honor each person's meta-program *and* find a way to be loving and in sync?

The Modus Operandi Game

Is your style to Operate from the Mode of Necessity, Possibility, or Desire?

People differ in their Modus Operandi. *Modus operandi* describes a person's style or mode of operating in the world. This is actually reflected in the words that we use, words which linguists call modal operators. These words reflect our model of the world and describe our reasons for acting as we do.

> Necessity words like *must, have to,* and *should* imply operating from a model of law, rule, and control.

> Impossibility words like *can't, shouldn't,* and *must not* indicate a world of what can't be done, constraints, problems, and blockages.

> Possibility words like *can, will, may, would,* and *could* reflect an optimistic model of what we can possibly do.

> Desire words like *want to, love to,* and *get to* indicate a model of desire.

> Choice words like *choose to, want to,* and *opt for* indicate a model of choice.

Find out by asking any question about a person's motivation: "Why did you choose your present job? Or, Why have you chosen this school, that schedule, etc.?" Then listen for reasons (possibility, wants to) or no reasons (he has to).

- Are you and your lover in sync in your *modus operandi?*
- Do you know your preferred style and that of your loved one?
- Do you know how to pace your lover's style?
- Is there a conflict or unresourceful pattern regarding this meta-program?
- What do you need to do to honor each person's meta-program *and* find a way to be loving and in sync?

The Convincer Game

Is your style to quickly believe things or do you need lots of evidence?

People differ in what convinces them about something. You may believe, decide, and act because that thing *looks right.* You may need it to *sound right,* you may because it *feels right,* or you may because it *makes sense.* To tell, ask questions presupposing decision-making:

> Why did you decide on your present choice of car?
> What helps you decide where to vacation?
> Which mode does he sort by?
> How often does it take to become believable?

Now for the personal questions for you and your loved one:

- Are you and your lover in sync in becoming convinced?
- Do you know your preferred style and that of your loved one?
- Do you know how to pace your lover's style?
- Is there a conflict or unresourceful pattern regarding this meta-program?
- What do you need to do to honor each person's meta-program *and* find a way to be loving and in sync?

The Primary Interest Game
What are you mostly interested in: People, Places, Things, Activities, or Information?
People differ about their primary interests and focus of attention. Some focus on people (the who), place (the where), things (the what), activity (the how), information (the why), what (the information), and/or time (the when).

Find out by asking your lover about a favorite way to take a vacation, kind of work, best life experiences to evoke the preference filter. "What's important to you in choosing how to spend two weeks on holiday?" "What kinds of things, people, activities, etc. would have to be there for it to be really great for you?" Listen for what matters most:
   Who they are with (people).
   Where they are (location, place).
   Things involved (objects, things).
   Kinds of behaviors/activities to do (activity).
   Kind of data available or experienced (information).

Now for the personal questions for you and your loved one:
- Are you and your lover in sync in your interests and preferences?
- Do you know your preferred style and that of your loved one?
- Do you know how to pace your lover's style?
- Is there a conflict or unresourceful pattern regarding this meta-program?
- What do you need to do to honor each person's meta-program *and* find a way to be loving and in sync?

The Going After Goals Game
Is your Style to Reject, be Perfectionistic, or Optimize Goals?
People differ in how we go after their goals. How do you and your partner go after a mutual goal? You may aim for flawless perfection and you want it just right. Nothing less will do. You may go for the best that you can do and leave it at that—optimizing your skills and opportunities without any need to be flawless. Or you may doubt whether striving for any goal has any

value or merit and so avoid goals altogether as you skeptically call everything into question.

Perfectionists are never satisfied with performance. The voice in their heads continually shouts, "It could have been better! It was not good enough!" They make their goals unrealistically high which leaves them constantly frustrated as they over-value the end product and discount the process of getting to goal. *Optimizers* seek to optimize things to do the best they can, and leave it at that. They set goals in small steps and appreciate the little stages of success along the way. *Avoiders* discount goals, refuse to admit wants, focus on spontaneity, the now. They are often burned-out perfectionists.

This meta-program enables us to predict and understand when a person will stop persevering, how the person will set goals, strive, recognize attainment, motivate self, and work together. Perfectionists begin well, then get bogged down in details and caught up in negative emotions. As they over-focus on end products, they feel overwhelmed and so procrastinate. Optimizers flow along, set more moderate goals, produce what they can, and enjoy the process.

- Are you and your lover in sync in goal setting and achieving?
- Do you know your preferred style and that of your loved one?
- Do you know how to pace your lover's style?
- Is there a conflict or unresourceful pattern regarding this meta-program?
- What do you need to do to honor each person's meta-program *and* find a way to be loving and in sync?

The Time Zones Game
Where do you mostly Live your life—in the Past, the Present or the Future?
People differ in how they process, understand, experience, and respond to time and time characteristics: direction, duration, orientation and continuity. You may be oriented to the past, present, or future. You may live in the past —thinking about where you have been and then get caught up in your history. When you use past references, you will speak in past tenses and find the past recruiting you to return again and again. When you live in the now, you will use present tenses and references. This will recruit you to enter into *today*. You may also speak about *the now* to such an extent and so exclusively that you may not think consequentially. This can lead to impulsiveness. You may also live in the future, using future tenses and references, and be forever planning for the future and never getting down to

do anything *today.*
* Are you and your lover in sync in time?
* Do you know your preferred style and that of your loved one?
* Do you know how to pace your lover's style?
* Is there a conflict or unresourceful pattern regarding this meta-program?
* What do you need to do to honor each person's meta-program *and* find a way to be loving and in sync?

The Time-Lover or Lost in Time Game
What's your relationship to Time?
Do you Love it or do you keep Forgetting about it?

People differ in their sense of time's duration. You may perceive time from within it as if being *inside* it. This mode of *in time* means you are *in* it —associated, present, and participating. Time seems to be a line behind you with the future out in front of you. This allows you to live in *the now,* to be random about how you operate.

Through time describes you if you are *out* of time and experience time consciously so that you see "time" as if from a distance. You experience "time" as if continuous, sequential, linear, and our memories sorted out. This enables you to operate sequentially and linearly.
* Are you and your lover in sync in time?
* Do you know your preferred style and that of your loved one?
* Do you know how to pace your lover's style?
* Is there a conflict or unresourceful pattern regarding this meta-program?
* What do you need to do to honor each person's meta-program *and* find a way to be loving and in sync?

The Emotion Recharging Game
What's your style for Renewing your Batteries—With people (Extrovert), by yourself (Introvert), or it doesn't matter (Ambivert)?

People differ in how they seek to renew their batteries when they are down or discouraged. You may be *extroverted* and turn to others for support, encouragement, and personal renewal. You may be *introverted* and turn inward to get off by yourself when you need to deal with stress. If you are an ambivert, you can shift back and forth in a balanced way. When you need your batteries recharged do you want to be with others or get away by yourself?
* Are you and your lover in sync in recharging your batteries?
* Do you know your preferred style and that of your loved one?

- Do you know how to pace your lover's style?
- Is there a conflict or unresourceful pattern regarding this meta-program?
- What do you need to do to honor each person's meta-program *and* find a way to be loving and in sync?

This meta-program is crucial for coupling because you need to know when your loved one needs your presence or the presence of others (extroverts) and when your lover may need some "space" and distance apart (introverts). These are battery recharging issues. And as such, they have nothing to do with love, although lack of attention here or mis-interpretation can do damage to your love life.

The Valuing Game
Each meta-program indicates a preferred or valued way of thinking which governs how you pay attention to things and what you sort for. In this,*each meta-program reflects and/or sets a "value" frame.* Each reflects what you value as important and significant. This also indicates that *everything you value* operates as a meta-program in that it becomes a filter or lens through which you see the world.

What you value, you esteem as significant and meaningful. In this way, you magnetized your values with emotion. You invest emotion by appreciating, enjoying, caring, and desiring them. Conversely, when you dis-value you feel negative emotions toward the things that threatens what you value. In this sense, *values* provide a basic perceptual and motivational structure in our mind through which you can invest your time, energy, and resources.

Abraham Maslow created a hierarchy of needs and wants which reflect our values as human beings and which are our biological inheritance. He classified the lower needs into the classes of survival, safety and security, love, affection, and belonging, and self-esteem. He classified all of the higher and uniquely human needs into the category of self-actualization. Within this list are the values that drive us as human beings: power, control, achievement, affiliation, transcendence, ease, pleasure, romance, sex, knowledge, religion, harmony, challenge, love, peace, joy, happiness, success, achievement, trust, relationships, being healthy, etc.
Find out by asking:
- What is important, valuable, and meaningful to my lover?
- What does my lover mostly value and adore?
- What does my lover go toward?
- What does my lover move away from?

Now for the personal questions:
- Are you and your lover in sync in the way you value and in what you value?
- Do you know your preferred style and that of your loved one?
- Do you know how to pace your lover's style?
- Is there a conflict or unresourceful pattern regarding this meta-program?
- What do you need to do to honor each person's meta-program *and* find a way to be loving and in sync?

Summary

- To play *The Getting in Sync Game* enables you to match and connect with each other for a deeper and higher sense of bonding. Connecting in how you and your loved one operates in the world will in turn govern your level and quality of being *in sync* with each other.

- Your natural energy levels and expressions creates one of the most basic connections and you can learn to adjust them so as to not mis-interpret them in a way that dis-bonds. Some bonding is more physiological than psychological.

- Meta-programs explain how you connect or don't connect with your lover in how you filter and sort for things. This affects your psychological bonding. It also suggests things that you can do about the mismatches you find. The natural connections that put you in sync are made up of the meta-programs that you share.

- The meta-programs in which you differ describe the challenges to your bonding connection with your lover and your flexibility to stay connected in spite of having different styles.

End Notes:

1. For more about meta-programs, see   *Figuring Out People* (1997) and *Words that Change Minds*. These NLP books present the meta-domain of the Meta-Programs Model. For more about self-actualization, see *Self-Actualization Psychology* (2007).

Chapter 9

THE DANCE OF
CONSCIOUS LOVING

- Can we love intentionally and mindfully?
- Does intentionality change the quality of love?
- Does a loving relationship involve planning?
- Must love be spontaneous and without any planning at all?
- How do our ideas and feelings about the future effect our feelings of love and connection in the moment?

These are but a few questions that we can ask about how Great Lovers frame things and the games that they play in their relating, giving and receiving of love, and their planning for the future. There are many more. The following questions orient us to *taking an intentional and purposeful stance in our relating* and the possibility of becoming more mindful about where we are going with each to enhance our bonding.

- What goals do you have with your loved one?
- Where are you going as a couple?
- What visions and dreams unite you?
- What values and meanings galvanize you in your future plans?
- What happens when you find, discover, create, and/or implement your visions and values into your relationship?
- Do you feel that you are going somewhere and that the relationship is working, in being purposeful?
- Or do you feel stress and pressure that you have to accomplish something?

When you fall in love, it's most natural that you entertain ideas about the future that you will create together. Falling in love usually motivates us to want to be with that person and so we begin planning how to live together and how to share our lives. Typically, this leads to many other plans and sub-plans. Traditionally it means creating a home, having and raising children, growing together, sharing life's challenges and joys. People who do this then feel that they are living in a purposeful way—that they are going somewhere. It gives them a reference point for evaluating where they are at and how they are progressing in their life journey together.

The Forecasting a Future Together Game

The best way to live more purposefully and intentionally is to begin with a co-created outcome. "What is our preferred future?" Starting with an ultimate outcome in mind gives you something to guide your everyday actions. To create this preferred future, use your vision to develop what we call in NLP *a well-formed outcome.*

Then you can use that vision to navigate your everyday pathway into the future. This lets you orient yourself in terms of your direction, of where you want to go, and of the kind of life you want to experience. Developing a visionary outcome connects your relating and bonding to your values and highest meanings. Failing to do this, you will drift along with circumstances life throws at you and react when you face unpleasant situations.

Developing a well-formed vision of your preferred future enables you to articulate your sense of mission about your relationship and to base your relating on the meanings and values you care about. To do this you have to use your meaning-making powers to describe what you want.

The Preferred Future Game

To forecast where you are going and how you will get there, you speak about moving from your present state to a future state. By contrasting how your preferred future differs from your present state clarifies the specific steps you need to take to move to your mutually created outcome. This contrasting process also helps you to specify the resources that you will need to move forward.

- What outcomes do you want for yourself and your loved one?
- What goals and dreams are you dreaming together?
- How well formed are those dreams?

The nice thing about forming your well-formed outcomes is that you can use them as guiding principles for making decisions in your everyday lives. Then you can use them as your criteria:

- Does this contribute in a meaningful way to our vision?

- What am I doing that moves us in the direction of our dream?
- What else could we do that would support our long-term goals?

As you develop and define your intentional objectives, you can use those very goals as your frame of reference for evaluating what you can do to translate them into reality. Envisioning your objective with clarity and precision gives you a clearer understanding of what to do today. It exercises your proactive powers to specify your desired outcomes. In this way you can use your preferred future to prevent you from getting caught up in the activity trap or running on the treadmill of "busyness." Many fall into the busyness trap by working harder and harder without moving any closer to their goals. They may be efficient, but they are not effective in actualizing their goals. Being truly effective begins with making sure you are headed in the right direction.

- What is your definition of relational success?
- How will you know that you have accomplished your objectives with your lover?

Dreaming and planning to make dreams real activates your creative energies and puts you in the driver seat. Conversely, when you don't plan, you default to let circumstances, events, and emotions determine your future. This undermines your sense of being in charge of your own life and fuels dis-empowerment. It invites you to live your life by default. When you do not set goals and directions, you choose to live without direction. And by failing to develop your own desired outcomes and the self-awareness to proactively take responsibility for it, you give your power away to others. You let circumstances shape your lives. You live in a reactive way to the scripts handed you by family, upbringing, others, and circumstances. In actuality, failing to plan is planning to fail.

When you plan together for where you want your relationship to go, you are co-leading your relational lives. Such co-creating and co-leading enables you to set the vision that inspires you and to identify your goals. From there you can set out together and do the things that will enable you to achieve that. After setting the vision, you are able to co-manage the everyday activities and tasks to endow your dreams and goals with specific action plans. This empowers you to make them happen. In managing the specifics you operate efficiently and effectively. As a couple, your mutual *leading* establishes your preferred future and your mutual *co-managing* engages the action plan.

It takes some active initiation to set well-formed outcomes. Begin by using your imagination and design your mutually compelling vision. Then, execute that vision day to day. By regularly stepping back from your maps and quality controlling them, you can keep refining them. This allows you to continually update the maps for your journey as a couple. It enables you to develop the *self-mastery* of designing and implementing well-formed outcomes as a couple.

What skill do you need for all of this? One skill is that of *stepping up* in your mind to a higher perspective. Then you can look at the quality of your thinking-and-feeling and to quality control it.

- Are they appropriate, wise, useful, enhancing?
- Is our vision empowering or toxic?

Designing Well-formed Relational Outcomes

Suppose you are highly reactive to your partner's bad moods. Suppose you have learned to quickly tense up, feel defensive, and respond in kind? Suppose you get into battles with each other in this way. What can you do? How do you go about creating a well-formed outcome?

1) Write a description of your present state.
> What is currently going on?
> What are the triggers that set it off?
> What thoughts and feelings are activated?

2) Quality control your present state.
> Does this enhance your life as a couple?
> Does it empower you as individuals?
> Does it make your life loving, passionate, and exciting?
> Does it make our love life stable, solid, and strong?

3) Design a new pattern and outcome.
> What would you prefer to do as a more enhancing way to relate?
> What resources would you prefer to access and operate from?
> How could you relate in a way that would be more empowering, acceptable, and enhancing for both of you?
> What can I do to take proactive responsibility for my actions?
> What shifts would I need to make in my self-image and self-definition that would allow me to make this transformation?

4) Step into that desired future.
> Begin with the end in mind by stepping into that imagined future and notice what it's like.
> Do you like that? How could you make it even better?
> What matters most to you when you are here?
> What are the critical values that you want to cultivate in this relationship?

(Menu: dignity, calmness, working things out, maintaining relationship, love, compassion, gentleness, thoughtful, etc.)

5) Edit your desired future until it becomes more and more compelling.
    What ideas are you now going to make part of your vision?
    How will you make these qualities part of the way you respond?

6) Step back to the now to let that future pull on you.
    Do you now clearly see a better way to respond?
    How compelling is that cinema in your mind?
    Are you willing to let this pull on you and influence your thoughts and feelings and actions today?
    Do you want to become that person in your future cinema and experience the resourcefulness of that movie?
    Are you willing to do what it takes to get there?

Once you have designed and installed several well-formed outcomes for your journey of love, use them to write a longer document that expresses your personal vision of your preferred future as a couple. As you do, you will set an even larger direction for your life that balances your purposes and goals from many different areas.

A preferred future vision statement allows you to chart out a direction that integrates all of your roles, functions, and purposes in life. It helps you internalize your meanings and values so that you can best choose the behaviors and responses that truly serve your values.
•   What is your overall mission for relationship together?
•   What are your goals and objectives within this larger vision?
•   What kind of a character do you want to develop?
•   What do you want to achieve and accomplish as a couple?
•   What do you want to experience?
•   What values and principles do you want to live your life by?
•   What legacy do you want to leave?

You can then incorporate your desired outcomes into your relating as you use it as part of your intimate talk with each other. You can use it as part of your nightly pillow talk. After all, being able to internally see-hear-and-feel the future gives you a map for how to get there. Writing a preferred future vision about your mutual love helps you to integrate things because writing itself is a psycho-neural muscular activity. Writing helps to integrate the conscious and unconscious parts of your mind-body system distilling, crystallizing, and clarifying things.

Actually, the very *process* of designing your vision is as important as what you produce. The thinking, writing, imagining, etc. invites you to think through your priorities, align your behavior with your beliefs, and integrate your goals. All of this makes you more conscious in your loving and relating. The process allows you to become centered in your values and meanings as a couple and to feel that you are driven by your mutually created vision of your life together. This makes you less dependent upon circumstances. It makes you more self-directed and congruent, more aligned and focused.

Summary

- When you love consciously and intentionally you discover the joy and magic of loving with purpose and focus. This lets you manage the relationship with more intention and translate your highest intentions into actual loving behaviors on a day by day basis.

- Loving consciously and intentionally enables you to become a much greater lover as it puts the art of love into your hands and not at the mercy of the fates.

Chapter 10

THE DANCE OF
PLEASURE
AND PLEASURING

- How much pleasure do you want from an intimate relationship?
- What kind of pleasures mean the most to you?
- How much pleasure do you think is possible?
- Can the pleasures of sensuality and sexuality last?
- Do you want the pleasures to last or to get better over the years?
- What pleasuring skills do you have that enriches the pleasures that you share together?

We bond and connect for the pleasure it gives us. *Pleasure* is what draws us into bonding relationships. There is the primary physical pleasures of touch, presence, companionship, affection, desire, passion, sensuality, and sexuality. And there's more. There are the higher level pleasures of what all of that *means* to us—love, connection, appreciation, support, etc.

The Games of Pleasure
Far too many people live miserable lives of quiet, and not-so-quiet, desperation in their closest and most bonded relationships. Yet that's not why you connect and relate, is it? You connect in order to increase your pleasure, delight and enjoyment, do you not? Isn't it for pleasure and fun that you want to find a loved one to be with and enjoy life with?

Pleasure (as in joy, delight, fun) is what we experience at the primary level and *happiness* (as in joy of joy, fun of fun, the joy of delight) is what takes place at the meta-levels of our mind-body-emotion system. This means that happiness, as a meta-state, is a higher level awareness.

Pleasure, as a primary state experience, operates as a function of our senses —the pleasures of sight, sound, sensation, movement, smell, and taste. *Enjoyment* or happiness, operates as a higher-order phenomenon. To experience *pleasure*, you only need the sensory equipment of your eyes, ears, nose, and skin. That will do it. To experience enjoyment, you need to bring your mindfulness to your experiences and embrace the experience with a special way of thinking—with *happy* thoughts.

To experience the higher levels of pleasure, you have to apply pleasant, accepting, validating, loving, appreciating, and enjoying *thinking-and-feeling states* about the first level experiences of sight, sound, sensation, smell, taste. That's why your enjoyments differ so greatly. We differ in our thoughts about the sensory experience. We do so by using different belief frames, understanding frames, and conceptual frames. You may give it pleasant meanings, another says that he finds it boring, dull, unpleasant, nasty, and obnoxious, and yet another finds it an ecstasy!

So while we all have a similar enough nervous system and sense receptors to commonly find the same kind of things generally pleasurable (within neurological limits), it is in the wide range of our meta-thoughts (beliefs, values, understandings, criteria) about our pleasures that creates an incredible amount of variety in how we experience happiness.

The structure of happiness involves bringing happy thoughts and applying them to some pleasure and framing the experience with thoughts of delight and pleasure. It's for this reason that in human experience, any of us can learn to feel "happy" about almost anything.

Figure 10:1
The Meta-Levels of Pleasure

Meta-State: "Happy" thoughts of Validation, appreciation, love, joy, value, etc.

↓

Primary-State: Some sensory Pleasure   →   Event in world

Happiness results *not* so much from more primary level experiences, but from *the ability to appreciate*—that is, to see value, to endow with meaning, to give more importance and significance to something. What this means in your everyday life is absolutely incredible. It means that the more significance you give to an experience—the more pleasant and enjoyable you make it. Then so it becomes to you. You fill your mind-body-emotion system with much more pleasure. *The secret of pleasuring is as simple as that and as profound as that.* As such, this provides a secret avenue for increasing your happiness and enjoyment in life, does it not? Actually, you have fantastic powers of pleasuring. You only need to discover them and begin to use them.

Exploring Your Pleasures Game
This pattern enables you to take a primary level pleasure and use it to discover your meta-level strategy for inducing higher level joy.
1) Make a "fun" list.
>What do you have fun doing?
>What are some of the things you do *for fun?*
>How many things can you list that give you a sense of delight and pleasure?
>Make a list of all the things that make you happy and include in it anything that gives you a sense of enjoyment, happiness, thrill, pleasure.
>"What I have fun doing, experiencing, seeing, etc. is ..."

2) Identify one pleasure that you really enjoy.
>What is one small and simple thing that you can describe in empirical terms that gives you lots of pleasure?
>We will use it to elicit your structure of happiness and meta-pleasures.
>Test to make sure you have a sensory-based referent (i.e., running, soaking in a hot tub, back massage, watching a sunset, playing with a kitten, reading a book, taking a walk, sexual intimacy, etc.).
>Can you see, hear, feel, smell or taste it?
>Can you make a Movie of it in your mind?

3) Exploring the internal world of your pleasure.
>What is this pleasure like? Describe it fully.
>Describe it in sensory based terms. What do you see, hear, feel, smell, taste, etc. when you are experiencing this pleasure in just the way you really like it?

4) Explore the meta-levels of pleasures about this pleasure.
> What is so pleasurable about this experience?
> Why do you like it so much?
> What does it do for you?
> How do you value and appreciate it so much?
> What is its meaning and significance to you?
> What else do you enjoy about this primary pleasure?

5) Elicit a first row of meta-pleasures then go up the levels.
> Ask questions until you have three to six first level pleasures of value and significance about the pleasure experience.
> *   What else does this mean to you?
> *   How else is this valuable and significant?
> *   What other meanings do you give to this?
> *   What positive meaning of value and significance do you give to this pleasure?
>
> *Diagram* the meta-levels of meanings as you go up the levels in order to be able to track the words and terms of pleasure about the primary pleasure (see Figure 10:2). Remember that as you go up the levels, your awareness shifts from the primary pleasure to the joy and delight in each higher level meaning. How is this pleasurable or meaningful to you? What do you get when you get this pleasure fully and completely in just the way you like it?

Figure 10:2
Example of the Meta-Levels of Pleasure

Meta-State	Be a sane person
	↓
Meta-State	Greater Self-Control
	↓
Meta-State	

	Relaxation	Health	Quiet Time	Cleanliness
	↓	↓	↓	↓

Primary-State	Taking a Hot Shower Or Sitting in a Hot Tub

6) Continue the upward exploration until you get to the top.

Continue with the questioning until you begin to loop around some of the responses or until you hear a lot of "edge of the map" type words and phrases, "only, just, absolute," "It's just this." "That's just the way it is." "There's nothing more above that."

7) Step into the experience of your highest pleasures.

Take a moment and just be with these pleasures and joys and let them inform your mind and body ... and radiate throughout your entire neurology because these are your values and meanings that give this experience so much significance and creates these feelings, is it not?

8) Sit back and appreciate the entire pleasure gestalt.

Now sit back for a moment and just notice the power and wonder of this entire experience ... notice it perhaps for the first time in life. Notice all of the joy that it creates in your mind-body-emotion system.

Appreciate that these are yours and that you created them. And allow yourself to recognize that these meanings *drive* your pleasure. They give it its meaning, energy, motivation, and power. Now you know *why* it holds so much meaning for you.

9) Begin to spread the highest pleasuring around.

As you step into your highest meta-pleasure states and access them fully so that you let them do their work of delighting and making you feel great, just enjoy the feelings for a moment ... That' right ... hmmmmm... and begin to wonder... to really wonder where else you could spread this pleasure, because you might want to spread it around and attach it to other primary experiences like shaking someone's hand, talking on the phone, taking a walk, the range of possibilities are endless.

As you become more fully aware of these pleasant and even ecstatic meanings that fill you with so much pleasure, just imagine taking these feelings into more and more of your everyday activities. How does that feel?

What other everyday sensory-based activities can you creatively imagine using to trigger these feelings?

Imagine fully being in this state in some particular context doing a task that you know is important but that you don't get all that much pleasure from ... That's right... and just *feel this*. There you go.

And now scan around in your mind about those everyday tasks of relating to your loved one and *feel this* as you take care of the small things that need to be attended to.   That's right.

The "Having Fun With My Loved One" Game

By taking just one pleasure in this way, and eliciting your meta-level thoughts-and-feelings about that pleasure and then meta-thoughts and feelings about those states, etc. enables you to build up a multi-level structure that reflects your highest pleasuring states. This invites you into a pleasure matrix. This process also allows you to map out what we pleasure and then *how* you pleasure that pleasure. This structure specifies your happy thoughts —the value thoughts, thoughts of significance and appreciation, etc. about the pleasure. It describes your motives for engaging in the experience. It specifies *what you get out of* the experience—conceptually. It identifies your neuro-semantic world.

Now we can ask other highly important questions about those pleasures:
•   Do I have *enough* meaning and value built in it to get me to use this behavior for triggering my sense of happiness?
•   What other meanings would I like to attribute to the pleasure?
•   Do I need to turn up my awareness and meanings of the pleasure?
•   Have I over-loaded the experience or behavior with too many meanings?

Is all of this really that important? If so, why is this important? Yes it is important. For intimate bonding relationships it is important that you have plenty of pleasure in being with your loved one, that it delights you and delights your loved one. And, once you know *the process and structure of pleasuring*—of endowing behaviors and experiences with pleasant and powerful meanings, then nothing can stop you from doing this with anything and everything in the relationship.

Imagine this!
     Do you want more pleasure, fun, and motivation in seeing your loved one at the end of the day?
     Would you like to attach more enriched meanings to taking a walk, talking about something you've read, or planning a trip?

You can. You can attached more pleasure to the daily chores, to all of the details that make life easier, and to the significance of just holding and cuddling. Too often we get so caught up in life's everyday tasks that we forget to enjoy ourselves along the way. Has that ever happened to you? What if you took time to pleasure yourselves with a walk, a date, soaking in a hot bath, a candlelight dinner for no particular reason, or a hundred other pleasures? Would that enrich things?

This pleasure pattern gives you a way to increase your motivation and desire for any activity. I have noticed that I can *amplify my pleasure*, my joy, my happiness, and my motivation in things as simple as taking a hot shower. I do that by simply getting into the shower and bringing my senses to the experience. What a concept! It's amazing how much joy we can experience of simply *slowing down and showing up to be present in life*. So first I just notice the hot water, how it feels on my skin. I then notice the smell of the hot water, and then the sound, the view of the steam, etc. Then I can use my pleasuring language, "I love this heat." "I love the smell of the soap." Then I can shift logical levels, "I love feeling clean." "I love the relaxation." "I love these moments alone." "I love the health effects." Etc.

Playing Pleasure Games with Your Loved One
What do you think about turning your love life into an experience of pleasure? You don't need to go on holiday or expensive night outs. That's the great thing about pleasure. Just as your body is wired for a thousand pleasures, so is your mind-and-emotion system. You only have to know how to trigger and stimulate your neuro-semantics for pleasure. You only have to make a decision that you will stop and smell the roses and enjoy the thousands of small pleasures in each day.

Doing this invites you to a new level of awareness and a special kind of awareness. It invites you to an *appreciative and valuing awareness* of all of the good things that you can delight yourself in. From smelling coffee brewing in the morning, to stretching and feeling your body move and wake up, to opening your eyes and experiencing the gift of sight. Here accessing the state of appreciation is the key to letting appreciation truly fill your eyes and mind so that you see the world afresh with the naive and wonder-filled anticipation of surprise and delight.

To play such pleasure games with your loved one, bring those eyes of appreciation to him or her and practice remembering all of the *whys* that thrilled and excited you from the beginning. Practice rehearsing all of the things that you adore and appreciate in your loved one today. Can you keep romance alive? The way to enhance romance is precisely in this way —pleasuring yourself in all of the little things that you adore. Enjoy feeling your fingers slide together in an embrace. Give and extend yourself to do something special that delights your loved one— call him or her during the day just to say "I love you."

Summary

- Pleasuring is primal. You have a body and nervous system wired for a thousand pleasures. Learning how to use your pleasuring powers and skills effectively put you in charge of your life, your choices, your motivation, your passion, and your happiness.

- By sorting out primary pleasures and meta-pleasures, you will begin to recognize the higher enjoyments that give the greatest pleasures.

- Discovering your neuro-semantic meaning-frames enables you to discover your pleasuring strategies. This enables you to experience more pleasure in your intimate relationships.

- Relating to your loved one can be an experience of ecstasy and enjoyment. And why not? It can give you a lot more fun in life and fun to share with your loved one.

Chapter 11

THE DANCE OF
SEXUAL PLEASURING

"Once you're made love, sex is never enough."
Stephen Bittoff

- How much sexual pleasure can you have?
- Can the sexual pleasuring last in an intimate relationship?
- Can you learn to develop and sustain your sexual pleasuring?
- How can we develop and increase our sexuality?

In a book about *Games Great Lovers Play,* you would think that sex might get a billing closer to the front than chapter 11, wouldn't you? Have you been wondering when I would ever get around to the intimacies of sexual bonding?

It's not news that sexual intimacy lies at the very heart of the coupling relationships we enter into with our loved one. We all know that. In fact, it's the sexual pleasures that often create much of the initial attraction and interest for us. This holds true for most of us regardless of age. It's the sexual intimacies also that deepen the bonding that we have with our loved one. There's something about being close both sensually and sexually that keeps the warmth, affection, and fun in the relating. So, no wonder sexual vitality, vulnerability, and openness play a central role in being a great lover.

The Game of Sexual Pleasuring
- What are the sexual pleasures?
- Why are they so compelling?

- How can we develop and cultivate these pleasures so that they serve to enhance our bonding?

At a most fundamental level, our sexuality arises from the fact that we are a sexual beings. We are sexual beings because we have sexual organs that differentiate us as male or female. We also have differentiating hormones that gives us primary and secondary sexual traits. Our sexual organs serve as the basis of our physical sexuality.

At the physical level, our sexual organs function like most of our organs through stimulation. This triggers good feelings. These good feelings excite our organs so that we become aroused. At the physical level this means nothing more than arousal and good feelings. Yet because this arousal occurs in those organs that are private and not public, we humans have generally come to treat them as special and only share that kind of arousal and pleasure with the one with whom that we are in a special and intimate relationship.

Yet our sexuality goes beyond the physical level of our sexual organs. Our sexuality involves our psychology—all of the thoughts-feelings and responses involved in being male or female, and expressing our sexuality. Sexuality involves our attitude, style, and way of being in the world. For this reason our attitude can make us more sexual or less.

Sexuality is not only about, or limited to, our sexual organs, our sexuality includes our whole being. We can be sexual in our everyday actions in the kitchen as well as the bedroom. After all, "Sex begins in the kitchen." It starts as flirting, being playful, being seductive and then it eventuates in desire, lust, and sex.

Permission to Play the Sexual Game
Are you comfortable with this discussion about sex and sexuality? If there's any discomfort, you might want to check to see if you have permission to be sexual and to more fully explore your own sexuality. Just go inside and say, "I give myself permission to be sexual" and notice what thoughts and feelings arise within or come to you.
- I give myself permission to share my sexuality with my partner in an open and vulnerable way.
- I give myself permission to be open to growing in my sexuality so I can give and receive more pleasure with my partner.
- I give myself permission to be *conscious* of my sexuality and the sexuality of my loved one and to talk about it.

People who uncomfortable with their sexuality typically suffer from the lack of permission. In some way they have had permission taken away from them. Perhaps parents or teacher tabooed sex, "sex for pleasure," or even talking about sex. Or a person may have had a negative sexual experience and then mapped sex as something he or she is not supposed to enjoy. However the tabooing or forbidding occurred, it's possible to live in an intimate relationship and not have permission to be fully present sexually or seductive with one's lover. Of course, to do that is to undermine the full intimacy that's possible for a couple.

You can even take permission away from yourself. Many do that. Many do so *after* they enter into a committed intimacy with another. Perhaps the intensity of the strong feelings scares them. Perhaps a partner wasn't in the best states at a given time, and felt overwhelmed, scared, or pressured, and so a person tabooed the experience. Perhaps a person feared not measuring up sexually. Precisely because a person can shut down or inhibit sexuality in so many ways, it's important to check and to give yourself permission to be sexual, to be fully sexual, to enjoy your sexuality, to feel passionate about your loved one's femininity or masculinity. Keep adding new frames of meaning and value until it "takes." It's your right and privilege.

When the Sex Police Stop the Game

As sexual beings we have bodies that are made for sexual stimulation. In this, *sex* is just that—the delight that you enjoy as you experience your partner's sexuality and play with your loved one's body and sexual organs. It's about loving, supporting, pleasuring, and stimulating each other's body about enjoying and giving pleasure to your partner.

By way of contrast, when a person uses sex for other psychological objectives, that person misuses sex and corrupts it. When you eat food for love, reward, fulfillment, satisfaction, having the good life, etc., you engage in *psycho-eating* (see *Games Slim and Fit People Play*). A similar thing can happen with sex. If you use sex to *prove* your masculinity or femininity, for dominating, controlling or being controlled, de-stressing (relieving tensions), settling an argument, making the marriage work, proving the validity of the marriage, etc. then you are *psycho-sexing*. You are no longer experiencing sex for what it *is,* but for what you can use get out of it psychologically. To that extent you pervert and distort sex, and in misusing it, you undermine its true use.

Psycho-sexing occurs when you give *meanings* to the experience of sex and sexual love which the experience cannot bear. This is the actual cause of much of the sexual impotency that many men experience. Whenever a person over-loads the experience semantically, it will come to mean too much.

Many men, for example, over-load it so that it defines their sexual identity and powers. Therefore to be aroused, or to "come," makes or breaks their sexual self-definition. They think of it in terms as "being a man." Within their self-talk there's lots of pressure and demandingness to reach orgasm. They don't desire to come, or get to come, they   *have to.* Now it is a compulsion. They are only as good as their sex organs and functioning. When this happens, sex ceases to be about *giving* of yourself to your loved one, it becomes about *proving* your identity or masculinity. Yet when it is about proving yourself, it is no longer about giving and receiving pleasure, it shifts to a psychological issue.

Neuro-semantically, this kind of over-loading of meaning takes on a seemingly paradoxical feel. The more you *try*, the less you are able to feel aroused or to come to an orgasm. What's wrong? The problem is that you have invested too much meaning into the experience. The solution lies, counter-intuitively, in letting go and reducing the semantic load of meaning. The solution is to *not care* if you are aroused or not, if you reach orgasm or not, and to care that you are lovingly attending to your lover and making your partner feel good. When you do that, arousal will come. Yet if you use this as the trick to come, it will only work for a short period of time, and you'll find yourself back in that paradoxical loop.

A great deal of the pleasure in shared sexuality with a lover is that you experience your own maleness or femaleness. It allows you to know and disclose yourself and your lover as a sexual person. This enables you to then be spontaneous, emotionally open and available, and uninhibited.

Let the Sex Games Begin!
Once you have permission within yourself to be what you are, sexual and to behave seductively with your loved one, several of these questions arise:
* How can you pleasurably enrich your sexuality?
* How can you enrich it so that being sexual makes sense, supports your loved one, and enhances your relationship.
* How can you enrich your sexuality with pleasure?

Adopt a more sensual attitude
In answer, the first thing you can do is to change your attitude so that you seek to be more sensual in relating to your loved one. By accepting and appreciating your sexuality, and your partner's sexuality, you can increase

your sense of permission for enjoying and exploring each other's bodies. This will enable you to adopt a more sensual attitude toward your own body, to enjoy your male or female sex organs being touched and stimulated by your partner. You can also become more sensual in your attitude toward the sexuality of your partner, wanting to touch and stimulate his or her body and make this a part of the giving-and-receiving that you share as you relate.

- Do you have a sensual attitude toward your body?
- Do you like your sexual parts?
- Do you get lots of sexual stimulation and delight from being touched, kissed, stroked, and petted?
- Do you have an enhancing self-definition as a sexual being?
- Does giving and receiving of sexual affection and stimulation seem like a gift of love from each other?
- How much more sexual will you become with your partner?
- What sexual delights would your partner love to receive?

Be more playful and experimental
By fully accepting your sexuality, you can more easily adopt an open and accepting attitude of your loved one and his or her sexuality. Doing so allows both of you to become more playful, more experimental, more open, and more vulnerable. These are the attitudes that make you, as well as the whole experience, much more sensual. Part of keeping the passion alive in relationship entails trying new things and adding surprise and variety into your love making.

- How playful are you currently in sharing your sexuality?
- What would help you to become more sexual?
- What sexual games would you enjoy playing?
- What sexual games could you invent with your partner to keep the excitement and thrill in the relating?

Seek first to please and then to be pleased
Isn't half of the fun of relating the experience of *giving pleasure* to the other person? There's a special pleasure of being able to induce your lover into the most pleasurable and ecstatic states. When you do this, the principle of reciprocity kicks in. Then you enjoy the pleasures involved in both giving and receiving because as you give so you receive in return.

- How much reciprocity is there in your sharing of affection, flirting, and sensuality?
- To what degree do you thoroughly enjoy giving pleasure as much as receiving sexual stimulation from your loved one?
- How thoroughly acquainted are you with what your lover loves and joys?

- How willing are you to extend yourself in simply giving pleasure?
- How free do you feel to talk about what you like sexually and giving your lover specific feedback about what to do?

Use affection as foreplay

Sex is not just intercourse. That's why you can experience and express your sexuality in flirting and being playfully seductive. Foreplay is not only where it all begins, it is what excites your sexuality. Truly pleasurable and playful sexuality is not just about the sex organs, it's about who and what you are sensually with your partner.

- To what degree do you and your loved one continue to flirt?
- How much flirting and playfulness is in your everyday encounters?

Add lots of variety and play to your love making

To a great extent you enhance your sexuality by adding variety to not only what happens in the bedroom, but also in all of the other parts of life. Being fun and playful in one environment then extends back to the bedroom. You can do this in many ways:

- How can you create an environment that supports intimacy?
- What environment variables assist you and your loved one?
- Would candles or dim lights, soft music, films or videos, sweet smells or incense, soft colors (pinks) or bright ones (red)?
- How can you use clothes to elicit more seductive feelings?
- Does dressing in a sexy way turn you or your lover on?
- Does getting all dressed up as if for some occasion or undressing and dressing very casually?
- What about picking a theme and dressing to that theme?
- What about having a fantasy night with your lover and invite each other to share a fantasy and act it out or act out part of it?
- What about reading or inventing a sexy story together?

And what about your frames of mind? What frames of mind support being sexual, being sexy, and enjoying flirting and being seductive with your lover? Certainly wanting and enjoying having fun is involved in letting yourself feel sexy and seductive. So is feeling free and willing to explore each other's body, being creative, open, valuing sex as a bonding activity. Conversely, what frames stop you from being sexy? These can involve negative experiences from former relationships, negative conditioning about sex, shyness, fear of embarrassment, etc. Identify what stops you and then change the meanings of those experiences.

The Bonding of Sexuality

There's a special bond that you share with the person that you love as you share your physical and psychological nakedness. With the undressing of the body, you are seen. And what does *being seen* stimulate? For most of us, it makes us vulnerable to the other's sight and judgment. Yet it is in this physical undressing that you can facilitate you and your lover to become more open and vulnerable within the higher levels of mind, heart, and soul. This leads to and encourages you to disclose your mind, heart, and spirit as you make yourself open and vulnerable in these dimensions. In this way, being physically naked can lead from one level of bonding to higher and deeper levels.

In sexuality, all of these facets of self come together in a unique synthesis. You can experience a rich bonding as you share your body and sexuality with your lover. This sharing involves many dimensions. It involves the fun and excitement of sexual arousal. It involves the trust and sharing of your lives. It involves the connection of commitment.

In fact, *how* you relate and handle your lover's body and nakedness says a lot about the nature and quality of your relating and sets a pace for how you handle each other in the dimensions of mind, emotion, and person.

- Do I handle my lover's body with care and respect?
- Or do I consume it for my own lusts irregardless of his or her feelings and responses?
- Do I think about pleasing and delighting my lover?
- Do I check things out and make sure that she or he enjoys and is okay with being touched or stroked or kissed in a certain way?

Our physical bodies are made for a thousand pleasures. Touching, stimulating, kissing, stroking, sucking, licking, and fondling creates the sexual and sensual stimulation. We feel aroused and excited and want to connect, bond, and experience the penetrating and being penetrated of physical love-making. In developing this you need an explorative and playful attitude so that you learn how to touch and pleasure each other in ways that your lover wants and desires.

It is now well known that men and women typically differ in the order of physical and emotional love-making. Various cultural phrases summarizes this knowledge:

- "Women need a why; men only need a place."
- "Men, like micro-wave ovens, are only a button away from being ready. Women are more like conventional ovens; they need to be

warmed up first."
- "Love begins in the kitchen. If you're not making love to her with your words in the kitchen, you won't be making love to her in the bedroom later."

These statements about men and women at best only serve as general guidelines. *Typically,* men are more ready and willing to engage in physical and sexual love-making at a moment's notice and often don't need a relationship to do so. *Typically* also, women need the safety of a loving relationship first. They do not only need a relationship, but a warm, caring, and emotionally safe and supportive relationship. Generally, women will only open up physically after they first open up emotionally. Again, these are generalizations, not absolute rules about "the way it is."

Numerous theories have been postulated to explain these male-female differences around sex. There's the evolutionary idea of man as hunter and warrior who wants to plant his seed in as many women as possible. This model views the woman as the one in charge of nurturing, protecting, and finding a protector and so much more picky about who she mates with.

Another theory describes these dynamics as culturally conditioned. We have simply been trained and conditioned to so think and feel about our physical sexuality and could have just as easily been trained to do it in a reverse pattern. We *learn* to be sexual in the ways that we now experience it.

There are also some psychological theories about the differences in masculinity and femininity. These describe what is common in most Western and industrial countries. Here men define their masculinity in terms of achievement, accomplishment, and actions. By way of contrast, women define their femininity in terms of connection and relationship. You can demonstrate to yourself the general truth of this by asking a man, "Tell me about yourself. Who are you?" The typical man will tell you about what he does, his achievements, his best accomplishments, status, standing, money, etc. What is the significance of this? It shows how doing, acting, achieving, and performing serve as the typical frames governing male self-definition and understanding.

Ask a woman the same question. "Tell me about yourself. Who are you?" You will undoubtedly get a very different answer. She will speak about family, loved ones, who she's connected to, her relationships, and her lover. Even highly successful and professional women will generally tell you who she's related to—her lover, children, friends, etc.

Summary

- Physical attractiveness and sexual stimulation obviously create a significant bond between lovers. In fact, most of us tend to confuse "love making" with sex. Yet sex is so much more because we, in our whole being, are sexual beings.

- While being a great lover involves so much more than sex, it certainly does not exclude sex and sexual skill within its scope. Great lovers appreciate and attend to each other sensually and sexually. They experience the full human range of emotions about their sexuality and this adds tremendously to the bonding pleasures that they discover with each other.

- Are you ready to let the sexual games begin? Are you ready to use the physical bonding of affection, sexual play and stimulation, and the discovery of what excites you and your loved one? May you and yours enjoy.

Chapter 12

THE DANCE OF
HEALTHY FIGHTING

If you love, you'll fight; so make it a good one!
"You never know someone until you've fought them."
(Bodyguard of the Oracle to Neo in *The Matrix Movie*)

*L**oving and fighting—do they go together.* If they do, exactly how does loving and conflicting go together? When you are a great lover, is your relationship conflict-free? Is your relationship so harmonious that you never experience conflict? Or does being a great lover transform the way you argue and conflict so that it deepens your bonding?

•	Is it possible to be conflict-free in that you never experience hurt feelings, disappointments, tension between in having different styles, disagreements of opinion and such like?

•	Could conflict actually be a healthy sign of two thinking-and-feeling human beings and a fact of life to be negotiated with graceful skill?

•	What's your style of fighting?

•	Do you know how to turn your fights from being destructive into being positive so it serves your connection?

•	Is it possible to work out conflicts and differences in a loving way that protects your relating and loving?

•	Is it possible to reduce arguing by simply acknowledging each other's feelings? Could more than half of most fights be done and over by simply acknowledging your lover's feelings?

•	Could you use your arguments to discover more about each other *and* strengthen your loving?

•	How do great lovers handle challenges, differences, conflicts, and such like?

Put any two thinking humans together for a period of time and eventually there will be differences of opinions, ideas, feelings, wants, and choices. What each wants and desires, the style that each takes will eventually find points of conflict. The question then is not *whether* conflict will occur, but *how* you will "fight" and be respectfully loving. Is that even possible?

- Is it possible to "fight" in a healthy and loving way?
- Can you disagree with respect, curiosity, and playfulness?
- Can you work out conflicts in ways that support your love?
- What skills do you need to conflict in a way that enhances your relationship rather than undermine it?

The Game of Positive Fighting

What's your attitude about conflict? Do you fear it? Hate it? What do you think about the existence of differences? Do you view conflict as being nasty, angry, and yelling? Could you view conflict in terms of being curious, respectful, explorative, and playful? Is that possible? The fact of conflict and difference only means that we have *two* real live human beings with minds and emotions of their own, and not one human with his or her clone.

"Conflicting" becomes problematic only when *the way* and *the style* of how you conflict becomes insulting, defensive, and aggressive. Conversely, conflicting becomes an expression of love if you do so with respect, honoring each person, seeking first to understand, and searching for the higher values and intentions above and beyond the conflict. So, suppose there are ways to conflict that actually support and protect relationship. Suppose that you conflict in a way that actually strengthens your bonding, that makes you more understanding and appreciative of each other, and enables you to grow.

- Would you like *that* kind of conflicting?
- Would you be interested in learning the skills for how to conflict in that manner?

To face issues and concerns in a straightforward way and go for the heart of an experience is to have a *fierce conversation* (Susan Scott's phrase). A fierce conversation is one that's robust, intense, strong, passionate, and eager about getting to the heart of things. In this way of talking you come out from behind your masks and roles and fully enter the conversation. This makes it becomes real—authentic, caring, and human. Engaging in fierce conversations enable you to work through conflicts with respect and love, to speak the truth in love. Of course, this raises many questions:

- How do you manage your states when you experience hurt in relating to your loved one?
- How do you learn to stop hurting each other?
- What models or tools can you use to manage our conflicts so that you do so with respect and honor?
- How can you stay open and resourceful during a conflict so that you can co-create creative solutions?
- Does conflict and even hurt have to dis-bond?
- Can you take a healing and loving approach even in your disagreeing and conflicting?

That you can, and do, get your feelings hurt as you relate to each other is nothing new. We all know that. It happens all the time. But why? And, how does it happen?

> *It happens because you are a semantic class of life who give meaning to things.* You invest ideas, things, people, values, etc. with *meaning.*

When you enter a inter-relational bond, you do so with needs, wants, expectations, hopes, dreams, and thousands of ideas and concepts. You enter with your meanings. You have meanings about the relationship and what you hope to experience through it. You have meanings about what it means to invest yourself in your lover. You have meanings about the things you want to experience with your loved one: conversation, dialogue, being real, companionship, friendship, emotional support, affection, sexual activity, play, etc.

Yet in inter-relating you often do not get what you want. Sometimes this occurs because of limited resources involving time, money, energy, ability, and understanding. What does it mean to you at that point? What do you feel? Typically people feel   *hurt* in some way—disappointed, empty, betrayed, angry, afraid, embarrassed, etc.

Perhaps you even let your lover know of your disappointment or displeasure. In doing this, you could just simply *report* your distress. More frequently, however, you *complain* or *blame.* Yet these are not the games that support love. You let your lover know of your grievance against what he or she has done, or failed to do. If you're smart, you also ask for the new and different response that you want. Or, you may ask your partner to stop giving you some old and hurtful response.

Does this communication succeed in changing things? No. It hardly ever succeeds. Typically, it only creates another hurt or want. You want your loved one to listen, to attend to you, to your hurt feelings, to work things out reasonably, to stop feeling and acting defensive, etc.

- How can you communicate your grievances without making things worse?
- How can you bring up unpleasant issues and work them through to resolution without the other feeling attacked, insulted, put-down, accused, blamed, etc.?

Noticing Hurts While They're Small **Game**
An essential resource for maintaining loving and bonded relationships is to notice hurts before they grow too big, or get to a threshold.

- What is a "hurt?"
- How do you recognize that something (a word, an action, a tease, etc.) will "hurt" someone?

Like communication, you never really know what will, or will not, hurt your loved one. Until you pay attention to the response that you get. The response begins to inform you as to what the other person thinks and defines as a *hurt.* So like love and beauty, *hurt* lies in the eyes of the beholder.

So as you have to learn your loved one's behavioral equivalents of *love* (those behaviors and actions that make deposits in his or her emotional bank account) you also have to learn your lover's behavioral equivalents of "hurt."

- What *hurts* you?
- What are you sensitive to?
- What makes "withdrawals" from your emotional bank account?

If I don't know what might *hurt* your feelings, *wound* your sense of feeling dignity, *traumatize* your hopes, dreams and visions, or in any other way *violate* your values and beliefs, then I might go about my business doing all kinds of harm, and never know it!

Doesn't this happens all the time? Psychologists see it every day in therapy. I have done it in my own life. We go about relating with others, thinking, "All goes well!" Then suddenly, our loved one reaches threshold, and then,

"Thar she blows!" "Wooah!" we say, "Where did all that come from?"

No wonder it is a critical strategy for protecting love to see hurts as they happen (calibrating in the moment), and to deal with them while still small and manageable. If you wait, if you put it off, discount it, the hurts can fester and grow and become so bigger they become unmanageable.

Is that what you want? Of course not. The solution is to develop the relational and communicational skills for dealing with hurts as they happen. As you adjust yourself to this aspect of relating, begin by expecting hurts to arise from time to time. Expect your own emotions to get hurt. You can expect that there will be times when your loved one will get his or her feelings hurt. Expecting and anticipating that this happens then prevent you from feeling side-swiped.

Embracing Negative Emotions as Just Emotions **Game**

After adjusting yourself to the fact that we all get our emotions hurt in relationships, you need to *develop a good adjustment to hurts when they happen.* Due to the cultural frames in which males typically are exposed to, this new game will be more challenging to guys:

> "Have a stiff upper lips—boys don't cry."
> "Be strong and take it like a man."
> "Don't be emotional, you'll lose control."

To the extent that you think that emotions are *not* okay, not valid, that you shouldn't experience them or acknowledge them, that "talking about emotions only inflames them," to that extent you will not be able to play this game. These are the ideas that undermine your ability to effectively handle your emotions. They exclude you from the game.

Embracing hurts means welcoming the negative emotions that you feel *as emotions* and as just emotions. That's what they are. Emotions—somatic registering in your body of the values and meanings that you compute in your heads. That's why,*as you think* (and the meanings you make in your heads) *so you feel and register in your body.* Emotions are not strange and mysterious forces. They make perfect sense. You don't go into fear states without thoughts of dangers or threats. You don't experience anger without a thought that your values have been violated.

Emotions communicate to you about yourself. They identify*the relationship* between your map of the world and your experience in the world. This makes each and every emotion you experience completely appropriate. It makes them fully understandable. It doesn't make them all equally useful, appropriate, or enhancing. You have to check them out. You have to check out the map that you're operating from and the skills and responses you use in encountering the world.

When your lover gets his or her feelings hurt, check it out. Welcome those emotions for the purpose of understanding them. What thinking and thinking patterns creates them? What experience has he or she had? Create a regular time for clearance with your loved one. This helps to clear the air and keeps things current. To play this *Love Game,* ask:
- During this past week have I hurt your feelings in any way?
- Did you stuff some feelings of anger or frustration with me that you feel safe in sharing at this time?

This allows you to feel safe when you communicate grievances while they are still small and manageable. Then they won't grow up into mega-demons. In this process you develop greater confidence in your ability to work things out. You come to believe in the power and value of having fierce conversations to flush out concerns and create positive resolutions.

The Fair Fighting Game

What's the criteria for having a good fight? In workshops on Conflict Resolution Skills I usually identify seven criteria. Gauge yourself on these indicators of effective conflicting. What's your skill level with these? How many would you like to add to your repertoire of skills?

1. I can *engage* another person about issues I feel strongly about.
2. I can engage the other person in a *respectful* way.
3. I can make the communication *safe* for the other person.
4. I can move through the stages

of conflict resolution effectively (the emotional, dialogue, and negotiation stages).

     5. I can co-create *an agreement frame* with others.

     6. I can co-create *a mutually agreeable solution.*

     7. I can *strengthen the relationship* in the process of conflicting.

Several factors come together to make conflict inevitable: the fact of differences, the conditionality of relationships, the systemic nature of communication, and that we more easily *mis*-communicate than sympathetically understand. Conflicting makes up a large part of relating. We conflict to merge our personalities, wants, and lifestyles. All too often we avoid conflicting when we can still access states of caring, motivation, calmness, etc. and we wait until we don't care, lack the motivation to try anymore, feel defensive and stressed-out. This is not a good choice.

In healthy relating, you take a proactive stance with regard to differences of wants, emotions, values, lifestyle, etc. You bring up things when you can access a spirit of sweet reasonableness. You proactively take responsibility for your own responses, for communicating love and integrity in the midst of emotional storms, for controlling when to talk as well as when not to talk. You initiate from a win/win perspective. You seek to create and build patterns of collaboration. You seek to keep communicating until all parties feel heard, understood, respected, and out of an ongoing dialoguing to create synergistic solutions.

The best foundation for having a good fight is having proactive and independent persons who are committed to communicating clearly and willing to heal issues in a loving way, even through difficult emotional storms. This is the foundation for being respectful in resolving conflict positively. This strategy for effective resolution of conflicting differences focuses on maintaining respect, thinking win/win, and keeping the communication going until you synergistically create workable solutions.

Embracing Conflict **Game**

Some conflicts are inevitable. Conflicting is the natural arena within which we all do the work of relating. It is in conflict that we work out mutually satisfying arrangements. This is our purpose in positive conflicting.

•   How have you mapped "conflict?"

- Does it appeal to you?
- Do you conflict positively with your lover?
- Or, do you fear conflict?
- Have you only seen hurtful and disrespectful conflict that ends in hostility, violence, insult, and rage without resolution?
- What experiences have led you to the maps you built?
- Who do you know (or know about) that would provide an excellent model of conflict resolution?

When you can conflict in a positive and loving way without blowing-up at each other, your bonding becomes stronger and more durable. Positive conflicting works out differences, meshes your wants, resolves the issues that otherwise gets in the way of your bonding, induces a sense of closeness, and raises your confidence in working things out. Because positive conflicting is respectful and productive, it is healthy. These skills make your relationships more durable. Those who lack these skills live on the edge of fear, forever avoiding the rough and tumble of interpersonal conflict. This leaves them with fragile relationships that lack the inner strength and endurance to dovetail each person's wants.

To play this game, begin to think about conflicts as giving you the opportunity to be real in your conversation with your lover. A conflict does not have to be unpleasant. It can be a call to authenticity. Conflicts can help to knock off your rough edges as you learn to become more human and compassionate with each other. It can challenge selfishness so that you get out of yourself. People who avoid conflict like the plague take on a sober and gloomy seriousness about it and so get into bad states from the state. And, of course, that won't help.

Summary
- Great lovers know how to fight *for* the relationship, the bonding, the loving, and the nurturing. They conflict about things of importance that nurture the relationship and they do so in respectful, loving, and compassionate ways.

- It's not a case *whether* you will disagree, differ, and conflict about things, but *how* you will do so. You can play the dangerous games of fighting *with* and *against* your lover or the loving games that fight *for* the relationship and for win/win solutions.

- Fighting *for* love and bonding keeps the relationship front and center and necessitates two people mature enough, skilled enough, and caring enough to have fierce conversations that get to the real issues *because* they love and value each other that much.

Chapter 13

THE RULES OF
THE FIGHTING GAME

• If there is a way to have healthy and fair fights that deepen the bonding and strengthens the love, then what are the rules for that game?

• How can you learn to play this new game with your lover?

In the previous chapter I began the exploration of how to work through "conflict" in such a way so that you will be able to play the *"Let's Have a Healthy Fight" Game.* To do that requires several things: you have to make it your aim to create some great rules for "fighting" in a loving way *for* the relationship. Then, when you really do know how to fight in a respectful way, you can have those fiercely loving conversations whereby you strengthen your love while dealing with the issues that you address. That's what this chapter is all about.

Rules for the Fair Fighting Game
The Fair Fighting Rules Game offer a way to work things out as you structure a methodical way to grapple with ideas, feelings, and wants so you don't become intrusive, ugly, or hurtful. Such rules offer a process for positive conflicting so that you can fight *for* the relationship in a way that allows each person to feel loved, respected, and understood. How does that sound?

Do you know what the word *argue* means? The word originally meant "to make things clear." How about that!? "Argue," from the Latin word *arguere,* meant "to make clear." Is that what *argue* signifies to you? *To make things clear!* That sounds like a pretty positive aim. Yet in Middle French, the word *arguer* came to mean "to accuse."

• Can you make something clear without accusing?
• Can you make something clear without it coming across as condescending or speaking down to another?

The "fighting" describing here are those in which we fight *for* relating, connecting, bonding, and perhaps for a thought, idea, feeling, want, hurt, consideration, etc. In this fight, you respectfully hear each other out. You work through conflicts until you get to a satisfactory resolution. You know that you've had a "great fight" when you do the following:

1) Create a positive resolution.
    Do you work through the differences and come to a resolution that you both can live with?
2) Maintain respect, honor, and dignity throughout the process.
    Do you feel respected, understood and loved when you're done?
3) Strengthen the relationship by the dialogue and solution.
    Have you made your relationship stronger and more durable?

Great lovers seem to know how to make positive conflicting an art. Do you know how to do that? Anyone who does not is always just one step away from the relationship dissolving. Relationships become fragile if you don't know *how* to communicate around differences. If the conflict of differences *per se* threatens the relationship—then you will be "walking around on eggshells" and treating each other as fragile. This isn't a good thing if you want to play a new game with conflict.

To play *"Let's Have a Healthy Fight" Game,* commit yourself to moving to a win/win position so that you keep yourself engaged in an open discussion, separating person from behavior and validating your loved one as you wrestle with the issues.

In a way, resolving conflict to a positive end is like navigating a storm. When two people with strong raging emotions like storm systems collide, the waters can become highly agitated. That's no time to start learning navigation! Is it? The best time for learning to navigate is during smooth sailing times, when winds are gentle and the sun balmy. Then you can study the storm dynamics and how best to respond. Similarly, what follows is a set of navigational rules for those storms.

Rule #1: Reframe Yourself about Conflict
- Is the idea of conflict unacceptable to you?
- Does it evoke feelings of vulnerability and reactivity?

Your thinking about conflict determines how you experience it. Any experience that you think, feel, and evaluate as unacceptable or even threatening will feel anxiety provoking, fearful, and threatening. You will then respond by entering into states that are unresourceful and ineffective for handling conflict. Identify your current frames about conflict.
- What does conflict mean to you?
- What's the first thing that comes to mind?
- What feelings and associations do you have to conflict?
- Where did these meanings come from?
- What other meanings could you give it?

If you attach "Destructive differences!" to conflict, then a reframe might be: "It's not the differences that threaten relationships, but intolerant and unloving attitudes and responses to differences."
- "I give myself permission to differ, even to differ strongly, and to understand my lover's differences without letting them push us apart."
- "I will view conflict as normal, not abnormal or bad."

David Mace (1975) offers this reframe:
> "Interpersonal conflict, far from being an extraneous element in modern marriage, actually represents the raw material out of which an effective marital partnership has to be shaped."

Your feelings about conflict indicate the belief frames that drive your experience. So when you install a new belief, you install a new way of thinking, emoting, communicating, and behaving. Since shifting frames is an art that develops through practice, practice writing some new and empowering reframes for the common limiting frames:
- Conflict means I'm being personally attacked.
- Conflict means she doesn't like me.
- Conflict always leads to violence.

- Nice people don't differ or collide over issues.

Possible new reframes:
- Conflict doesn't have to end with a winner and a loser; both can win if there's love, respect, and quality conversation.
- My self-esteem is never on the line; only a particular issue that we both feel strong about.

Distinguishing person and behavior protects you from personalizing— a destructive thinking pattern in negative conflicting. After all, aren't you are more than your behaviors, ideas, emotions, and experiences? *Self* differs from all of your expressions of yourself. Your lover is more than his or her behaviors. Separating person from behavior also helps to avoid moralizing the issues over which you differ.

Conflicts can arise from many sources: differences, frustrations (stresses), misunderstandings, imperfections, faults and mistakes, power struggles, wanting your own way, etc. These things are not bad *per se,* but are simply things to be dealt with. When stressed, most of us move into a moralistic (or judgmental) way of thinking and communicating which, of course, only makes matters worse.

Rule #2: Create an Atmosphere for Fighting
The atmosphere within which you conflict makes all the difference in the world between conflicting that resolves things and that which makes things worse. What is the right kind of atmosphere? How is it created? It's created as you communicate lots of love, affirmation, and care for your loved one and do so every day. This develops the kind of relationship that you will also want to fight for.

To build this foundation, you can actually structure a ten minute "Stroke/Hug Time" every evening. Call it your "Relationship Nurturing Time." Tell yourself, "I want to give myself ten minutes every day for accessing feelings of extravagant pleasure with my loved one."

The structures you live within greatly effect your thinking, feeling, and behaving. Creating good conflicting structures can avoid unfair and unproductive fighting. Define the arena in which you're going to fight respectfully. Stake out an area where you can give and receive lots of feedback and dialogue. As you do more attentive listening and paraphrasing back to clarify messages, be sure to eliminate any and all *telling* statements. Create ground rules about planned breaks. After all, even in boxing, the bouts only go for three minutes. The more intense the conflict, the more important to do it in small doses.

To create the right atmosphere, you will want to work on your own internal state:
•   Am I in the right state?
•   Do I have a sweet spirit with my loved one?

Resolve to never try to resolve things when your spirit is out-of-control and you want to return hurt. Would you want to be confronted by someone in that state? Take time to get into a more resourceful state so you can control yourself from labeling, blaming, judging, or blowing-up. A conducive atmosphere is open, honest, and genuine. It is safe for trust, acceptance, good-will, patience and calmness.

Explore wants and concerns of each other to create an agreement frame. By finding, creating, and building on commonalities, frame your interactions in terms of seeking a mutual agreement that makes for a win/win relationship. To do this you only need to assume that you both want to do something valuable and positive for yourselves and to then explore the higher positive intentions that you can agree on.

Rule #3: Go at it Gracefully and Respectfully
Having a good fight means knowing   *when* and *how* to go at it, how to flush-out issues while they are still small and manageable, and not waiting until they are of overwhelming proportions. Make this great pre-fight decision, "I will always treat my lover sacredly —with respect and kindness." In going at it, make it your policy to keep things current. Don't let the problem grow through neglect by resolving them soon.

It's important to make sure that the time and place is right. Conflicting can be emotionally exhausting so you need to be up for it. It is inappropriate when one person is feeling ill, stressed-out, or has a splitting headache. Give each other permission to check whether they are up to it. If one says "No, I'm not up for it," then wait. Do it later.

The place should also not be out in public and usually not in front of the children. While children need models for good conflict-resolution skills, they also need only limited doses. Set an appropriate example by making sure the subject is appropriate for their ears. In keeping it private, don't use the bedroom for fighting, save that room for love-making. The place itself should give some privacy and quietness.

Develop a good style of *problem reporting.* Some people report problems in such an emotional state that their problem-reporting comes out negatively as griping, fussing, badmouthing, criticizing, bitching, etc. This doesn't help.

Develop an objective problem-reporting style. State dispassionately what you think is the difficulty. Do this in *descriptive language* (see-hear-feel terms). Hold back on your *evaluative words* (judgments, interpretations, evaluations, meanings, etc.) until at least the problem is clearly described and both can agree upon it. Then move into identifying what the problem means to you. The ability to distinguish between description and evaluation language is itself a powerful verbal, thinking and communicating skill. Why? Because we can say almost anything to anyone when we use descriptive language.

Refuse to allow your mind-body-emotion system to polarize. Under stress most everybody polarizes and shifts to black-and-white thinking. De-polarize by asking gauging questions. Identify where on the continuum you are and at what stage or step is the problem to make the conflict more reality oriented.

Regarding emotions, simply *report how you feel.* As you own the emotion as your own, simply register your tension level in a non-judging and non-accusing way. Emotions, as just emotions, reflect your thinking. Give each other permission to have emotions without acting on them. You are more than your emotions, so don't over-identify with them. Experiencing an emotion isn't a moral or immoral issue, but an emotional one.

STAGES OF CONFLICT RESOLUTION
Stage #1: The Emotional Stage.
> Register your emotions, identify feelings, ventilate, own, and disclose whatever you feel. When the other is in this stage: defuse, pace, listen, understand.

Stage #2: The Discussion Stage.
>   Talk about what things mean to you, affirm, validate, and make statements of assurance to the other. Explore ideas, possibilities, and alternatives.

Stage #3: The Negotiating/Resolving Stage.
>   Avoid rushing into this problem-solving stage too quickly, if you do, you will bypass much of the work of relating, discovering, and creative possibilities with which to negotiate.

Owning the emotion distinguishes between the trigger that evokes your emotional response and your emotional response. These are two entirely different phenomenon. Become skilled in making this distinction and put an end to the old nonsense, "You make me so angry!" Nobody can "make" you feel anything; your feeling response is precisely that, a feeling response that arises in your nervous system, brain-body. Because it comes from your internal model of the worldj, it is always your creation. Knowing what evokes it and what you want from the other is an entirely different matter.

To slow down the conversation and truly understand the messages going back and forth, paraphrase what you hear and reflect it back to the person. Ask your loved one to gauge the accuracy of your understanding from 0 to 10. If you aren't even getting a 5 on the accuracy scale, then have the other person clarify his point again.

These navigational tools help allow each person to become aware of the other's internal world. As empathy tools, they enable you to enter knowledgeably into the other's world to see, hear, and understand with accuracy your lover's perspectives.

Go slowly to give yourself thinking time so you can use your mind rather than merely react. Call mini Time-Outs since knowing when to fight and when not to fight is critical. It needs to be a good time for both. "Be slow to speak, quick to listen." In listening— learn to listen with your heart. Such listening is not trying to show the other how unreasonable he is, but trying to understand the Matrix of his or her mind.

Target one issue at a time. You will be more resourceful when you deal with one thing at a time. Use a pad of paper to keep track of other issues that will need to be dealt with later. To avoid getting lost in content and missing the real issues, take a meta-position to the content. Of the many meta-perspectives you can go to the perspective of the other's feelings, intention, meaning, memory, the relationship, etc. What does it all mean to your lover? As you develop a sense of wonderment about the other's model of reality to deepen your understanding, say:

> "This must mean something pretty important to you. I tend to want to dismiss it, moralize about it, condemn it, etc. so tell me what meanings you are experiencing about this."

As you talk, say things that match what the other feels and perceives. This will enable the other to feel understood. and give him or her the experience of feeling heard. Asking lots of questions will enable you to curiously explore the other's intentions and meanings. Find out what you are dealing with before responding. What is the issue? We often fight about things that there's no need to fight about, like "the past."

There are numerous behavioral styles and modes that can assist in giving you more control of your conflicting. You can talk things over while taking a walk. Or if you can whisper, that will change the feel of things. Imagine discussing something while hugging or embracing. Or suppose you discussed the conflict while holding hands and looking into each other's eyes. You could sit at a table and communicate everything by writing on a tablet. You could lower your voices and even play out the conflict by switching roles so that each argues the other's side.

Communicate in face-saving ways that nourish and cherish and when in a state of disrespect, take a time-out. Always be respectful because as psychologist Dr. Harry Stack Sullivan wrote:

> "Every human encounter is an emotional experience in which we risk some of our self-esteem."

Rule #4: Keep your Objective continually before you
- What's your intention in working through a conflict?
- What's important about finding and creating positive resolutions for you and your lover?

Once you know your objective, keep that intention before you as you engage in the dialogue. Set your goal to clarify things, to understand your lover, to support and respect, and to resolve things in a positive and resourceful way. Any other battle aim than these will probably be destructive.

Especially fight to deepen your understanding of each other. Most conflicts are resolved with a little bit of understanding. It's amazing how many conflicts melt away by adding a good dose of understanding. The problem may actually only be that of hurt feelings or some form of negative emotional build-up (i.e., fears, angers, guilts, etc.). Frequently, just letting person express his and her feelings will bring resolution.

You undermine good conflicting by operating from insufficient intentions like wanting to conquer or defeat the other person, intending to win or dominate. Resolve to put aside all competitiveness, comparisons, desires to conquer, crush, or dominate. Also, refuse to defend yourself. Defensiveness, even if accurate in content, is usually ineffective. To stay on target, keep asking yourself:
- What am I trying to accomplish?
- What am I trying to prove or say with these communications?

Old programs and inferior intentions can come into play outside of your conscious awareness and ruin the relationship or communication while trying to get some need met in an inauthentic way. Communicating, discussing, problem-reporting, problem-solving and negotiating can be engaged in for many different purposes:
> To deepen understanding, to validate another, to win over, dominate, conquer; to blame, hold another responsible, to dump; to express frustration and/or anger; to think aloud and de-stress self, to work through ideas, to brainstorm, to bond, to lash out and hurt, to pick the other's details apart, to refute her logic, to correct his inaccuracies, etc.

In communicating that seeks to understand and negotiate, adopt a learner's position to your lover. That is, adopt a teachable spirit and give yourself permission to not always be right. What's destructive to arguments is trying to prove yourself right. If you moralize about chores, wants, emotions, etc. you confuse morals issues with other issues. Do you know how to be wrong graciously and to be right and quiet about it? If you *have to* be right or win, it may very well cost you the relationship. Is "being right" that important?

Richard and Mary Strauss write,

> "If I want him to understand me, I have to make myself understandable. I must be willing to answer questions, to share my mind honestly, to avoid becoming defensive, to make myself vulnerable, and to listen and think before I speak. And I must be willing to look at things from his viewpoint."

Rule #5: Check all Weapons at the door

Your desire to win can become too important. Many have won an argument and lost a relationship. If you fight *for* the relationship, *for* understanding, *for* love, good resolutions, then check your arsenal at the door. Make the policy absolute: no destructive weapons allowed.

Below-the-belt punches are disallowed in boxing. Do the same at home with your loved one. Identify all below-the-belt areas that are forbidden: sarcastic tones, attacking motives, name-calling, mocking, labeling, judging, discounting, contempt, etc. If you lower yourself to such, the interactions will not be fun. Call a Time-Out when any of these occur. "Dirty fighting" between lovers is typically involves fighting over unchangeable things like the past.

Let there be *no threatening*—accusing, judging, demanding, or blaming. Don't push with parental tones, criticism, teaching, or anything that pushes buttons. Avoid anything that triggers defensiveness. To learn this, watch your tone, cussing, and name-calling.

You can threat simply by using the "you" word. Exchange all "you" statements for "I" statements to report how you feel. If there's something you respond to as a trigger, identify it and acknowledge how your own thoughts create it. If a dysfunctional conflicting style from an old program or automatic defense mechanism occurs, give each other permission to flag the other's attention and reflect on the other's communication. Do this to update your skills.

> "I want to hear what you're saying, but *how* you're saying it (your tone, facial expression, posture, words, etc.) are preventing me. It's my limitation and prevents us from really communicating. Would you please repeat yourself in another tone (posture, words, etc.)."

Rule #6: Know How and When to Call it Quits

Good discussions often go awry because you don't know how or when to quit. You keep at it with emotions heating up until emotion-laden words are said that really heat things up.   The solution is to refuse to let the communication go that far. So call a halt to your conversation before it gets there. As you develop a time-out procedure, you will learn to keep a cool spirit.   Do this by gauging your stress level (from 0 to 10) and calling Time-Out whenever either person reaches a level of 6.

If you don't, do this, if you keep at it while getting more angry, fearful, stressed, one or both persons will hit threshold and will attack. The signal that this has happened is when angry words begin to fly. When you're in the hurt mode, you return the hurt. The problem is the defensive state itself. If you are skilled in how to defuse your loved one, you will handle it. Yet when you do, don't aim to do problem-solving. It's not time for that. Aim only to help the other to ventilate the emotional tensions.

Calling a *Time-Out* prevents things from getting worse. By stopping to take a break every thirty-minutes, you prevent your state from escalating out of control. Agree to a no-escalation rule: "No physical or mental pushing or shoving is allowed." Flag when you feel pushed and then explore, "Is it your intention to push or am I misreading your communication?" If "Yes that's my intention," call Time-Out. If "No," then ask, "Tell me what you're trying to communicate to me that I'm not hearing."   Identify what the other person can do to help you feel safer.

A forgiveness ritual is also important. Do you have a ritual for forgiving and releasing, a ritual so you can kiss and make-up? It's pitiful to not be able to reconcile. Keep shorter accounts and prevent grudges from building-up by saying, "I'm sorry that I didn't conflict in a more productive way; tell me what would have been more useful."

Now, Imagine the Great Fights you Can Have!

How you respond can either provoke or defuse. After all, there's great power in your words and behaviors.   An old Jewish proverb says, "A soft answer turns away wrath, but a harsh word stirs up anger."

You can now aim to persuade without manipulating.   Communicating "negatives" is where most get into trouble. So confront in gentle ways that provide caring feedback. Learn to balance your speaking of *truth* so that it is with *grace and love.* If you over-emphasize truth, you may become brutally honest so we have to know when to shut up. If you over-emphasize love, you may not speak up and be heard. The balance is to "speak the truth in love." This allows you to always speak graciously with a wisdom that adds value to your relating.

Summary

- There is an art and form to having a "fight" *for* the relationship that's positive and loving. It's an entirely new game—a way to deal with things when they are small and manageable. It's a way to get things "on the table" while you still feel resourceful, loving, and thoughtful. The game is to explore each other's desires and understandings and work through to a win/win arrangement. It's as simple as that; it's as important as that.

- Learning to play the *Let's Have a Healthy Fight* Game takes commitment and practice. Yet this kind of conflicting that leads to satisfactory resolution is worth the effort. If you care enough to connect and bond, then you can learn to care enough to confront early, to manage your states, to stay flexible and open, and to translate your love into loving actions.

Chapter   14

THE DANCE OF
A LOVE THAT HEALS

M argery Williams tells a delightful story in her book, *The Velvelteen Rabbit.* It begins late at night in a child's bedroom. There a skin horse and a stuffed rabbit sit up and talk about what it means to be real. The Skin Horse begins:

"Real is not how you are made; it's a thing that happens to you. When a child loves you for a long, long time, not just to play with but *really* loves you, then you become real."

"Does it hurt?" asks the Rabbit.

"Sometimes," said the Skin Horse, for he was always truthful. "When you are real, you don't mind being hurt."

"Does it happen all at once, like being wound up, or bit by bit?"

"It doesn't happen all at once. You become. It takes a long time. That's why it doesn't often happen to people who break easily, or who have to be carefully kept. Generally, by the time you are real, most of your hair has been loved off, and your eyes drop out and you get loose in the joints, and very shabby. But these things don't matter at all, because once you are real, you can't be ugly, except to the people who don't understand."

When you open your hearts, you become receptive and vulnerable to experiencing love and hurt, connection and disconnection, attraction and aversion. You open your hearts to extend your love to others, to invest yourself in the lives and fortunes of others, to care, to love, and to rejoice. Yet in doing this you open yourself to caring enough to hurt when the other hurts, to feel loss when your lover leaves or dies, to feel disappointment, stress, concern and the whole range of emotions. This kind of "hurt" is built into the human experience.

Hurt—this refers to feeling with another and being sensitive to the fortunes and misforuntes of life. This ability to *hurt* distinguishes us from rocks, cars, and other inanimate objects. They are insensitive to both love and pain. Their inability to register such makes them incapable of knowing love. We are able to love because we are able to sense what the other feels.

Hurt isn't a bad thing, yet it is unpleasant. Hurt refers to *how* you register harm, threat, or violation to your being and to your emotional investments. Hurt makes you more authentic, real, and loving. Would you or could you ever trust a person who couldn't feel hurt or be affected or moved emotionally? We describe such individuals as cold, hard, closed, defensive, etc. —words that describe persons who are unlovely and unloving. This is the drama that every robot, android, and Vulcan in sci-fi films goes through. Can you be *human* if you can't experience both the positive and the negative emotions?

When you extend your heart and soul to care about another person, you open yourself up to the most glorious and transcendent emotions *and* at the same time, to the backside of those, the negative and distressing emotions. Yet whether you experience the negative emotions as hellish, gut-wrenching, and despicable depends on *how you frame them*. Are they just "negative" emotions that alert you to threat, harm, or loss or are they demonic and bad in and of themselves?

Recognizing emotions as *just emotions* empowers you to welcome all emotions just as you welcome all thoughts. Thinking-and-feeling is how you process and represent things inside your mind-body system. They are not absolutes, nor are they things. Your thinking-and-feeling is only as good and valid as your thinking-and-emoting which creates them. To the extent that you were using inadequate, or even toxic thinking patterns, your emotions will be off-base and erroneous. That's why it is wise to check out your thinking-and-emoting to make sure that you're not doing yourself harm by how you're thinking.[1]

All of this means that you cannot have deep and lasting relationships without experiencing hurt. It comes with the territory. For anyone well-adjusted to human reality, it is not only *okay*, it is something to celebrate, something to embrace. It's by your emotions that you *come alive* to reality.

If hurt is inevitable then to make your relationships more enjoyable and exquisite you need the abilities and skills to effectively handle hurts. If you experience hurts and wounds without dealing with them effectively, if you try to ignore them, stuff your negative emotions, and/or fight about things with no satisfying resolution, then your emotional bank account will become increasingly depleted. You will become unresourceful. Eventually you will feel overdrawn in your account with your loved one. Then, when one or both persons reach a threshold, something will snap. One or both will pull back, stop connecting, and refuse to extend oneself. Typically this is the beginning of the end. To prevent that requires that you learn how to be healing in your communicating and relating.

When Love Gets Wounded
If there are behaviors that communicate and signal "love" (e.g., the sensory-based behaviors that you use to know when you are loved, respected, valued, appreciated, that deepen and amplify the sense of being loved), then their opposites will undermine, dampen, and destroy your sense of love. These behaviors and actions *dis-bond.* These actions make withdrawals from your emotional bank account, and when continued will bankrupt the relationship.

Too much of this dis-bonding and you will hit a "threshold." You will get to the limit of how much displeasure, hurt, pain, stress, or emptiness you can stand. The threshold is your limit. You hit the threshold when you can't take anymore. You sense that you are living a life that you don't want to live. You will feel that "Nothing is working" and "I can do nothing to make a difference." This sense of powerlessness and inadquacy weakens your bonds of love and connection. At this point you need the dis-bonding actions to stop. You need to find what has gone wrong and chart a new course. The new course may be to find your way back to a loving relationship with your partner or to leave the relationship entirely. Yet, when there has been a lot of hurt in the past, how do you move yourself and a relationship back to an authentically loving one?

The Problem and Danger of Threshold

We often talk about "getting to our threshold." It happens with things that we have dealt with, and coped with, and yet for all the coping, we are unable to effect a change. Typically when we hit our threshold, and "can't take anymore," we become reactive and default to our reactive default patterns. Threshold occurs when we reach our limits (the limits and edges of our map, etc.) and can no longer cope.

Threshold here refers to a stress-overload "the last straw" phenomenon.

• Have you ever experienced threshold with some behavior?
• Have the negative consequences of the behavior lead you to, "Enough of this!"?
• "I will never again smoke (chew, over-eat, be cussed at, be left hanging on the weekend, etc.)."?

Some people will reach and go over threshold several times before it becomes "the last straw." They have natural "threshold reducers" inside the Matrix. Others hit threshold so quickly that it may only take a time or two, and pow! They're over the top with one experience. Threshold involves experiencing too many disappointments or negative symptoms. An old proverb describes this poetically:

> "Hope deferred makes the heart sick, but a desire fulfilled is a tree of life." (Proverb 13:12)

Does hope deferred sicken your heart? *Sick* here literally means "to be weak, diseased, grieved, or exhausted." The spirit feels fatigued, unable to go on, and wiped out. We "lose heart."

To the real and authentic requires the punctuating of illusions. When your expectations are unrealistic, false, and mythological, your maps misguide you and set you up for disappointment. Because unrealistic expectations orient to non-reality, they invite emotional problems. Conversely, aligning your hopes and dreams with reality creates a healthy realism. Here's more of the old Proverbs that summarize such internal *hurt:*

> "A man's spirit will endure sickness; but *a broken spirit* who can bear?" (18:14)
> "A brother *offended* is like a strong city, but quarreling is like the bars of a castle." (18:19)

When your heart breaks because some hope is deferred or some expectation continually falls to the ground, you experience *a wounding of our heart or spirit*. When this happens, you're not only offended, you are grieved and violated, and so become defensive. You become hard to deal with. Do you know this one? Typically when you hit threshold, you become highly defensive and then from that hurt, so you hurt back. You strike out in retaliation. That's why dealing with a hurt and defensive person can be like trying to work with someone behind the walled fortress of a castle who's throwing stones and launching catapults at you. It's not an easy task to get through such defenses.

What is this internal brokenness or hurt like? Here is more poetry:
"A downcast spirit *dries up the bones"* (17:22)
"A glad heart makes a cheerful countenance, but by sorrow of heart *the spirit is broken"* (15:13)
"All the days of the afflicted are *evil* (bad)" (15:15)

This is not a pretty picture! Talk about having a really bad day! Multiply many experiences of disappointment where hope, desires, and expectations are deferred or crushed and watch a person's heart become sick, distressed, wounded, and offended. This is the kind of thing that creates "mental illness" as coping resources are devastated. In this context, you begin to distrust your own mind, emotions, sense of reality, and ability to relate. You become distrustful and cynical about the world, about people, about human nature, about women and about men. Your grief and disappointment leads to a deep sorrow that breaks your very spirit. In that hurt and disillusionment, you then go over threshold.

Seeing the Invisible
When your lover is physically wounded, you can easily detect that hurt and shift your responses to be more caring, compassionate, and gentle. It's easy. Why? Because the damned casts are right in front of your eyes. Anybody can see that. A person would have to be a card-carrying Jerk to act as everything is normal and expect your loved one to do the dishes, take out the garbage, or make wild passionate love. Seeing that she is hurt and not feeling good, you become more thoughtful and considerate. If your lover is sniffing and sneezing, vomiting, or suffering from the flu, you know better than to push for romping in the bedroom.

If you can be so thoughtful and loving when your lover is physically hurting, what interferes with your compassion when the hurt is *emotional*? The problem is that you don't see it! The hurt is less visible. Internal psychological hurts are not so easily seen. While physical ills signal you to go easy, psychological wounds can be hidden under a facade of "normality." The person can act perfectly normal. So without external stimuli reminding you, it's easy to forget to go easy, to be gentle.

Thresholds can be "person specific." That is, a person can be "at threshold" with one particular person (or situation, or event), while able to give and take normally with others. To handle this, you have to see into the matrix. You have to learn to see what's invisible to the physical eye. Such deep perceiving, like deep listening, means becoming more attentive to the other's state and cuing yourself that the person is at threshold.

Falling in and Out of Love
Consider how a person falls in love in the first place. *Valuation* is the first step to falling in love. Love flows from valuing. You can't love something unless you see something to value. So in loving you value and appreciate. From a state of appreciation you recognize value. Knowing what you value and specific behaviors that express such gives you greater power to pursue those values.

When falling in love, you do so from *a state of appreciation.* That's why you notice, recognize, and express appreciation for the qualities, traits, and behaviors that you adore in the other person. Prior to experiencing these strong feelings of appreciation, did you not *value* something in them that fit with your world of values and needs? You love the valued behaviors. Those valued behaviors attract you and create the magic of bonding.

The attraction of values is the magnet that pulls you into relationship. In valuing and appreciating you move closer and closer—and with the the mutual giving and receiving of things you value—you experience intimacy. You then generously give compliments and affirmations, and say endearing things to each other. What an incredible experience! It's ecstasy, romance, and transcendence.

Will it last? Will the excitement and appreciation endure? Typically it will cool as you get used to the glory. Things will habituate. As habituation sets in, you experience a demon called *familiarity*. Is this good or bad, a blessing or curse? It's both. It frees your attention for other things. Yet it also introduces the danger of losing awareness of what you value in each other. No wonder *habituation* threatens relationship. The subtle seduction of simply getting used to your loved one weakens your appreciative valuing. You may even completely stop seeing the other's sacredness and your lover's wonder-filled mystery.

What's the solution? *Keep redirecting your attention to what you can and do appreciate in your lover.* It's to keep making new discoveries about that person. If familiarity leads to a boring stagnation, then when you stop noticing and appreciating, you weaken the bonding. This begins a negative downhill cycle of dis-attraction. Yet there's something else that's even more lethal than familiarity. *Expectation.*

The Eliminating "Expectations" Game
Whenever you fall into the mental dis-ease of setting up expectations about your lover, you introduce a very toxic element into your relationship. With expectations, two things occur:
*   First, you put our loved one "under the law" to your expectations and demands.
*   Second, you set yourself up for disappointment.

Expectations marks a transition point in how you relate to your loved one. When you *expect*, you introduce demands, rules, laws, shoulds, musts, have tos, should nots, etc. into *the Love Game*. Prior to this you simply *desire*. You hope. You want. And with that, every response is a delight, a surprise, a gift.

When you get used to the gifts, familiar with them, you slowly slide into expecting them. Now romance becomes a duty. Before, romance was the excitement and attraction, now law, rules, and obligations govern. Now you "should" on your loved one with a list of your demands.

This will not bring out the best in your loved one, as you well know. Your lover will feel unappreciated. What had been a gift no longer seems like a gift. This is when lovers becomes defensive and argue and set counter-*expectations*. This begins *the Downward Spiraling Game*.

Three things elicit un-romantic states: familiarity, getting used to each other, and expectations. These, in turn, elicit other unresourceful states: impatience, neediness, demanding-ness, sarcasm, anger, and judgment. You reach *the expectation phase* of the relationship when you notice and focus on what is *not* there. As things continue to spiral downward, it invites a negative perspective. It comes out as nagging, fussing, and criticizing. It's not long before you experience more complaints than compliments. All of this sets in motion a dis-bonding as each person feels more and more unloved, unvalued, and unappreciated.

With the negation of love, you feel less respected and less honored. You begin to increasingly notice what you dislike. This initiates a perceptual shift that does the relationship tremendous harm. The disappointments, hurts, and spiraling of negative emotions lead to more complaints, and then complaints about the complaining, until all you can *see* and *perceive* is the other as "the bad guy" the source of pain and hurt in your life.

The Art of Staying in Love Game
What's a couple to do to avoid all of this?

> *You stay in love by reducing your load of expectations, turning up your ability to appreciate everything that you receive from your loved one as a gift and releasing your loved one from your demands. You stay in love by texturing your expectations with appreciation and freedom.*

If *expectations* kill appreciative relationships, then at the heart of the secret of staying in love and experiencing a renewing love is reducing the semantic load on your expectations. Loading up your expectations with far too many meanings is what I mean by "the semantic load." It's a load that burdens the relationship. It does not free you for appreciation, and it certainly does not put more energy or vitality into your relating.

- Does the idea of *not* expecting seem like a strange request?
- Does that seem contradictory to the way you have always thought about relationships?
- Aren't you free, even obligated to *expect* and even *demand* that your lover do the things promised and desired?

That's what we think, isn't it? If they promised to love and honor us, if they promised to meet our needs, then doesn't it follow that if they don't come through, *we can demand it of them*? Don't we have a right to *expect* it? It seems that way. Let's run an ecology check on our expectations to quality control them:

* Do expectations enrich your relationship?
* Do your expectations make things better?
* Do they bring out the best in each of you?
* Do you function better when someone perceives you through the eyes of expectations?

Expectations create and invite a *demanding-ness* into your relating which then undermines the very heart of loving—valuing and appreciating. To reduce the expectation load, shift your thinking:

> "My loved one does not *owe* me anything, but is *free to respond* to give me in whatever way seems appropriate."

If you believe that your partner *owes* you, challenge that thought, "Why does your lover *owe* you? What is the basis for this *owing*? Notice your responses. Usually, it is something like:

> "Because I want her to."

Ahhh, you *want* it! Yet that's an entirely different matter.

> "Because she promised."

Yes, *she* promised. That's her desire. She *wants* to give and extend to you. She plans to be responsive. The question is not what she "owes," but what's interfering with her current desire? What's wounded or hurt that passion? What dampened or killed the passion she once felt?

The secret is to reduce the pressure of expectations on your lover, to release your loved one from your rules. It is to put your lover under your grace and benevolence, and to freely give. It's to return to valuing and appreciating and to rediscover what your lover truly wants and what fits his or her world. What are the behaviors that your lover equates with being loved, respected, close, and bonded? As you rediscover the heart of your loved one, you can then gently deposit these behaviors—expecting nothing. The way of healing is to simple meet his or her needs.

The secret for you is to do this knowing and believing that *when* your lover feels full, loved, safe, valuable in your eyes, appreciated, cared for, listened to, treated as special, etc., the responses you want will come. They will come easily and naturally. It will be spontaneous. Out of abundance comes abundance. All of this necessitates a very loving spirit on your part. It also calls for lots of personality growth in patience, true concern, willingness to be self-giving, gentle, and non-demanding.

Summary

*   In loving and caring and extending yourself, you make yourself vulnerable and that invites the hurting and wounding of love. In relationships, this is inevitable.

*   Yet this "hurting" is not necessarily a "bad" thing. It is what makes you alive and authentic. It is what makes things matters. To avoid being hurt is to avoid entering into *the Game of Love* in the first place.

*   To be in the Game of Love requires that you develop skill at healing wounds that occur. You choose to respond to hurts you receive and to own and correct the hurts you cause your lover.

Chapter 15

THE DANCE OF
HEALING WOUNDED LOVE

If you have ears to hear, you can hear *threshold* in everyday language. To tune your ears to relational thresholds, pay attention to such statements as the following:

"You have pushed me too far this time with your drinking (cussing, ignoring, snide remarks, etc.)."

"You went over the line one too many times."

"That's one time too many!"

"I've had it up to here with your laziness (lateness, possessiveness, jealousy, etc.)!"

"I can't take anymore."

"I just can't love you anymore, I feel like something has snapped or broken inside me."

These words and phrases indicate the experience and process of threshold. They warn that a partner is moving to a threshold and that something is about to snap. *Relational thresholds* involve the repetition of painful things until a limit is finally reached. The person then says, "Enough! Never again!" This happens with regard to habits like smoking, drinking, and over-eating, and it also happens to *hurtful* relational patterns. When you are not being loved, respected, cared for, and nurtured in the ways that count.

What are these threshold patterns based on?

Anything that your loved one finds hurtful or undesirable.

Anything that your lover experiences as an emotional *withdrawal*. You can get to relational threshold with another's cussing, inattentiveness, critical complaining, over-spending, bitching about things, silent treatments, lack of affirmation, broken promises, drinking, financial irresponsibility, etc. Such things push a loving relationship to a breaking point and become the "reasons" as to why people break up or divorce.

"Logic" is not the point here, *it is about our psycho-logics.* You must ask about your lover's psycho-logical state of mind and emotion. Is there something your partner cannot take anymore? It's about the failure of effective communication. It's about your failure in attending and meeting each other's needs, in responding to each other's person and disclosures.

The Structure of Threshold
*   What is the internal structure that leads a person to say, "Enough! Never again!"?
*   What allows a person in love to so radically shift thinking, emoting and behaving as to fall out of love?
*   What does a person do within him or herself to accomplish this?

Steve and Connirae Andreas (1987) describe the *Threshold Pattern* as a tool for getting some behavior or response to go "over the top" so that you can be done with it. To do this, you only need to keep intensifying some thought, feeling, or response until your "response pops" (p. 116). There are numerous ways to do this. You can keep accumulating representations of the unpleasantness continuing (i.e., the pain, distress, etc.) until you reach and cross a threshold. While reaching and crossing threshold usually occurs over a period of time, you can speed it up by overloading, pushing, and amplifying your internal mental movie of what you don't want. When the movie is bad enough, you're out of your seat and the theater!

Natural thresholding occurs through exaggerating or catastrophizing. We all know how to do this, do we not? All you have to do is to stack an unacceptable consequence into the future so much and so fast (i.e., "She will always do this to me for the rest of my life!") that you go over the top. Then you won't be able to take it anymore. This stacking of examples and representations into the future causes your brain to go, *"Enough!"* and for you to feel an impatience about never doing that again.

When you go over threshold, there is almost always some representation of something popping. Something in the inner movie or some meaning frame snaps, breaks, shatters, or crashes. It's similar to the physical threshold occurs when you take a piece of metal and bend it back and forth repeatedly. Eventually a point will come when the metal reaches a critical point and something snaps. The metal breaks. To explore this with your lover, ask:

> "What do you need to do inside to get yourself to the point where you say or feel, 'Never Again!' 'Enough!'?"

Some people store up lots of pictures of failures, insults, etc. Others represent it auditorially as more and more noise, criticism, nagging, cursing, insulting, etc. Some have mental movies of their loved one flying off into infinity, others have it go blank or white out, or go dark. Others exaggerate their pictures. They "make a mountain out of a molehill." Some step back far enough (zoom out) until they can see how ridiculous the whole thing is and then go, "That's useless and stupid!"

After a person's representations shatter, it is usually replaced with entirely different representations. Often a person sees himself being more resourceful, hears himself managing communication more effectively, pictures himself alone, senses quiet and solitude, etc.

When a person goes over threshold, the brain swishes to representations of a different future—it may be of a more attractive future, or it may be of a blank or neutral future, one that is devoid of the pain. When people go over threshold, they go beyond the negative representations they hold about the relationship. They now think about getting out of the relationship. This is the perceptual shift. Prior to threshold a person thinks about how to make things better. Mentally and emotionally the person is still in the relationship frame, and want to make it better. After threshold, the person's perception changes. Now the person wants out. The person thinks about how to get out, not how to resolve things.

Going over threshold shifts a person's mental mapping. *"Never Again!"* we say. We then begin imagining how we will create a new life. Thresholding works by building up feelings through stacking cases, illustrations, pictures, sounds, etc. until we reach a critical mass. We ratchet an unpleasant experience as we loop round and round it. This amplifying process pushes us to a critical mass. When people collect injustices from the past they hit threshold; eventually it sends them over the top.

The dynamic is that your frames about your lover shift when you go over threshold. Steve and Connirae Andreas describe this in these words:

> "Before going over threshold, people usually see the old behavior in their present, and sometimes the future. After people have gone over threshold, that old behavior has usually shifted to the past on their time-line." (p. 126)

This makes the pattern more permanent. As a result, *how* you think about the past with your lover changes. If you think about something that you once were compelled toward, but are no longer, something to which you said, "Never Again!", notice how you represent that old desire. Do you not watch it as if you are a spectator to a movie? Have you stepped out of the movie so that you're no longer in it? Doing this creates the sense, "I know it was me, but it doesn't seem like it was me."

The Neutralizing Threshold Game
•   Can we neutralize a threshold experience?
•   Once a person reaches threshold with a lover about something (or many things), can things be reversed?

The amazing answer is *yes*. Things can be reversed. Yet be warned: the reversal process is a delicate process, and typically takes a lot of time, patience, and skill. Doing so is not for the faint-of-heart or the impatient. It takes a lot of E.Q. (Emotional Intelligence) to pull it off. Why? Because the one over threshold must be gently entreated to become willing to consider the possibility of going back.

At threshold no one is in a resourceful place to even consider that. If there are significant factors and consequences to breaking up (like the effect on the children, family, etc.), then it's at least worth putting in the investment to see what can be done. Actually, even if a couple will not stay together, it's good for the hurt partner to threshold specific behaviors, rather than the whole relationship. This will give more focus and clarity for the next relationship. Intimate relationships are so precious that it is good to neutralize the psychological shift that occurs in hitting threshold. The good thing about going over threshold is that it protects a person's sanity. Hitting threshold shouts that some pattern of relating was not working. It screams at us that put up with something far too long and didn't solve the issue earlier.

How do we neutralize the "mate dissociation?" It begins by *re-evaluating the relationship patterns*:

> "Yes, it's good that you've come to the point where you will *not* accept or tolerate being treated or talked to that way. It's totally unacceptable for a civilized adult person to treat anyone that way, let alone a lover! Now what I want you to do is to use your best assertive skills to confront it, establish a good boundary, set up logical consequences for the other to suffer if they violate those boundaries, and then stick to your guns."

Thresholding specific *behaviors* helps everybody. It breaks the dysfunctional and unloving patterns that created the problem in the first place and enables us to develop more healthy ways of relating. Those who go over threshold first are usually caretakers or rescuers and may have been "co-dependents" to another's dysfunction. Being naturally sensitive to people is both their gift and their curse. They operate in an other-referent way and overdo explaining away the unacceptable behaviors, thereby excusing their partner from responsibility.

When their spirit first gets wounded, instead of using that as a signal that something needs to be attended to—they ignore it. They do not confront. They don't even speak up. They opt for being "nice," and letting things go. Of course, this reinforces the unacceptable behavior and makes things worse in the long run. Others will confront. They will confront time and time again, and get a little response that satisfies them enough to put it off again—for a while.

Yet in the process of ignoring and excusing the source of the pain, their spirit breaks more and more. The internal hurt eventually becomes chronic. Then something more disastrous happens—they go over threshold. Often they try very, very hard to avoid it, but it happens. It is as if the unconscious mind finally forces the person to begin to dissociate from the hurtful behaviors since they do not create a healthy and appropriate distance or boundary.

The emotional dissociation puts them over threshold. As it does, a *belief change* occurs reflecting the perceptual shift. One's internal representations change as images about the lover swishes to negative images. They now believe their lover no longer fits them, their values, or their world. They now feel enough pain that they cry out, "Enough! I can't take anymore! I won't take anymore. I'm out of here."

When this happens, the person snaps. Inside it is nearly impossible to think of anything good or positive about the other person or the relationship. Everything goes blank, bleak, hopeless, useless, worthless, etc. In this way, *thresholding* causes the future to be colored dark. At one level of awareness the person may even want to feel close or positive about their mate again, but at another level can't. (This psychological 'can't' speaks of how the person has shifted inside and has become organized in a different way.) This is a signal of threshold that needs to be neutralized.

The Threshold Game: *"I've Had Enough!"*
Many at threshold desperately "try again." Yet when they do, they find themselves only going through the motions and not feeling love or attraction. Often this "trying again" actually makes things worse. The threshold person's "tries" are ineffective, and only add more "failure" to their list of failures which gives them yet another thing to feel bad about. Sometimes this becomes the "proof" that the relationship can't get better.

What happens at threshold is that a person *cannot* try. The person is not in the right state to give it a good try. The person is not resourceful enough. The threshold experience prevents the person from being effective. It prevents one from seeing the partner through unprejudiced eyes. The perceptual shift prevents one from seeing one's loved one in a fresh and unbiased way. There's too much hurt inside that needs to be addressed, healed, and released.

Many things have to be addressed—the patterns that have not worked and the negative beliefs. So before "trying" to work on the relationship, the threshold person needs a break from trying. Release him or her from all of the normal relationship pressures—from even the basic expressions of affection (like hugs and kisses).

Because going over threshold triggers a perceptual shift, it is harder to win him or her back than conquering a fortress. Why is this? Because all of the person's defenses are up. The person "knows" that his or her lover is hurtful and causes pain, that everything in the past has been terrible, and that there is no hope in the future. The person's hopes have been deferred so often and so much that the person's heart and soul is "broken." That's why the person cannot see good in the one once so attractive. Attraction has turned to aversion.

When this happens to us, then typically we demonize our partner. We no longer see our partner as sacred. We see him or her as an enemy to our happiness, an opposer to everything sacred (i.e., our talent, growth, hopes, needs, etc.). Nor can we order or demand this to go away although I have actually seen partners try such ... to their own detriment. It doesn't work. They only confirm their mate's worst nightmares.

Once at threshold, numerous limiting beliefs that sabotage the relationship itself arise:

> "The relationship is over."
> "It's not worth having."
> "My partner cannot and will not provide the desired and necessary fulfillment of those behaviors that I highly value."

You can verify for yourself that your lover is at this stage if he or she perceives you in this way. Are your behaviors now experienced and perceived negatively? "My mate is stupid, dishonest, ugly," etc. Behind all of this, the threshold person is inwardly bankrupt of those highly valued behaviors that would have allowed them to feel loved, respected, wanted, etc. When these behaviors do occur, they are discounted. The threshold experience's perceptual filter prevents that.

Neutralizing Threshold

The design of neutralizing the threshold experience is to gain sufficient clarity to evaluate the relationship and to negotiate a better arrangement. The first thing about someone at, or over, threshold is that the person is stepping *into* painful memories about the partner and stepping *out of* past pleasures. Pain and dissatisfaction is now attached to the loved one. Negative emotional states are linked to them which darkens of the past.

The Neutralizer Pattern is designed to separate the pain from the partner without dismissing the pain of the behavior. It allows us to regain access to the pleasant memories. After all, they are our memories and should be used for feeling good, not bad. There's no need to lose them or let them become darkened. Before re-evaluating the relationship, regain the lost resources. The following is Leslie Cameron-Bandler's "Threshold Neutralizer" pattern.

Step 1: *Establish a Self-Appreciation State*

In the process of recovering those resources, allow yourself to lean back in a comfortable chair and find yourself getting relaxed and comfortable. Allow these words to elicit your resources for a new sense of identity.

For now, just pay attention to yourself. Rather than working on the one with whom you feel so hurt. Now is the time for you, for self-healing. After all, hasn't this been a difficult time for you because you have suffered from deferring your hopes for so long and because you haven't really taken good care of yourself? That's what we want to do now. For right now, regardless of what you eventually decide, know that it will be in your best interest to learn how to *feel good* about yourself.

The ability to love anyone begins with the ability to appreciate your own dignity, qualities, gifts, skills, and person. If you are ever to love anyone in a healthy way, it arises from the foundation of being able to validate yourself and to keep all of your good feelings with you. Doing so allows you to feel more full. People give when the are full, not when empty. Fullness brings out our best, not emptiness.

If you go back to your partner out of guilt, how productive will that be or if you go back out of fear and insecurity? Both you and your partner deserve to have a relationship in which you are loved, wanted, and cared for, do you not?

So just for right now pull out of your memory banks a time and place when you really appreciated yourself. Recall a time when you paid attention to yourself and to the relationship you have with yourself. From that, *make a check list* of those things that you appreciate most about yourself.
* What are the qualities that you cherish most about yourself?
* What are the qualities that you want seen and valued?

Take a few moments and give yourself this gift of appreciating something about who you are.... And as you do this you can anchor these good feelings of appreciation, because they are yours and they enable you to be full—inwardly rich and able to give.

If this is difficult to do, then think about someone who you know loves you. Think of someone who you know, without a doubt, loves you. Who is this person? Perhaps a parent, spouse, friend, child, or God. Or you may want to think about someone who you know appreciates something about you or something that you've done. Allow yourself to enter into their eyes so as to turn, and look at you through the eyes of appreciation.

You can *relax* into that feeling of self-appreciation even more than you have before. Perhaps you are seeing yourself in a past experience where you demonstrate some highly valued quality. Perhaps you are seeing what you were seeing and feeling in a cherished memory. Allow yourself to get fully in touch with what it is you appreciate about yourself. *Appreciate* yourself in a way that sustains you and assures that you will express your best qualities in your future. See yourself in every time zone (past, present and future) from this appreciative view. Because this appreciation is yours and not dependent on anyone, it can't be taken away from you.

Isn't it worth holding onto because it is such a powerful resource? And it's worth taking with you as you look into your past, your present, and your future. For with self-appreciation you can see mistakes, and successes while still caring for yourself. With appreciation you can encourage yourself and others without collapsing into negative feelings.

STEP 2: *Mentally Dissociate From Your Partner*
Now feel this rich and full feeling of appreciation for the person you are and begin to carry it with you as you begin to turn the clock back and to recall another memory. Begin to recall this memory as just an image of how your partner first looked to you in the beginning. Let it be just a still shot, like a snapshot. And the only thing that's important now is that you can still *feel your feelings of self-appreciation* as you see him.

Hold on to feeling good within yourself and about yourself, at the same time that you begin to see him as he was in the beginning of your courtship. Now while you know that other things have happened between you, from this point of view with self-appreciation, you can begin to see him as separate from you, as a separate person in his own right. See him over here, separate from you and while you do you can continue to *feel those feelings of self-appreciation*, and look at him for who he is.

As you begin to see him as an independent person, separate from yourself, you can realize that in the beginning of your courtship, he must have been seen as special to you. He was important to you then. Good and bad, his qualities, his style and his attributes once attracted you, and were cherished by you. Are you willing to think of him at that time long ago when you first met him? You may or may not see all his talents, the things that make him who he is that you can appreciate.

While you do, *feel* those feelings of self-appreciation while you see him as his own person, begin to identify what it was that drew you to him in the first place. What was it? What did you love about him then? Until now, it's been hard for you to step aside from him as you can now. And being able to maintain that kind of psychological distance enables you to maintain your own integrity and individuality, it enables you to do good boundary work, and that gives you just the kind of strength that you're going to need in order to speak up in a kind and yet assertive way, so that any relationship can be straight, healthy, and satisfying.

STEP 3: *Reconnect Yourself to Some Positive Memories*
I want you to now find and reconnect with some positive memories that you both shared together. Because those too are yours, and because it would be a shame to lose them, it's important to realize that it would be a lie if you let your current perceptual shift to blacken your past.

So when you have taken a look at him from those eyes . . . so that you can see him clearly as you would see another person, keep your own sense of yourself securely in your own hands with appreciation, go ahead and pick one pleasant memory that was good for you which you shared.

Now pick some memory where there was more than would have been if either of you alone. Allow your unconscious mind to pick a time in which his presence contributed and brought forth more out of you than would have been possible by yourself. Explore that memory with your self-appreciation feelings to discover what other good feelings are there.

Enough time has passed that you can now reminisce and feel nostalgic with that someone from your past that you cared about. You cared enough to have such a pleasant experience in your memories. This is your memory, no one else's. It would be a shame to lose your precious memories and its good feelings. As you do this always continue to feel your own sense of appreciation for yourself as you are reminiscing through a past experience, or more than one, that you shared with him.

Allow yourself to feel how much of that experience comes back to you even now and you can feel how good that was now. You can remember that it is yours, and you can come back to it anytime . . . leisurely, taking all the time you need to hold onto feeling yourself as whole, secure in your sense of self, appreciating who you are and who you are becoming. And when you have done that allow your unconscious to consolidate these learnings so that they will be with you."

Debrief Explanations

Your past resourceful experiences are yours, so wouldn't it be a robbery to have the pleasant memories from your personal history taken from you? If memories were pleasant in the past, then they are pleasant. And that makes them innate resources. To deprive yourself of them only darkens your state of mind and makes you less resourceful for relationship. Since those memories are yours, let's proactively refuse to let them be contaminated by bad feelings. This is one way you can be more kind and gentle to yourself as you move into your future.

Summary

- Love can be wounded so grievously that winning back the offended person can become a major task. Yet dealing with the problem of a person who has gotten to a threshold level and can't take something any longer can be learned.

- Reducing the wound calls for patience, understanding, resourcefulness, and the ability to reframe.

End Notes:

1. See Appendix B, *Thinking Patterns.* The more your thinking is formed and governed by cognitive distortions, the more your misery and problems.

THEORETICAL FRAMEWORKS

FOR

GAMES GREAT LOVERS PLAY

You have explored *the Games that Great Lovers Play.* While there is some information there, some of which may be new, my focus has been on setting forth the Love Games so that you can quickly step in and begin playing and enjoying them.

What follows differs from that. Here are some of the more theoretical foundations and frameworks for the Games.

Chapter 16

CONNECTING

The Bonding Game

The invitation to bonding says,
"Come in and make yourself at home."

- How do people connect?
- What creates the feelings of connection?
- How does love bond people together?
- How is it created, supported, and developed?
- What skills are needed to create a lasting and loving bond?

Lovers are *lovers* precisely because somehow, in some way, they have become *bonded* to each other either in mind, heart, body, and soul. Typically, it starts with the physical bonds of attraction and desire. From there it moves to the emotional bonding of heart to heart, and then to the mental bonding that leads to commitment bonding. We describe this psychological state as bonding, connecting, and closeness. This describes the very heart of greater lovers—creating a feeling of connection with each other.

- Yet what is this thing that we call *"bonding?"*
- What do we mean when we say we are bonded to someone?
- How does bonding work?
- What are the factors involved in bonding?
- What factors create a dis-bonding?

•   How does the *lack* of bonding affect a couple?

Acknowledging that *bonding* lies at the heart of loving and connecting, we want to explore how great lovers create the significant bonding of mind, body, heart, and soul. How does bonding work? If you want to become great lovers, you need to be mindful about how these processes work. To play well you need to know how the Game works. You will then love consciously and be able to mindfully improve it day by day.

Bonding as Emotional Connecting

In woodworking, metal work, and other facets of physical materials, we speak about the forging of the materials as creating *a bond*. There are glues and apoxies that create such bonding. Super-glue is a great bonding agent in the physical realm and you may know that all too well if you have ever gotten some on your fingers. That's the bonding of tangible things.

Psychological and personality bonding begins very early. In fact, *we are born to bond.* The bonding of our lives, minds, hearts, and souls begins with birth. Part of healthy development depends on the mother-child bond, the bond with our caretakers, the bond with our siblings and friends. And, as we are social creatures, this continues throughout life. Our connection, closeness, and bonding with others is what allows us to become fully human.

We are not born fully human—we *become* human. Young children separated from a human community and raised by animals become *feral* children. Typically they miss the imprinting of language, symbolism, and culture during critical developmental stages. In missing these critical imprints, they miss key ingredients in the experience of becoming human. They may never discover how to enter into the symbolic world of language and tools that make us human.[1]

The most primitive bonding occurs around our survival needs. We depend on those who take care of us to keep us warm and fed, and to protect us from harm. And even at the survival level, we also need to be touched, stroked, noticed, talked to, played with. Without such we literally and physically shrivel up and either die—we "fail to thrive." Those taken hostage by armies or kidnappers often experience this kind of bonding. They may forge bonds with their captives, sometimes even shifting identities to fit in with those who control them, as Patti Hearst did when she joined her kidnappers and fell in love with their cause.

More advanced forms of bonding occur. Simply being around others in close proximity can create a bond. Your original friendships with associates arise in this way. You bond with those with whom you play, interact, and associate. This bonding of activities explains why we revert to these factors in many team building processes like rope courses, outbound adventures, river rafting trips, etc. It explains the bonding between rescuers and survivors in a disaster. Working together to achieve an objective brings people together and creates a bond.

This is especially true for play. *Playing bonds.* We bond with those with whom we play. This explains the prominence of sports, teams, athletics, etc. and why and how we can become so attached, so devoted, so emotionally invested in "our home team." We connect and bond when we do things together and are in close proximity. Realizing that putting people together offers an opportunity to connect lead to the 1960 efforts in the USA to integrate the black and white communities.

The next highest level of bonding occurs through *similarity of ideas and beliefs.* It is in this way that you connect, bond, and feel invested mentally with others. This shifts the relating from mere physical activity and proximity to sharing a similar point of view or better yet, a world-view. This explains the bonding and closeness that occurs in clubs, associations, churches, and civic groups. It explains the influence groups in an entire culture can have when they unite around "an idea whose time has come."

Emotional bonding comes next and yet often arises through the previous forms of bonding. You experience the connecting of hearts as you invest your emotions. This is obviously true of the positive emotions: caring, compassion, love, sympathy, empathy, joy, fun, pleasure, celebration, etc. It is also true of the negative emotions: anger, fear, sadness, grief, regret, guilt, shame, etc. There are groups that form around these emotions. Many of the anonymous groups build a whole program around a particular negative emotion. That's what bonds the participants. They know that emotion, and that emotion forms a great part of their self-definition and identity.

Psychological Bonding

While I have spoken of mental and emotional bonding as if these are separate, they are not. While we use different words and terms, *mind-body-and-emotion* work together as one *system*, the same neuro-linguistic system that describes our brain-body functioning. Actually, we can only separate these facets in language—it is only a way of talking, the separation is not real. Where there is mind, there is body. There are no dis-embodied minds except in sci-fi movies. Where there is body, there is mind, and with mind, there is emotion.

This mind-body-emotion system is what we mean when we use another term, a more holistic term, "psychological." That's what we're talking about, *psychological bonding*. How you use your speech and behaviors, your activities, and lifestyle to effect the sense on the inside that you are invested and connected, or *bonded* with another.

Psychological bonding involves framing—how you frame yourself, others, ideas, the world, meaning, etc. When you frame something as essential to your survival needs or to your psychological needs, you typically connect with that object, person, activity and may even *identify with* it. This is the foundation of your sense of self, your sense of self-definition, and what we call (or miscall), "identity." Who you "are" becomes highly related to who, and what, you bond with.

Isn't that true for you? "Who are you?" As you identify who you are, notice how your answers specify the people, experiences, and ideas with whom you have identified.

The deeper or more intimate or closer the connection you make with a group, an idea, a belief, a set of activities, a lifestyle, a person, a family, a race, a nation, a country, etc., the more *bonded* you feel. And the more you will *identify* with that object. This mental-emotional or psychological bonding explains how you can bond with real and unreal things, tangible and intangible things, actual and imaginary things, people living and dead.

Bonding and the Ego
Psychoanalysis explains bonding in terms of ego, ego-extension, and ego-incorporation. We are born without an "ego," that is, a *self-aware sense of self* (a "me" or "I") that can face reality. We begin without a sense of self, without personal boundaries, without knowing who we are, what we are, without a differentiation from others. The best we can tell, the newborn infant experiences no discrimination between self and other, especially mother. Self-and-mother; having been part of the same system for nine

months is undifferentiated. In time the newborn will learn to make the first primitive discriminations as it discovers itself as an organism separate from mother—with its own fingers, arms, feet, stomach, mouth, eyes, etc.

We call this separation process, *individualizing.* This refers to the process of how you become a separate and independent individual. In this you become more and more *aware of your self* and construct your first mental maps about your self. You do so in very primitive terms: you feel good or bad; you trust that your needs will or will not be taken care of, you sense stability or chaos, you learn to self-nurture or you remain helpless and needy, etc. No wonder your first impressions set the frames for how you experience the world.

Ego, in this sense, is a neutral term simply referring to your ability to face reality for what it is, that is, to use your eyes, ears, skin and other senses to represent reality. You represent the world and then deal with it. Ego is to your orientation to the world, your reality orientation. You develop a strong ego as you learn to trust your basic visual, auditory, and kinesthetic senses. This enables you to trust your representations of what you see, hear, and feel. At first you cannot hold your internal images constant. So, when "out of sight," mommy is also "out of mind." This creates the delight of peek-a-boo, and the horror of mommy going out for the evening with daddy.

With time, "constancy of representation" allows you to carry your see-hear-feel world *in your mind.* After that you begin to manipulate the internal world on the theater of your mind. This gives birth to ever higher stages of cognitive development as described by Piaget. It gives your first sense of who you are, your sense of self. This is a neutral term that simply describes your self-conscious awareness of yourself and your ability to accept reality for what it is.

Bonding occurs as you *open up* your "self" (your sense and definitions of self) and brings other things, people, experiences, ideas, etc. *into it.* As you bring in you mom and dad, they become part of your internal world, your internalized others. You bring in brother and sister and puppy dog and your toys and your favorite foods, etc. Opening up your ego boundaries and bringing things in describes the process and dynamics of "bonding."

These processes continue into adult life. You buy a new car and "bond" with it. It is "your" car. You bring it into your mental world. It enters into your "ego space." Which is why you can feel your very "self" violated when someone scratches your new car.

"Hey, it's just a car, chill out!"

While you may agree, "Yeah, I know!" on the inside, at the level of bonding, *you* somehow, in some way, feel that *you* have been violated. It's the same way when you *bond* with your jobs, job titles, degrees, family, loved ones, pets, etc. You bring them into the mental world of who you are (your Matrix), what you like, what you're about (your inner "quality world" or model of the world). It's as if you open your ego boundaries, incorporate the person, thing, event, or idea, and then set a boundary that protects it as "yours."

Usually you experience emotional bonding as a wonderful and ecstatic experience. When you bond with someone or something on the emotional level, "you" become more in your sense of self. You feel *more* of who you are with this person, with this job, this car, this child, this title, etc. Your world expands. As you transcend your old definitions of self, you emotionally experience this as transcendence. This explains the headiness and "rush" of infatuation at first love.

In dis-bonding the reverse happens. In dis-bonding, you have something inside your quality world in your mental theater that you find painful, distressful, untrue, or unuseful. So you seek to expel the pain and shove it out beyond your ego-boundaries. You discharge it. You de-commission it. "No longer mine." "I don't want it." "Take this job and shove it." You experience this as *grief*.

Emotionally, you find this painful. You label and experience it as *loss*. You are less for it. That's why most people find it hard, difficult, painful, and time-consuming to dispel something from their internal quality cinema world. In divorce, mid-age crisis, identity crisis, job loss, bankruptcy, etc. you expel whatever thing creates tremendous pain inside your world. Yet at the same time, to rid yourself of it without having something to replace it feels like a bleak emptying of life.

The Mechanisms of Bonding
With this description, you can now identify several of the numerous

mechanisms involved in psychological bonding:
- *Representing:* Representing something in the theater of your mind and incorporating it inside your "quality world."
- *Valuing:* Giving value and significance to a person or thing.
- *Owning:* Claiming ownership of the object of the connection.
- *Identifying:* Identifying yourself with that object so that it becomes part of your self-definition, part of your "identity" and yourself.
- *Opening:* An opening up to the influences of another person.

You use and apply these mechanisms whether the bonding is based upon survival needs, proximity, activity, giving and receiving emotions, ideas, etc. In this you see the extent to which bonding is neuro-semantic. Bonding involves the meanings (semantics) of value and significance that you give to an object, person, experience, or idea and how that meaning affects your entire brain-body neurological system.

You cannot *not* bond. It's only a question of *what* you bond with and *how* you engage in that bonding. Bonding is a game we all play. The question is whether your bonding is healthy or toxic, whether it supports your development or undermines and limits it. Hitler obviously bonded with some pretty toxic ideas, race superiority and blood purity. He identified himself with the Aryan Superiority myths and made them his purpose and his mission. Mother Teresa bonded with ideas and emotions of empathy and compassion and brought that into her Matrix. Soon it became her neuro-semantics and fully entered into her neurology and her muscles becoming her "way of being in the world."

The same happens when you bond with those you love. You bring your loved one into the quality world of your Matrix ... into the cinema that you constantly play in the theater of your mind. In this way your connection to them becomes a key part of your model of the world—who you are and what you're about. When that happens, you become highly invested in those you bond with. The fortunes and misfortunes of the others affect you as if they were your own because at the neuro-semantic level, they are your own. You have made them your own. That's why their departure or distress is your pain.

The Principles of Bonding
How do we bond? What are the principles of bonding?

- *Representation.* Bonding begins by representing someone in your mind. It initiates your connection with your images of that person. This is so powerful, you can bond with someone not present and not even real. Presence isn't necessary for bonding. You can feel close to someone who has died.
- *Heart opening.* Bonding occurs when you open your heart to another and let the other in.
- *Emotions.* Bonding occurs through investing your emotions. You can bond by hate, anger, resentment, pity, fear, etc. and you can bond with love, compassion, play, and attraction.
- *Involvement.* You bond as you get involved in another's life.
- *Opening boundaries.* The best bonding occurs when your boundaries are permeable rather than rigid. The more you have walls rather than boundaries, the less you're able to bond.

The Game of Bonding

Given the fact of bonding, we can now identify the Rules of the Game and learn how to play *the Bonding Game* mindfully and intentionally. Here are the rules if you want to play this game:

1) *Be supportive.*

Give of yourself in ways that supports the other's survival and emotional needs. The more you provide a positive support to the other, the easier it will be for you to bond with that person and for that person to bond with you. Let your heart by your loved one's sanctuary.

2) *Spend quality time.*

Spend lots of quality time together doing things that are fun, pleasurable, valuable, and meaningful. Use proximity to get to know, attached, and invested in the other. The more you relate in ways that evoke positive emotional states, the more you will bring the other into your quality world and feel connected. Neglect this, and the bonding weakens.

3) *Disclose your heart.*

Share ideas, values, understandings, visions, hopes, dreams, etc. The more you share your mental world, the more understand the other and can appreciate the other.

4) Share your emotions.

Give and receive empathy, compassion, love, affection, wonder, curiosity, fun, playfulness, etc. The glue of your bonding gets stronger as you share your emotions and weaker to the extent that you don't.

5) Be open and vulnerable.

Make yourself open and vulnerable to the other. When you extend yourself, and invest your hopes and fortunes, this makes relationship possible. Disclosure of yourself as being real, authentic, honest, etc. also allows the other to trust you more apart from the roles that you play.

6) Be available.

Give your presence to the other person. Give your ear in attentive listening. Give your eye and heart in providing your presence and countenance. Be present when you are with your loved one and be nowhere else.

7) Make it safe for others to connect with you.

Provide assurance and a non-judgmental response pattern so that others feel safe and secure in your presence and in your eyes.

Meta-Rules of the Game

If these are the first *Rules of the Game* for getting close, connecting, and becoming deeply attached to another, then by implication there are frames above these that are equally important. These higher frames operate as the meta-rules of the game. [*Meta* refers to something that is "above and beyond" or "higher" to something. Hence, meta-rules are rules about rules.]

1) Develop a strong sense of independence.

Are you ready for the first paradox of relationship? It takes a lot of independence, a lot of ego-strength, self, self-esteem, etc. to open yourself up to another. All of this enables you to be vulnerable in a healthy way. You can only *give* in this way when you have enough of yourself to give. You can only bond and connect when you're not afraid to open your ego-boundaries and let another in. When you are okay with your own humanity, fallibility, and vulnerabilities.

2) Develop a strong sense of abundance and resourcefulness.

> To give in a healthy way, your giving must not deplete your resources. Giving and extending yourself must come from the sense that you have plenty to give, from a sense of abundance. When you have a full and rich sense of self, you relate, not in order to become a somebody, but to express that you are a somebody.

3) Develop the self-trust to open and share your internal world.

> It takes a lot of trust and openness to chase away the fear of opening up your ego-boundaries. Only then can you let another in. You do so in belief that it is by giving that you become richer. Obviously you do not do this with everyone, wisdom enables you to know who is trustworthy and who is not.

Summary

- Bonding is your heritage as a human being. It is the way you connect and create healthy relationships. In bonding you open yourself up to others—to the influence of others.

- In this it takes a lot of resourcefulness to bond in an open and healthy way.

End Notes

1. There's a lot of literature on Feral Children, I wrote about it in *Languaging* (1996) in describing human consciousness as a languaged phenomenon.

Chapter 17

CENTERING

Independent Enough to Bond

The Inter-Dependence Game

Great lovers bond because they know how to give themselves to each other. Seemingly, *connecting* comes easy and natural to them. They seem to possess a magical quality that reaches out and invites the other into their world. They fully experience the quality and richness of the bonding process.

- How do they do this?
- What are the secrets to this bonding magic?
- What preparations have they made that allows such bonding richness to emerge?

Quality bonding does not happen for the unprepared. There are certain prerequisites and preparations that allow you to bond with your loved one. Bonding with a lover involves numerous factors and makes certain demands of you.

To bond in a healthy and vigorous way you have to prepare yourself and you have to be very centered. After all, bonding means investing your minds and hearts. You have to prepare yourself for this kind and quality of bonding. You need certain skills and resources if you want to connect in this way for this game. Without adequate preparation for bonding, you fall back onto an infantile bonding seeking another to take care of you.

- So, how do you prepare for the bonding of intimacy?
- What are the foundational qualities?

Would you like to play *the Bonding Game*? If so, you need to be solidly grounded in a sense of who you are. This grounding or centering enables you to mindfully use the principles and processes of bonding to connect with another. This grounding involves becoming centered in your internal powers, in a solid sense of self, in a healthy sense of independence, and in distinguishing responsibility *to* and *for*. This grounding prepares you for the wonderful world of inter-dependency.

Alone Enough to Bond

There's a strange oscillation in our experiences. When we are conceived, we develop in a context of complete connection, and yet we are born to individuate so that we can connect again. Paradox. Via our psychological birth onward, we experience a consciousness that is immutably private. Ultimately, we are alone. We are alone with our thoughts and emotions, our mappings of the world, and our self-awareness. In the last analysis, this is our glory and our agony. Our aloneness enables each of us to develop a strong sense of self, a sense of *me*. It also allows us to connect again from the richness of our self endows us with a sense of *we*.

It is in this sense that it takes a lot of self-esteem and independence to healthily connect with another. Until you come to terms with yourself, your ultimate aloneness, and your willingness to be yourself, you will seek to use others to feel okay rather than to give yourself. This is the basis of unhealthy bonding. Independence is the foundation for bonding.

The Grounding or Centering Game

To become independent enough to bond each person of a couple has to be solidly grounded in a strong sense of self. If your sense of self is resourceful and independent then your connecting will use each person's strengths and fullness. This allows each to extend self in a mutual giving-and-taking interaction that supports each other. This eliminates the desperate neediness of feeling empty from infecting the relating.

It takes a lot of self-esteem to relate to another in a healthy and straight-forward way. To love someone out of your emptiness turns the "love" into a clinging, childish neediness. That kind of "love" will only last as long as the two people play the *Rescue Game* with each other. As soon as one person tires or grows up, the game is over.

To relate in a warm and loving way to another we first need a solid sense of your own strength and independence. Does that strike you as strange? It will if you don't know that love is about giving, enriching, enjoying, and blessing another. True love is not about getting. If you want to be in relationship with another to feel full, to be more of who you are, to fix your problems, to be okay within yourself, you are looking for a therapist, not a lover. Doing so mis-uses the relationship and is not the design of a healthy coupling relationship.

How you relate to yourself sets the course for how you relate to others. Your self-relationship establishes your style and reasons for relating to others. It answers the question about your motivations and intentions in relating. *Why* are you seeking to bond with another? You can do so in healthy and in unhealthy ways, for legitimate or for illegitimate reasons.

Unhealthy reasons: to become a Somebody, to fix yourself, to finish "unfinished business" of your history and previous relationships, to fix someone else, to prove something, to make up for your inadequacies, to have someone take care of you, etc.

Healthy reasons: to express yourself, to extend yourself for the other person, to give and receive love and affection, to enjoy companionship, to co-create a life together, and to grow together into new and higher levels of purpose, cooperation, and fun.

Connecting with another to get the love that you didn't get during childhood or to become a somebody, or to prove that you are lovable *uses* the other person. It confuses relationship with therapy. Connecting to fix them, to straighten them out, to help them, etc. similarly confuses relationship and love with consultancy. "Co-dependent" relationships arise from these kinds of arrangements. In co-dependence, you need the other, not as a healthy expression of your mutual needs, but for some individualized agenda: to get a new mommy or daddy or to be a new mommy or daddy to the other. What is the solution to this?

Being Independently Centered

The solution to co-dependency, to *using* another person for your undeveloped issues, is to develop your own *independence.* It is to know yourself, to operate out of your own strengths, to feel self-assured, to know your own mind, and to have sufficient confidence in your personal powers to take effective action.

Healthy inter-dependency first moves from being dependent to being independent. Only then can you move to inter-dependence. Without this step, you move from dependence to co-dependence.

Healthy *independence* involves autonomy, assertiveness, and a strong sense of individuality. Independence allows two people to effectively share and interact in a mutually beneficial give-and-take manner. Their responses come from their strengths and are expressions of their resourcefulness. When you *give and receive* from a state of personal strength, you can do so in a straightforward way. It allows you to level with the other respectfully.

By way of contrast, when you are dependent, you are more defensive, needy, and unable to stand on your own. You then focus on everything being precisely fair and equal. You become demanding. This makes you less able to extend yourself when circumstances call for it. In dependency, you are less able to get out of yourself, out of your ego. You easily feel and quickly become defensive.

Inter-dependency is based on healthy independence—upon differentiating yourself from others and becoming self-contained as an individual. Centering yourself in your own values and principles, you have healthy ego-boundaries and can exercised your right to say "Yes" as well as "No." You have the personal strength to give out of your resources and to extend yourself for the sake of another.

Independence enables you to know and own your own response-abilities, assume complete responsibility *for* yourself, and assume responsibility *to* others. When you are independent, you can easily share your independence with another because you recognize and accept that relationships are conditional. Love may be unconditional, but relating is highly conditional (more about this later on). You can give-and-take with others in non-competitive ways.

The Challenge of Independence

When I first met Janet, she very much lacked personal independence and was very dependent on her husband John. She didn't feel that her opinion counted, that she could cope with life, and that she would be nothing and horribly lost if anything happened to Bill. This, of course, led her to act in very clinging and possessive ways. When they first married, Bill loved that. He took these responses as being "loved." But after a few years of it and with all of the other demands on his time, energy, and efforts, he became very tired of it.

"Let me see if I understand where you both are, and what you want. Bill, you are feeling that you want Janet to be less clinging and possessive. And Janet, when you hear this, it feels like Bill is pushing you away and rejecting you? Is that an accurate assessment?"

> "Yes, she just needs to grow up and realize that I can't baby her all the time."

And when you say "grow up," what does that mean? How do you see her "growing up?" What would that involve?

> "She's always wanting me to tell her that I love her, and she can't seem to make any decision. I have to do everything."

And Janet, does that make any sense to you or do you have a different perspective on it?

> (Sniffing and quietly crying) "If he really loved me, he would tell me, wouldn't he? That's all I'm asking."

Is that how it feels, that he doesn't love you?

> "Yeah. Of course, he keeps pushing me away. What else am I to think?"

So on the emotional level, it feels like rejection and the lack of love? [Yeah] If you step back from that and look at Bill, what do you think? Do you think he's trying to get rid of you or do you think he loves you?

> (Crying) "I don't know. I just don't know."

Really? You really don't have a clue ... if you did, and I know this sounds kind of crazy, but if you did know the truth ... if you could step back and look at Bill with objective eyes, what would you then know?

"Well, I know he loves me, but I just don't feel it, and especially when he gets frustrated with me wanting more time for snuggling and kissing."

Janet, what's your worst fear? Just say anything that comes to mind, no matter how crazy it might sound.
"I'm nothing; there are so many other women that Bill could have who are more pretty, stronger ... (crying)."

Janet, it sounds like you want and need Bill's love to be okay. To feel good about yourself. To feel validated as a person. Does that seem true for you? (Yeah.) So, you need his love for your own sense of validity, do you love yourself?
"What?"
Do you love yourself? Do you love and appreciate yourself? Do you feel okay in and of yourself?
"No. How can I when I'm being rejected?"

So there's an emptiness inside and you look to Bill's love and affection to fill ... Do you love him?
"Well, yes, of course."
Really?
"Yes."

What is that like ... on the inside? How do you know you love him ... you don't need to say anything or explain it, just be with those emotions of love. Good. And do you love your children (shaking her head 'Yes') ... Good ... you really do? Then be with those feelings too. Because you know how to love, don't you? To want the best for your husband and children, to extend yourself for them, to want to be with them ... right? Good. ... Now feeling all of that, *feel that love for yourself* ... let it reflect back onto yourself. Hmmmmm. You don't need to understand this ... just feel this for yourself as a human being, as a precious and valuable person.

This was just the beginning, applying the thinking-and-feeling of "love" to herself to build up self-loving, self-esteeming, and self-validating. This eventually led her to being able to let the feelings of love from Bill to "count" and to stay with her.

Three Game States
Dependence, Independence, and Inter-dependence

When we are born, we are born totally dependent and in absolute need that someone take care of us. We are born *needy*. We need someone to take care of our survival needs, to protect from harm, and to introduce us into human culture. Not a single one of us could have made it on his or her own.

Consider *how* we are born—the state and condition we're in when we first arrive in the world. We are born ignorant, undeveloped, undifferentiated, unskilled, and inarticulate. We know nothing, we can do nothing, say nothing, we don't even know that we are a separate self. These traits of immaturity call for development and describe our utter sense of dependency.

Yet with time, growth, and training, we become less and less dependent. Growing up is a growth into personal independence so that we can stand on our own two feet and become a contributing member of a community. This independence may be healthy and productive, it can also be unhealthy and counter-productive.

A *counter-dependent* person rejects dependency altogether and so cannot be dependent even in a healthy way. As a result this leads such persons to polarize to anything that resembles dependency. They do such to demonstrate that he or she will not accept any dependency. Because the counter-dependent person utterly fears needing another person or depending on another, he or she will have semantic reactions to dependency, even to the thought of such. This forces him or her to opt for a hermit type of life to get away from human interactions.

Those who differentiate themselves in healthy ways from parents and peers, and who develop autonomy center themselves in their own sense of self with their own values and visions. This gives them good boundaries with others, with events, and with experiences. It allows them to enter into inter-dependent relationships with appropriate trust, faith, love, and wisdom. They have moved through and negotiated the developmental tasks that psychologist and theorist Erick Erickson described, namely, trust, initiation, autonomy, independence, faith, etc. They develop self-confidence which allows them to truly be him or herself in relation with others without dominating or being dominated.

This allows us to trust easily without being naive and gullible. We are able to take ownership of our own powers and initiate action in a proactive way to make our hopes and dreams come true. Because we have come to terms with our own autonomy and can stand to be alone, we differentiate solitude from loneliness.

Figure 17:1
Interpersonal Bonding States

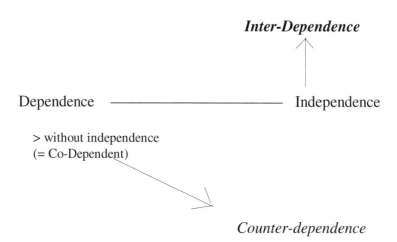

Exploring Your Readiness
* Are you ready for *the Bonding Game*?
* How independent are you?
* In what areas are you independent?
* In what areas are you dependent?
* How do you feel about your independence?
* How grounded are you in your values and in your visions?
* Why do you want a coupling relationship?
* What do you hope to get, achieve, and/or experience?
* What do you have to give and contribute?
* Do you have these qualities for a healthy inter-dependent relationship?
* Are you resourceful enough?
* Are you whole enough in yourself?

The Game of Loving
Consider the state of feeling love. Step into the state of loving yourself, enjoy it fully, then step into the state of loving another. Isn't that one of the most resourceful states that you can imagine? Loving self and other is comprised of many resources, resources which allow us to—
- Esteem yourself
- Extend yourself to reach out to another.
- Believe in the value and dignity of the other.
- Value and care for the other as you do for yourself.
- Give to enrich the other.
- Receive from the other.
- Delight in opening up and being authentic.
- Accept yourself and accept the other.
- Communicate your feelings of endearment and appreciation.
- Be patient with the other.
- Put up with the other's limitations.
- Give your presence when the other is hurting.
- Listen attentively and to be fully present.

If you have to be grounded in love and grant love to yourself first so that you can love others as you love yourself, are you ready? Do you love yourself in a respectful way like this? What frames of mind do you need in order to do that?

The Representations of Resourcefulness
Representation determines what plays in the theater of your mind. From the Cinema that plays in your mind, you experience various states, some resourceful and some not resourceful. This mapping of things into your mind as film clips about connecting, relating, others, love, respect, etc. determine what you think and feel about the bonding process.

Once you have mapped something onto your mental screen you can step back from it and notice where your brain goes and what state it elicits. If it doesn't put you in a grounded, centered, or resourceful state, you can use that as a learning. You can learn what movies to stop playing and which ones to play.

Do you have a mental movie of yourself as grounded and centered and independent enough to extend yourself as an act of love for another? If not, the following Swish Pattern gives you a way to create such a map as a new film clip for your mind.

The Swishing Game for a More Resourceful Self Image

Brains go places in wild and ungoverned ways until you take control and give your brain the needed guidance. Then establish the directions that you want to go. To develop your skill in doing this, first practice *noticing* where your brain goes. Don't attempt to do anything about it. Just notice. This will put you at a choice point so that you can do something about where your brain goes and the state it puts you in. You will then be able to work more methodically with your consciousness. What and how you think about your mate, relationship, love, emotional needs, etc., determines your feelings, experiences, and attitudes. Here's how to play the *Brain Swishing Game*:

1) *Identify the triggers that evoke an unresourceful state.*

Where does your brain go that puts you in unproductive, unresourceful and non-enhancing states?

Though this may induce some negative feelings, take a moment and notice where your brain goes when you think about your significant one. What are your internal representations?

What is a state that prevents you from being very warm, charming, kind, thoughtful, etc.?

What state or experience invites you to let your passions wane?

Notice the movie you have of this and the cinematic features of that movie.

We will use this as our "Cue" Picture later, so put it aside for the moment.

2) *Create an image of the resourceful you when you feel loved.*

What elicits you to feel so resourceful that the other triggers would no longer be a problem?

Create a mental representation of the *You* that would be so resourceful that these cues would not rattle you. They would not send you into an unresourceful state. Step into that movie and be there. Experience it fully.

Do you like it?

What does your partner do that really makes you feel loved?

It may be a look, a sound, a word, a touch, etc. Recall a specific time and place when you felt loved by them.

What will make your internal movie of this resourceful you even more powerful and compelling? Make the picture brighter, more colorful, closer, sharper, etc. Make the words, or music, more compelling and attractive. Continue until you edit it just right for you.

3) Link the two images together.

Are you ready to *swish* your brain?

Are you ready to train your brain to associate a powerfully positive movie when you are triggered to feel unresourceful?

Will you allow your brain to be swished in a new direction?

Take the first representation that cues you to feel unresourceful and into the center of that picture or to the lower right hand corner, shrink the resourceful you picture into a dot. Let it be encoded as no larger than a dot. Yet you know that the dot will explode in a moment and open up totally filling the theater of your mind.

4) Get ready, go.

When you hear or say the word Swwissshhhhh... the movie of whatever it is that makes you feel bad, negative, and unresourceful will fade into the background, zoom far. far into the background or just wash out and simultaneously the resourceful movie will explode onto the screen of your mind and fill the screen. It will become all encompassing—big, colorful, full of resourceful sounds and words, compelling.

Ready? Then as you look at that Cue Picture, see it fade out and Swwissshhhhh .... in pops the resourceful movie and it occurs in one or two seconds.

Good. Now clear the screen ... and starting with the cue picture, repeat the process.

Clearing the screen each time, repeat the process five times.

5) Break state and test

After you have repeated the process five times, take a break and think about something very different for a moment. What did you have for breakfast?

Now, what was that cue picture that formerly induced negative feelings in you? See if you can recall it and feel it and not think about the new resourceful movie.

6) Future Pace.

The Game of Self-Esteeming
- Have you mapped a frame about *self* that's enhancing and healthy?
- What kind of mental-and-emotional frames have you created for your sense of self?
- How well do these frames serve you?

Here's how to play the Self-Esteeming Game:

1) Access resource states and amplify these so you have a good dose.
Bring *acceptance, appreciation, and esteem* and apply to your felt sense of self. Access a small and simple example of thoughts, feelings, and behaviors of each of the following. Then amplify each of the states until it is amplified in just the right way.

> *Acceptance:* Acknowledgment and welcoming of what is without judgment nor endorsement, just witnessing and bringing into your awareness that you exist and have powers of mind, emotion, speech, and behavior.

> *Appreciation:* A gentle openness that finds simple delights and pleasure in existence, a warm welcoming that can magically find values in the simplest of things.

> *Esteem:* The feeling of valuing something highly as important, significant, and worthwhile. The sense of awe and honor at the value and marvel of something to be held as precious.

2) Upon accessing these states, apply them to your "sense of self" as a human being.

> Let acceptance first support and acknowledge your humanness. Say it out loud. "I accept myself fully and completely with all of my fallibilities." Feel the warming and welcoming feelings of accepting yourself as a *self*, as a human being.

> Next, apply appreciation to your *self*. Nourish and validate with appreciation yourself with your powers and potentials. What can you appreciate about yourself? As you take the feelings of appreciation and engulf your sense of yourself with those ... let specific appreciations emerge in your awareness.

> Finally, *esteem* self highly as having worth, value, and dignity in an unconditional way—as your birthright for being human. This separates and distinguishes your *Self* as a doer (your skills and competence, self-confidence) from a human being (yourself as a

person).

3) Let this highly valued, unconditional self-worth and dignity operate as your core self.

Apply these things to *the You* who lies beyond the specific conditions and environments of your life. Then, with a dignity that cannot be taken away from you, an honor that exists as a human being, you can now executively decide *how* you want to run your thinking and emoting, *how* you want to speak and behave, the kind of person you want to become, the kind of experiences you want to enjoy, etc.

4) Use your core state as your sense of value, worth and dignity.

When you feel this fully, notice how it transforms your posture, your gauge, walk, talk, how you hug, embrace, extend yourself, and give. Imagine doing this into the future months and years of your life.

Summary

- It may sound contradictory, yet it does take a lot of independence to move on to inter-dependency. *The Independence Game* allows you to love fully in giving and extending yourself. All of us relate best when we are operating from our best states. You do too!

- Stepping into the resourcefulness of independence and love allows you to access all of the resources so that you become more ready to relate. Claim your powers of self-esteeming, being independent, having your own voice, your own mind, your own values and visions, claim your power zone for owning your response-abilities *for* yourself so that you can easily and abundantly be response-able *to* the other person.

- Mindfully use your powers of proximity, sharing, communicating, giving your heart, being true and faithful to begin the bonding. Ask for a list of the things that really count for the other person. What really counts for them? What makes them feel loved, trusted, understood, valued, respected?

Chapter 18

CO-CREATING
A RESPONSIVE BOND

The Responsive Game

By esteeming yourself unconditionally as a valuable and precious human being and by seeing "the resourceful me for whom love and loving is no problem," you can center yourself in your powers to respond in ways that will increase your bonding and become a great lover. To do this will then empower you to feel completely grounded in your self so that you are focused and response-able. To do this also sets the foundation for intimate bonding, does it not? Yet this is not sufficient; more is needed.

What is needed beyond becoming personally resourceful in your own personal independence, empowerment, and self-esteem is *responsiveness*. A loving responsiveness. You need a special kind of responsiveness to your loved one—one that is responsible, proactive, able to initiate effective actions, and distinguish responsibility *to* and *for*. Do you know why? Do you know what's so important about this?

There are several things. One thing about great lovers is the degree and extent of their *responsiveness* to each other. Have you ever noticed that? There's an elegant responsiveness that is absolutely exquisite that makes the love relationship a work of art. It is passionate and yet solidly content to live in this moment.

• 	Where does this responsive come from?

- What is involved in it?
- How is it textured and qualified?

To explore this theme, consider what happens in a relationship between two people who fall in love. What's actually happening? They *respond* to each other. They relate by giving and receiving each other's responses. This actually is the very stuff of relationships. It is that simple.

Relationships arise, develop, deteriorate, flourish, and stagnate depending on *how* the lovers relate to each other in the exchange of responses. Give loving, thoughtful, considerate, and appreciative responses and the relationship will become richly enhanced. Give defensive, angry, distrustful, fearful, suspicious, and judgmental responses and watch the relationship shrivel up. Watch it become more distant, cold, and defensive. Herein lies a critical secret for enhancing your relationship.

> *The quality of your relationship arises from the quality of your responses to each other.*

Numerous actions, responses, and behaviors influence relationships. Opening up your ego-boundaries, extending yourself, seeking to understand, supporting, caring, giving your presence, appreciating, etc. are the magical responses that deepen love. These are *the Games that Great Lovers Play* and so will be our focus in the next two chapters and they all begin with being—

Responsive and Responsible
Let's start with the idea of "responsibility." Doesn't that word strike you as the most romantic word you've heard all day? It doesn't? Well just how romantic is that word for you? Did it cause you to think of your loved one and melt? No?

In starting with the idea of "responsibility" we have a problem. The word *responsibility* itself is problematic. It does not come with good press. Actually, it has a lot of bad press. For many people (perhaps most people), *responsibility* is semantically loaded with negative connotations. Typically it elicits heavy, serious, and foreboding feelings, doesn't it? People experience it as burdensome and unpleasant.

So does it surprise you that "responsibility" lies at the very heart of romance?

It does. And does not have to carry all of those negative meanings or emotions. Actually the word tellingly points in a very different direction. As a composite word, the term is comprised of two smaller and very dynamic words: *response* and *ability*.

> Responsibility is the ability, or power, to respond. If you are *able* to respond (with your mind, emotions, speech, or behavior), then you have some *power* to act, to exercise influence, and to effect things. This establishes what you are responsible *for* which creates your personal *accountability* since you can only be held account-able for the responses you are able to make.

Giving the actions (behaviors) and verbalizations (speech) that you are response-able *for to* another person creates *relationship*. What do you give *to* another person? You give speech (talk) and behavior (actions). You talk to another person in a certain way (desired or undesired) and you act, behave, and gesture in a certain way. These responses define and create the nature and quality of relationship.

Figure 18:1

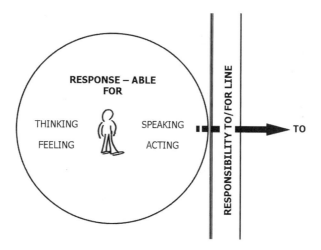

Responses are all of the ways that you respond when something happens. The private responses internal to yourself are what you think and feel. The public responses that impact the world and others are what you speak and do. This fully describes the range of responses for which you are accountable.

> You are responsible *for* what you think, feel, say, and do.
> You relate to, and influence, others through the responses you give *to* them.

Relationship arises from what you have agreed upon with another as to the responses to give *to* them and those you receive from them. It is your personal *responses,* with these personal powers or abilities, that make up your *responsiveness.* Because of your ability to respond, you do not act like furniture or have the life of rocks. You are *responsive* by nature.

When anything happens, you respond mentally as you think, wonder, explore, question, and conceptualize its meaning. You respond emotionally by caring, fearing, rejoicing, angering, grieving, playing, etc. Your emotions enable you to register *in your body* the significance of the meanings that you give to something. This makes emotions psychosomatic in nature.

You respond verbally by using all of your powers of language and symbol. You can ask questions, make statements, tell stories, create poetry, write music. You have so many linguistic powers by which you can encode the meanings you create and feel. You can respond in action as you do things that will translate your thoughts-and-feelings into effective behaviors that make a difference.

Of the *responses* you can make to the things that happen, you have four central powers. You can respond in the way you think, emote, speak, and behave. With these four responses you affect yourself and your world. They make up your Power Zone. No one can do these things for you. Ultimately your thoughts are your own as are your emotions, talk, and actions.

The Accountability Game
Of these distinctions, the difference between what you are responsible *for* and those you are responsible *to* offers the most significant one for loving and bonding in relating to your loved one. When you confuse this distinction, you undermine your ability to relate and your own personal sense of power, control, and being in charge of your own life. That's because *accountability* differs significantly from *relationship.*

In the main, you are responsible *for* yourself and what occurs within you.

And that's about it. So take your index finger on your right hand and touch your nose. As you hold it there realize that this points to your responsibility zone. And that's a full time job in itself, is it not? You are responsible for what you think, what you feel, what you say, and what you do. Yet your responsibility *for* all of these responses for the most part ends at your nose.

Each of us uniquely have control over what lies within—our thoughts, values, our feelings and emotions, our words and speech, our reactions and behaviors. Yet it is also obvious that this level of control is not absolute. You are not able to perfectly control all of your thoughts or emotions. Of course not. So even though fallible and limited, it is within your power, and no one else's. So in that, your responsibility *for* basically ends at the edge of your personal space.

If you do not assume responsibility for what goes on inside, you undermine your powers to be active and proactive. Failure to do that, you will seek to transfer responsibility by blaming, accusing, holding others responsible *for* your feelings, behaviors, etc. This begins the interpersonal craziness that occurs whenever anyone says, "You *make* me feel..."

After all, if I believe, talk, and act *as if* others are responsible for what goes on inside me, I make my emotions and responses dependent on what *they say and do*. That puts me out-of-control. It dis-empowers me. It pops the bubble of my Power Zone. Typically it will lead me to either play victim or seek to control them and what they do. You can image the games that this leads to, *The Blaming Game* full of accusations and counter-accusations, *the Victim Game* and *the Dis-Empowerment Game*.

No wonder the best pathway to a healthy inter-dependent relationship is developing personal independence. The essential requirement for this is simple, develop and own your ability to make mental, emotional, verbal, and behavioral *responses* that fit what you want, your values, and your visions for yourself. Own and claim your powers of response and welcome the sense that ultimately you, like the rest of us, is responsible for your own self. This is what leads to a sense of self-ownership and empowerment:

> "I am responsible for my happiness and my misery, my anger and joy, my success and failure. I can and will not blame anyone else for my responses or the results I get. If I get a response that I don't like or want, I will rethink things and respond in a more effective way."

It is in the very process of taking the initiative to change your responses that you don't like, and don't find productive, that you assume personal responsibility *for* yourself. In this way you accept your own accountability for what you think, feel, say, and do. In being accountable for initiating, disciplining yourself, managing your time and energies, controlling your states, and engineering your future you develop the skills and abilities for success in all of these areas.

Relationship as Responsibility *To* Another
Responsibility *to* creates and defines your interactions and relationships. If I am responsible *to* you, then my relationship with you is defined in terms of the responses that I give *to* you. The responses that I promise, or that are understood as belonging to the relationship, defines the relationship.

> So I say to a friend, What would you like from me?
>
> He says to meet him for a jog by the River Trail. So we agree upon a time and place. Then when I come through by taking ownership of my own actions so that I can give him what I said, I act in a way that is responsible *to* him *for* what we agreed upon. When I don't come through, that's my responsibility. And if I don't make it right by communicating, apologizing, showing that I care that I disappointed someone, etc., that will negatively affect the relationship.

Every relationship can be understood, defined, and even analyzed in terms of the actions we promise to give *to* each other:
- How would you like for me to talk to you?
- What tone or volume would you like me to use when I'm upset?
- What would you like for us to do together as a couple?
- What counts for you as an enjoyable evening out?
- What counts for you in the giving and receiving of affection?

Relationships emerge from these sets of actions that we give to and receive from each other. In the best of healthy relationships we joyfully accept that we are responsible *to* each other. We're thrilled to respond to each other.

This is true for every relationship. Even business relationships involve a set of actions that we have said that we will give *to* our employer to get the things that we want (employment, pay, benefits, opportunities, etc.). The *giving and receiving* dimension of any relationship is the dimension that we can see, hear and feel.

The inside dimension are all those *responses* of your thinking-and-feeling that make you responsive, or not-so-responsive, to each other. This is the dimension of attitude, disposition, mood, beliefs, and all of the other things that endow the relating with a certain feeling. In healthy relationships you are responsive, caring, respective, supportive, open, vulnerable, etc. Frequently you find yourself feeling these emotions, but unskilled or unable to translate these responses into behaviors that effectively transmit them. This is where you relate to your loved one by asking them what counts and even inviting that person to coach you into how to behave in ways that count for love.

Relationship are composed of sets of interactions. So you can now discover what will make the relationship work and what will make it not work. You can now make specific what you and your loved one is giving and receiving from each other. The verb at the heart of relationship is *relating*. In relating we respond to another, we give to and we receive from the other. Now we can directly ask:
•   How are we *relating* to the other?
•   In what are we *relating?*

The two small words— *to* and *for*—give us two very different concepts, each one critical for understanding our relationships. Your *to* and *for* responses identify your area of accountability and the nature of your relationship. Both of these emerge from your responses and yet both create very different experiences. Each creates a different Game:
•   *The Game of Accountability*— the game wherein you feel *able* or empowered to be ready for relationship with another because you know your powers of response.
•   *The Game of Relationship* — the game of giving-and-receiving which then makes you responsive to your loved one.

Kinds of Relationships
The kind of relationship you create with each other depends on the specific responses that you give to each other. Kinds of relationships arise from the kinds of agreement, commitments, arrangements, and negotiations that you agree upon. Accordingly, you can create dependent relationships, independent relationships, and interdependent relationships.

Dependent relationships

We all begin life in a *dependent* relationship to our parents. Yet total dependency only lasts a few months as we begin the process of becoming increasingly independent. The dependency during childhood to parents, teachers, and others in authority over us also sets the tone and attitude that we develop about *dependency*.

> Do we like it or despise it? Does it suppress and degrade us or does it support and nurture us? Was it loving and respectful or was it harsh, uncaring, and even disrespectful?

Many come out of the dependency of childhood vowing never again to experience any relationship where they are in a one-down position or dependent on anyone for anything. Others come out looking to replicate that childhood dependency. That's what they want and long for.

Independent relationships

During teenage years we begin to experience some of our first feelings of independence. As our understandings, skills, abilities, and personal powers for being accountable grow, we take on and try out numerous experiences of independence. Going out, taking trips without parents, taking a first job, etc. these are some of the first experiences of independence—of standing up on one's own two feet without having to depend on others.

We experience such independence as both exhilarating and scary. During our teenage years we often oscillate back and forth between sallying out to the world of challenges and opportunities to diving back to the homestead of safety and security. Independence brings with it the sense of using our own intelligence to think things through to make our own decisions and to act with mindfulness about the consequences.

During the teen years we move back and forth in this limbo-like period when we are still dependent in many ways and yet, in other ways, independent. This makes for instability, mood-swings, and ever-changing interactions. Yet as we develop various skills we eventually begin to become independent within ourselves, able to make our own decisions, to face results, to solve problems, to create our own pathway through the world.

Interdependent relationships

After independence comes the ability to truly connect with others, friends and associates first and then a special loved one in an inter-dependent way. The *inter-dependency* that characterizes coupling involves mutually reciprocal responsibilities. *We make ourselves dependent upon the other yet now with a difference.* It is not the dependence of weakness, but of desire and choice. And the other person now chooses to depend on us for the things that we bring to the relationship.

Inter-dependency can only work when two people are responsible *for* themselves and are able to be responsive *to* each other in a sensitive and caring way. Only when you are as good as your word can you make a promise and keep it. Or at least you will do everything you can to come through with what you say, and if not, you inform the other, make apologies or amends and make yourself accountable to the other. These are some of the things that indicate that you are ready for adult relationships.

- Are you willing to be accountable to another?
- Are you able to come through with what you said?
- Are you willing to be forthright and honest when you can't do what you said you would do?
- Can you be wrong with grace and gentleness and maintain your own dignity?

As a social creature, you live in close proximity with others, especially your loved one. Adult life is all about entering relationships with others, from friends, to associates, to employers, to lovers. Being *dependent* to, on, and with another is the nature of social life. We contract with an employer to be on the job from nine to five and to contribute our knowledge and skills as per the job description. We become dependent on that employer or company for our livelihood, status, employment, etc.

Distinguishing Responsibility To/For
Suppose you claim or take responsibility that does not belong to you? What happens when you do that? What happens is that you are *aggressing* into another person's area of response! You are intruding. Even if you are doing it because you are sincerely trying to be helpful, you are still aggressing. You are actually violating that person's sovereign rights to think, feel, speak, and act for him or herself. And that makes that response disrespectful and unloving.

Suppose, on the other hand, you do not take responsibility for what rightly belongs to you? Then you are *passively withdrawing* from your responsibilities and dis-empowering yourself as you are playing the victim's role. Most of us alternate between these extremes. And worse, those who take too much responsibility and those who take too little responsibility often get together as caretakers and care-receivers. In family systems these dynamics complement each other. Caretakers attract care-receivers. The givers seek out someone to rescue. So no wonder distinguishing response-ability *to* and *for* is so important!

In doing this you create the phenomena essential for healthy relationships. This includes good healthy boundaries for each person: accountability, the art of being kindly firm, trusting and trustworthy, and holding yourself and the other accountable without blaming.

I first saw Brenda for "stress management." That was her presenting problem. In fact, her employer sent her to me because she was increasingly anxious, overwhelmed, forgetting things, feeling unwell, worried, grumpy, and irritable. When I had her fill out a questionnaire for the stressors in her life and the signs and indicators of stress, it was clear that something was going on inside. As I explored the contexts of her daily life with her, I asked her about what was at the top of her list in terms of stressors.

> "I don't know. Everything. I am up to here (gesturing with her hand to the top of her head) with everything I have to do and all of the pressures I'm facing."

Like what?

> "It's everything. I don't know where to start. I used to could go home and get away from the stresses at work, but then there are stresses there."

Like?

> "Like Tommy's problems with his girl friend, Tammy. They are always arguing and he pushed her last week and she called the police, that was at some restaurant and then they came back home and continued arguing."

I must have missed something. How is Tommy's problems with Tammy a stressor for you? Isn't that his problem?

> "Well, sure, but it's mine too."

How does that work? How do you have to feel bad or frustrated or stressed about what he says and does and the way he relates to Tammy?

> "Well, I'm his mother. .. (Pause) ... I have to worry about his happiness."

You *have to*? That's "the Law?" And what will be the punishment if you don't worry about his happiness?

> "It sounds funny when you say that."

If we draw a circle around the *responses* you can make to things, your thoughts-and- feelings, your speech and behavior in this drawing ... and if that's what you are responsible *for* ... You are responsible *for* what you think, feel, say, and do, aren't you? (Yeah.) Then, if we draw a circle around Tommy for his thoughts, feelings, talk, and actions ... and he's responsible *for* those responses ... Isn't he? (Yeah.) Then how is it that you cheat him by trying to take away his responsibility *for* himself?

Brenda got it. I had to draw the line between responsibility *to* and *for* repeatedly throughout the session, yet in one session, she got it. She gained insight about how she was absorbing problems and heart-aches that were not hers. This was the cause for her to feel dis-empowered by the situation and it was actually making the problem worse. As she owned her own responses and gave herself permission to let others experience life as responsible persons, she found her stress level and symptoms melt away very quickly.

Good Healthy Boundaries
Responsibility *to and for* enables you to not react emotionally to every distress, upset, or pain. You can use this distinction to obtain the psychological distance from what you might otherwise personalize. When negative words are spoken, you can distance yourself from them.

> "I am not responsible for his words; his words are his. What does he mean? What state are they spoken from? Are they accurate or not?"

You do not have to immediately believe what is said, or disbelieve it for that matter. You can *just perceive* that it is the other person's belief, and allow that person to be responsible for those thoughts. You are only responsible for your response.

"Boundaries" refer to your sense of self in distinction to the other. Where do I end and the other begins? While you open your ego-boundaries to let the other into your world, this does not mean that you become so enmeshed that there is no self left. You are still there and so is your loved one. You are there as two individuals *and* you are persons in the new emergent experience of "we."

Without boundaries people become *enmeshed*. With boundaries you develop a flexible system of two people who join their lives, loves, and fortunes and yet who also have the sense of individuality within the bonding. In this, healthy relationships breathe. There's times when you come together and experience a merging, then there are times when you move apart. Then you experience your own individual lives. And from that you have many new things to bring back into the relationship.

Accountability

The responsibility *to/for* distinction enables you to be accountable *for* yourself and *to* hold another person accountable. While at first this may seem or feel frightening, it is actually one of the most enriching things about a relationship and it is an exciting thing. Being held accountable means. "There's someone who cares about my interests and goals and will support me as I seek to live up to my highest values and dreams." As a couple, when you share your dreams, you hold each other accountable to revisiting those dreams from time to time, and asking how each person is doing. No wonder communication plays such a crucial role in relating! It is another key factor that great lovers know how—to communicate effectively.

The Art of Being Kindly Firm

Responsibility *to/for* enables you to be kindly firm. If someone fails to come through, rather than reacting and jumping on him or getting emotional, you can simply inquire in a curious matter-of-fact tone:

> "I thought you agreed that you would do this or that? Am I mistaken about that or have there been some things that have come up that's made that difficult?"

In holding someone accountable, and in being held accountable, you communicate in a way that it allows your loved one to save face. No confrontation ought to disgrace or insult the other in a degrading way. That's not confrontation; that's simply being ugly and degrading. Done in the right way, even confronting the one you care about can be an indication of love and trust. Of course, you will want to do so when you are in a good state so that you can stay calm and gently supportive as you speak your truths.

Trust and Trustworthiness

Responsibility *to/for* also builds trust between individuals. How does this work? It happens to the extent that you eliminate trying to read the minds of others and simply take your loved one at his or her word. This encourages a forthrightness that allows each person to be responsible *for* what is said, promised, or done. Trusting the other person respects the right of the other person to handle his or her own thoughts and feelings and to take actions that will balance concerns for the individual and for the relationship.

The Holding Accountable Game

Responsibility is *not* the same thing as blaming. Blame radically differs from responsibility, although most people blur the difference. We seem to blur the difference especially when we experience conflict or pain with someone. Yet *holding* someone response-able for what that person can do is not accusing, threatening, or blaming. These are two very different set of actions.

What creates the confusion between *being responsible* and *blaming*? Thinking linearly. Thinking that the *relational inter-actions* between two people operate in a simple cause-effect way is the problem. This is a myth that we all have grown up with. We assume that relationships operate in a similar way that a billiard game operates. If a ball goes careening around the table, it is *because* someone hit it or another ball and *made* that happen.

That's *not* the way things work in a *system*. Newtonian physics gives us a good understanding of the transfer of energy on a pool table because the billiard balls are not sentient beings with responsive thoughts-and-feelings that can respond. Billiard balls can't even *react* in the strictest sense. They can only *be acted upon* by external forces. There are no internal forces *within* them, especially beliefs, ideas, memories, imaginations, hopes, etc.!

That's why kicking a soccer ball differs so much from kicking a man. Kick the ball and you can pretty much figure out the trajectory of the ball, where it will go, how quickly, and in what direction. But try to figure all of that out ahead of time what will happen when you kick a man or a dog. When you deal with a sentient being who has his or her own energy system, you're dealing with a much more complex system (Bateson, 1972).

The Inner Game of Systemic Thinking

You have to move beyond the simple cause-effect thinking that you can cause, or make, another person to think, feel, say, or behave anything. That is the delusion. You cannot. Others think and feel what they think and feel according to their representations, meanings, memories, hopes, etc. You do not *make* them think or feel anything. At best you *invite* them to accept certain thoughts or ideas, which if they do, then triggers their emotions and responses. But from beginning to end, their internal psychological responses of thinking, feeling, speaking, and acting is theirs.

No wonder *blaming* and *accusing* any other person for your thoughts and feelings, or for your external actions is irrational. At best, it is a reversion to the most childish of states and, at worse, it indicates a total lack of understanding of the systemic nature of *inter-actions* in relationship.

*   What *causes* you to feel bad in relation with another person?
*   What *causes* people to behave as they do in relationships?
*   Who is to blame when something goes wrong?
*   Where will *blaming* get you?

If each of us are responsible *for* our internal states of thinking and feeling and for the verbal and behavioral expressions that come out of out states, then *blaming* isn't the answer and won't solve anything. *Holding* yourself, and the other person, *response-able for* what each says and does, is not blaming. Judging and accusing will only make things worse. Exploring what a statement or action means, what the person intended to achieve by it, what state drove it, etc., these are much more constructive explorations and can lead to new negotiated responses.

By contrast, when you *blame,* you accuse and attack. This complicates things by adding a second problem to the first one. And because blaming, accusing, mind-reading, discounting, insulting, etc. eat away at the bonding, these behaviors and games create a more significant and destructive problem than the first problem. How is that?

> That's *because how you relate when you are in conflict and unresourceful* is more important than the particular problems you are working on and solutions that you create. (See chapters twelve and thirteen on how to have a good fight.)

The Mutual Co-Created Responsibility Game
In a loving bond of *responsiveness,* two people accept their own *responses* and willingly invite the other to hold them responsible *for* what they say and do. They know that it is through *saying and doing* that they bond with each other and that *the quality* of their speech and behavior determines the quality of their relationship.

They also know that their behaviors emerge from their states and that it is not a simple linear process, but non-linear and systemic. They know that their behaviors are actually influenced by a whole range of things from their health, states, memories, histories, learnings, skills, beliefs, understandings, level of development, goals, and much more. That's why they don't point the finger and blame. Blaming is too simplistic and unbalanced. Blaming doesn't take into account the previous steps.

Behaviors are *systemic* precisely because they come out of the mind-body-emotion system. And *systems* involve multiple interactive parts—feedback and feed forward loops. This is why systemic thinking eliminates simplistic linear thinking about the "cause." Linear cause-effect thinking in relationships lead to *the Blame Game* where judging and accusations are wildly flung around. That, in turn, leads to the deterioration of communication and bonding.

When you shift to systemic thinking, you shift to an entirely different way of thinking. You move to thinking about multiple causes and multiple contributing influences, and the system of interactive parts, and how to find a solution acceptable to all. Shifting to this kind of thinking empowers you with a richer map. After all, relationships are a system of responses, actions and communications within even larger systems (i.e., family, cultural, religious, belief, etc.) and involve *interactive patterns* that define, describe and create the relating.

What does this mean? It means that whatever happens in a system which I participate in—*I* helped in some measure to create it. I'm a participant. When I think in terms of systems (i.e., systemically), I can no longer blame, accuse, and point the finger. I cannot hold my partner to be exclusively at fault. Now I ask myself, "*How* did **I** play an active role in the shaping of this inter-personal reality and this problem?"

System understanding enables me to realize that I participate in every relational outcome that occurs. This allows me to assume my responseableness.

Linear thinking in a system always fails to see the influence of "time." Yet in systems, *time* always plays a crucial factor. Take the system of your mind-body and the occasion of a headache. Suppose you say, "I've got a headache, so I will take an aspirin and make it go away." Seems logical. After all, "taking an aspirin is supposed to make your headache go away." Yet the logic of the statement does not take *time* into account. The linear thinker will take an aspirin and then check. "Hmmmm, I still have a headache. I'll take another aspirin because aspirins make headaches go away." So he pops in another. He then makes another check. "I still have that headache," and takes another.

Obviously, the system of the stomach, digestive track, blood system, muscular tension, etc. operates in a fashion that we can describe as event after event (or "times"). It does not work instantaneously. One event stimulates and triggers another event, or series of events, and all of the factors contribute so that eventually the aspirin ingredients assists in the sense of release of tension.

Not thinking systemically can do you great damage. The delay factor within a system means that it takes *time* for events to move through the entire system and have their full influence. This comes true with a vengeance in a relational system. This explains why "things that happened a long time ago" sometimes takes a long time to "pop up" and create mental-emotional effects. And given the skill that some people have for "stuffing" things, repressing thoughts-feelings, not dealing with things, etc., no wonder some systemic factors takes years before the full effect begins to show up.

This *time factor* within the operation of systems explains the importance of *patience* as a great virtue and resource in systems thinking. Consider the "patience" of the farmer who reckons with the natural system of seasons, maturation of plants and/or animals, and who accepts the reality that you can't skip the planting season and cram in the fall in order to get a great harvest.

Ignoring the natural patterns, rhythms, stages, seasons, and processes within a system leads to an increasing maladjustment to reality. The reality of a system involves many factors. *Patience* is the perspective that takes the delay element into account.

This also explains the need to distinguish between systemic symptoms and structural causes. Otherwise you can get caught up with fighting mere symptoms and never addressing those factors that actually create the problems. The headache itself is but a symptom of other factors in the mind-body system. Thinking systemically enables you to recognize symptoms as a form of "information"—a "communication" from the system itself about something not working well. This structural focus enables you to not get caught up in wasting time and energy fighting symptoms and over-focusing on unpleasant symptomatic facets.

Exploring Your Current Game
- To what extent do I live reactively rather than proactively?
- What one thing could I do, which if I did regularly and consistently, would dramatically improve my effectiveness in the various aspects of my life?
- What reactive words or language have I used today?
- What proactive words and language have I used today?
- Has my focus and orientation today been more defensive or defenseless?

Pattern for Being Responsively Centered
Having spoken about getting centered in order to become ready to play *the Games that Great Lovers Play,* it's time to put the pieces together into a pattern. So here we go:

1) Fully acknowledge your core responses.
> Reflect again on your powers of mind-and-emotion, notice them and wonder at these basic powers by which you can respond to the world.
> Also reflect on your powers of speech and behavior. These are your public powers.

2) Frame with Ownership.
> Are you willing to take complete *ownership* of these responses and to own them as your own?

Think of several things that every fiber of your being knows is yours, something you own, something to which that you can fully say, "Mine!" Access this feeling of *mine* and then apply to your core responses of power (your thoughts, feelings, speech, and behavior). Imagine all of these powers in your space as a circle then as a sphere so that it becomes your sphere or zone of power.

3) Frame with Appreciation.

Access a series of things that you really appreciate and let that feeling of appreciation fill your body completely. As you do, keep amplifying and turning up the sense of appreciation as you apply that feeling to your Sphere of Power Zone. Do so until you see these responses through the eyes of appreciation.

*4) Distinguish your Responses **To** and **For**.*

What are you responsible *for?* Notice how you immediately begin to claim and own your response powers. Let this re-access your Sphere of Power Zone immediately.

To whom are you responsible? And about what? Notice how this brings your relationship into your view so that you notice the exchanges you give to each other.

5) Fill up your Sphere of Power Zone with your Values and Visions.

What are some of the things that you most of all care about?

Why is that important to you?

What are your highest intentions?

What is your highest dream and vision for yourself?

As you access these values and visions, let them fill up your Sphere of Power making it richer, fuller, and more compellingly pleasurable.

6) Coach your body how to feel these feelings.

What is it like when you let your body fully feel this?

How much more can you turn up these feelings so that they fill every cell in your body?

What kind of a stance does it *in-form* you with? Take that stance and begin to feel its strength and energy and power. Do you like that? Would you like to make this your way of being in the world?

7) Anchor this internal state of being Centered.

> What can you use to visually anchor this?
> What word will you now use to anchor this?
> With what tone, volume, pitch? Any other sounds?

7) Meta-state your centered Sphere of Power Zone.

> Access various resources so that you can enrich and texture this centered state with more qualities: Access respect and apply to it.
> Access glorious fallibility and apply to it.
> Access outrageous fun and apply to it.

8) Place into your Future.

> Imagine taking this with you.   Do you like it?
> Are all the higher levels of your mind aligned with this?

Summary

- What bonds you together as lovers? Is it not your *responsiveness* to each other? Yes, it is your responsiveness of mind-and-emotion, of speech, and behavior that creates the foundation for loving.

- Where does such responsiveness come from? It arises from your acknowledgment and ownership of your basic human *powers*. It comes when you fully accept and own your powers of mind and emotion, your powers of speech and behavior. These four powers make up your Power Zone and you can now access these as primary states from which all of the higher states will arise.

- Owning your powers *empowers* you. It enables you to step out of *the Games of Reactivity and Victimhood*. It enables you to step up to play *the Games of Responsiveness*.

- From your response-powers you can not only become responsive to your loved one, but accountable. This leads to holding each other accountable and for mutually co-creating a rich and meaning life together. All of the dances of intimacy arise from this one:
  > The Game of Accountability
  > The Game of Trust
  > The Inner Game of Thinking Systemically

Chapter 19

COALESCING
The Merging of Our Worlds

- Can we connect when we differ?
- How can you connect when you differ with someone?
- What are differences and where do they come from?
- How can we be great lovers when we are so different?

L overs often differ. Why is that? It arises from the fact that lovers have differences. They have and experience many kinds of differences. Some are biological, while others are mental and emotional. These differences involve likes and dislikes, habits and patterns, and styles and values. Most of our differences, however, arise from how we map things —from our matrix of frames. We differ because we operate from different maps.

The Map/ Territory Distinction Game
The good thing about differences in your mapping with your lover is that they are *just a map*. They are not real: "The map is not the territory." What you have mapped is just that, it is a *map* of the experience—a way of thinking and talking about things.

Map and territory distinguishes the two dimensions of reality you have to navigate. Territory is outside your skin; map is inside. The map is your associations, frames, beliefs, values, understandings, etc. These frames within frames define your sense of reality (or Matrix) which then governs how you respond to things.

Ultimately your subjective experiences of loving and being loved and experiencing the richness of being in a loving relationship arise from your maps. Realizing that the representations in your brain is a map empowers you to treat them as only useful when they allow you to experience what you desire. A map is only as good as it structurally corresponds to the territory it maps.

What is the value of the map/territory metaphor for relating and communicating? It enables you to not over-invest too much meaning or validity in your maps. It allows you to lighten up. Maps are maps and not absolute. They are not the last word about things. They are not real—at least not externally real. They are only real on your insides. When you forget that your mental maps are *maps,* you get serious. Then you will feel threatened by maps that differ from your own.

The map/territory metaphor does something else for you. If maps are just maps, you can appreciate a map without needing to use it or fight against it. You can also appreciate the power and value of changing a map. If you don't deal with the reality of the territory directly, but through your maps, *you change* as you change your maps. Changing your maps can profoundly alter your thinking, feeling, speaking, acting, and relating. That's why changing a mental map can lead to impactful transformations in personality and experience.

Conversely, if you confuse the territory "out there" with how you have mapped it, you create all kinds of problems for yourself and others. This confusion leads to arguments about whose version of the territory is "the right one" or "the real one." It leads to discounting and degrading the other's sense of reality. Then you forget that none of us are dealing with reality, but just our maps about it. Failing to recognize this, you become rigid, dogmatic, intolerant, judgmental, impatient, and aggressive. And none of this will improve the quality of your relationship. Actually, these are the very things that undermine and sabotage love.

If you fail to account for the fact that we all carry our Matrix world of frames around with us in our brain-body-emotion system, you will become blind to the "map filters" that we all use. None of us cleanly see, hear, or feel. We all hear and process our understandings through our frames. Without our frames, there's no meaning. It is our frames that create the meanings that we impose on things. Frames create our interpretative style.

What does all of this mean for relationships? It means that whenever you deal with a human being, and especially your loved one, you deal with your lover's subjective reality of meaning frames. Forget that and you'll *not* understand that person, let alone *appreciate* him or her.

Suppose you operate from the assumption that your lover thinks, processes information, and experiences reality exactly as you do. Assume that and you'll fail to recognize your loved one's wonderful uniqueness. You will then project your own maps of the world onto your lover. Doing that will blind you to your loved one and make you less and less able to adjust to the relational reality between you.

Now in the human activity of mapping, we all inevitably leave out things. We *delete* as we leave characteristics out. We selectively see, hear, and feel. This explains how we can live in the same world and yet have very different understandings and feelings about things. It's why two witnesses to the same event can tell completely different stories. Their stories actually tell more about them and their filters than about the event.

Differences can either pull us together and create deeper bonding or separate and dis-bond. No wonder handling differences with grace and appreciation is critical in being a great lover. If you want to coalesce in your love, you need to play certain games.

The Acceptance Game
Recognizing the presence of your subjective inner worlds of embedded frames enables you to understand that each of you operate out of your own model of the world. It's not the case that the other person "doesn't get it," or that "they are stupid," or that "they are bad," or that "they misunderstand." It's rather that the other person has mapped things differently ... mapped them in his or her own unique way.

This is true for everyone. Everybody has constructed his or her own sense and definition of reality. Each of us live in our own matrix of frames. We all have our models about what is real and true (our belief frames), what we pay attention to (our perceptual filters or meta-programs), what we deem important (our value frames), and how to make sense of things (our meaning and understanding frames).

What results when you construct your models of the world? Your unique experience of "reality," your truths, the things that feel real to you on the inside. No wonder *telling* and *lecturing* each other, or *arguing* with beliefs, values, and understandings results in fights, arguments, and conflicts, not understanding. Telling and arguing does not support any of us to feel understood or appreciated.

You now know what *not* to do if you want to be a great lover. Don't argue! Don't try to change your loved one. Doing so will undermine the very foundation of your bonding.

Arguing for our position and arguing against your lover's is the worst thing to do when there's a disagreement or conflict. This is especially true with the one that you love and adore. The worse thing to do is to tell them they "are wrong," to lecture them around how you are right, and to try to persuade them to change. Do that, and you won't make love that night ... and perhaps for many nights. It will not endear you to them!

Instead you will succeed in one thing—in creating lots of bad feelings. When you argue and tell, you will almost always trigger lots of tension, pressure, defensiveness, and conflict, and that will lead to dis-connection and the breaking of the bonds of love.

The Appreciative Understanding Game
What are you to do when you differ? To play the first Game of Love, play the *Seeking First to Understand* Game. Set out with an open mind to truly understand how the other is thinking, feeling, and perceiving things. Explore what the other means to expand your understanding. Ask respectful questions about the matrix of frames your lover lives inside, knowing that his or her thoughts are just that, *thoughts*—a way of mapping reality. Be respectful of the mapping, perceptions, and understandings. Do so with an appreciation that it all makes sense to them on the inside.

This is a key for understanding and appreciating others. The Matrix that each person lives in always makes psycho-logical sense *to the person.* No matter how irrational it might seem to those of us on the outside, inside that person's world of meaning, it makes perfect sense.

"But how? How does it make sense?"   Hmmmm, this is precisely why you have to seek first to understand and to give the other a chance to disclose his or her way of mapping and perceiving things. And your lover won't do that if you are not appreciating or open to those perspectives. And, if you don't know how it makes sense to your loved one, you really do not understand.

In relating, you always and only deal with *subjective* reality. For some, this seems to be a difficult lesson to learn. To the extent you do distinguish your mapping of things from the territory you map, you confuse your map with the territory. You then think that you can argue or reason the other into being "logical." Yet most of us know all too well, that "being logical" with others doesn't work for creating close bonds.

When you deal with people, you are dealing with their *psycho-logics.* You are dealing with the other's unique framing of meaning. This is the world from which the other operates. As you learn to appreciate this in your dealings, you learn how to value that reality, to enter it, and to adjust yourself to it. Doing so enables you to connect and negotiate effectively.

You first seek to understand the other's mapping. As this gives you the key for how the other thinks, feels, believes, values, etc., it improves your communications. It makes you aware of the other's language patterns, beliefs, values, thinking style, etc. It allows you to enter into your lover's world.

Entering the Matrix Game

To understand how anyone thinks, yourself or another person, you have to know a little bit about how *thinking* works. When you think about something, you make a mental snapshot or Movie of it. You do this on the inside using the same sensory systems that you experience on the outside. You use the sensory system of sights, sounds, sensations, smells, tastes, etc.

This means that you *think* by making pictures, hearing sounds, tones and words, feeling body sensations, recalling smells and tastes, etc. on the screen of your mind.   This is not a literal description of what happens in the brain. It is a phenomenological description. It *seems* as if you have an internal Movie playing in your mind, and that you re-present the activities and actions. You have a *MovieMind.*[1]

Most people also favor representing things in terms of sights and images (visually), sounds, music, and words (auditorially), or in terms of movements, gestures, and experience (kinesthetically). This creates different kinds of learning styles and representational strengths.

> *Visual preference:* Some people are better at visualizing pictures and images; others are better with sounds, tones, volumes, and melodies, and yet others are better at sensations, movements, and feelings. This sensory systems also affect the way we talk and respond to each other. People who prefer the visual mode tend to use visual terms and pay most attention to sights and visual images.

> *Auditory preference:* People who prefer the hearing mode use auditory terms and pay most attention to how something is expressed in tone and volume. They talk a lot inside their minds, say words, and may even have lots of chatter going on.

> *Kinesthetic preference:* Those who prefer the kinesthetic mode use terms of sensations (movement, vibrations, warmth, pressure, etc.) and pay most attention to tactile sensations or propriceptic feelings.

Each of these sensory systems creates a "language" of the mind. Each system functions as a language that you can and do use as you think and encode information. These processes of thinking lead to different mappings of reality and different worlds.

Yet it doesn't stop there. This is just the beginning. Above and beyond the Cinema that you play in your mind as you represent information are *your frames.* As you set *frames* of meaning *about* your Movies, these frames powerfully influence the movie and how you experience the movie.

Editorial frames
One set of frames has to do with the cinematic features that you use to frame the Movie. Framing it as a snapshot rather than a moving picture radically affects how you experience it. So with encoding it in black-and-white versus in color. So with close versus far. The same applies to how you encode the sound track and the other sensory tracks in your mental movie.

Conceptual frames
Then there are all of the conceptual frames: valued versus disvalued, believed

in versus doubted, identified with versus treated as just a movie, etc. There are hundreds of conceptual frames that you can set *about* the Movie that in turn affects how you experience the Movie. And we all differ in respect to the higher frames of reference that we bring to our Movies.

Yet as you think about yourself, about being loved and respected, about being listened to, nurtured, trusted, and all of the other behavioral components of the phenomenon called "love," so you experience. The way you experience love inescapably results from the way you mentally map things. It results from your primary level Movie and from all of the higher level frames you embed it in—from your Matrix.

The Taking Charge of the Internal World Game

Now what is the value of knowing how you think? The greatest benefit is that it empowers you to take charge of "running your own brain." It allows you to manage your own states. Or to put it in terms of frame games, when you control the frames, then you can more effectively manage the games. The games you play are the results of your frames.

If I know that I have mapped things in a certain way and that it is just a map, then I know I can re-map to expand my awareness as I develop more enhancing representations. Every map or frame leads to some action (or game). When I recognize a map and its representations, I can take charge of running my own brain—my own Matrix. In understanding yourself, you learn that you operate from your maps. Your nervous system feels and responds according to the signals that you receive from your representations.

The key to understanding people is not to know what has actually happened to them, but what they *mapped* from their experiences.
- What conclusions have you mapped from your experiences?
- What have you linguistically and semantically mapped about your maps?

This is why you can know where something came from (its source and origin) and still not be free from it. Knowing where you first began thinking or feeling in a certain way only informs you of the original trigger. It does not necessarily enable you to alter it. To transform your thinking and feeling requires an entirely different set of skills. There are times when knowing the original source of a problem can makes things better. Yet there are also times when that knowledge will actually make things worse. Awareness sometimes reinforces the old programs and makes them stronger.

What gets in your way to prevent you from experiencing full choice in your thoughts? *How* you think or map anything determines how you feel, behave, speak, cope, etc. This is true for how you think about others. Your thinking and mapping about others determines your feelings, experiences, behaviors, skills, etc. It's your thoughts that ultimately create your problems. It's the map that creates the limitations.

Summary
*   All of your maps about yourself, about love and loving, about others and about your loved one are just that—*mental maps.* They are not real—not externally. Yet they are internally real.

*   As maps *about* what's actually "out there," they are at best a set of representations that you have mapped that help or hinder you to deal with things. As such there is a great divide between map and territory. They are not the same.

*   Recognizing this frees you from having to defend your maps or to be right. You can keep mapping, refining, and developing new and more empowering maps that will help you to navigate the Games that Great Lovers Play.

*   And now— on to the Dance of Romance.

LET
THE GAMES OF LOVE
BEGIN!

We have no choice but to play games. So instead of asking, "Do you play games?" ask, "Which Games are you Playing?" And when we ask that question, you can now ask a whole series of other important questions:

- Are *the Games of Love* that you're playing working for both you and your loved one?
- Are you both winning at love in all of the ways that count for each of you?
- Are you experiencing the states and emotions of love so that you feel respected, adored, cared for, nurtured, etc.?
- Have you been playing any games that have undermined true love for you and your lover?
- What new games would you like to begin playing that will enhance your love life?

This book has focused on the following Games—those that reflect the way *Great Lovers think and feel and act.* Feel free to steal those that you find appealing so you can begin playing and winning at the Games of Love.

__ The Game of Attentive Listening (Chapter 1)
    __ The Listening to Understand Game
    __ The Defensive Listening Game
    __ The Leisure Listening Game
    __ The Analytical Games
    __ The Game of Focused Learning
    __ Letting Others Affect Us Game
__ The Game of Appreciation (Chapter 2)
    __ The Love Language Game
    __ The Love Strategy Game
    __ The One Thing that Makes You Feel Loved Game
    __ The Anchoring Game
__ The Emotional Bank Account Game (Chapter 3)
__ The Self-Disclosure Game (Chapter 4)
    __ The Communication Game

__ The Appreciation Game (Chapter 5)
     __ The Appreciating Differences Game
     __ The "There's Always a Positive Intention" Game
     __ The Valuing Game
__ The Rapport Game (Chapter 6)
     __ The Verbal Pacing Game
     __ The Game of Clear and Strategic Speaking
     __ The Game of Bonding with Loving Words
     __ The Sweet Nothings Game
__ The Game of Getting In Sync (Chapter 7)
     __ The Meta-Programs Games
     __ The Global / Specific Game
     __ The Sameness / Difference Game
     __ The Favored Representation Game
     __ The Experiencer / Observer Game
     __ The Motivation Direction Game
     __ The Adaptation Style Game
     __ The Information Source Game
     __ The Polarization / Holistic Game
     __ The Adaptation / Control Game
     __ The Attention Sort: Self or Others Game
     __ The Response Style Game
     __ The Authority Source Game
     __ The Modus Operandi Game
     __ The Convincer Game
     __ The Primary Interest Game
     __ The Going After Goals Game
     __ The Time Zones Game
     __ The Time Lover or Lost in Time Game
     __ The Battery Recharging Game
     __ The Valuing Game
__ The Conscious Loving Game (Chapter 8)
     __ The Forecasting a Future Together Game
     __ Well-Formed Outcomes Game
__ The Pleasuring Game (Chapter 9)
     __ The "Having Fun with my Loved One" Game
__ The Sexual Pleasuring Game (Chapter 10)
__ The How to Have a Healthy Fight Game (Chapter 11)
     __ The Game of Positive Fighting
     __ The Noticing Hurts While They're Small Game
     __ Embracing Negative Emotions as Just Emotions Game
     __ The Fair Fighting Game
     __ The Embracing Conflict Game

__ The Fair Fighting Rules Game (Chapter 12)
      __ The Game of Conflict Resolution
__ The Healing Hurt Love Game (Chapter 13)
      __ The Seeing "Thresholds" Game
      __ The Game of Avoiding Expectations
__ The Threshold Neutralizer Game (Chapter 14)
      __ The Giving Love another Chance Game
      __ The Game of Staying in Love

__ The Bonding Game (Chapter 15)
__ The Inter-Dependence Game (Chapter 16)
      __ The Centering or Grounding Game
      __ The Games of Dependence and Independence
      __ The Swish Game: "Directionalized for the Resourceful Me" Game
      __ The Self-Esteeming Game
__ The Responsive Game (Chapter 17)
      __ The Accountability Game
      __ The Responsibility To/For Game
      __ The Game of Systemic Thinking
__ The Game of Differences (Chapter 18)
      __ The Map/ Territory Game
      __ The Acceptance Game
      __ The Appreciative Understanding Game

Appendix A
Models Used in this Book

NLP AND NEURO-SEMANTICS

NLP — Neuro-Linguistic Programming

NLP is first and foremost a Communication Model that describes how we encode messages and transfer those messages within our mind-body system. It describes how our nervous system and brain as a system maps the world outside of our body and transforms the information from one level to the next. It originated from a linguist (John Grinder) and a pattern genius (Richard Bandler).

From their studies (*The Structure of Magic*), they provided a model of human functioning that essentially offered patterns for how we can *run our own brain*. We run our own brain by using "the languages" of the mind by which we create our internal Cinema (see *MovieMind*, 2003). These are the sights (visual), sounds (auditory) and sensations (kinesthetics), smells (olfactory) and tastes (gustatory) that we use to understand the world "out there." We "make sense" of things using our internal senses for mapping purposes. We also use the meta-representation system of language or linguistics.

This means we internally process information and represent such in the theater of our mind. When we do this, our internal movies induce us into mind-body-emotion states. This is crucial because the quality of our life is the quality of our states. This also explains why NLP is about *modeling* human experience, especially experiences of excellence, that is, best practices and expertise.

Meta-States®

Above and beyond primary states of mind-body-and-emotion are those states that we have and experience about other states. When we feel joy about learning, playful about being serious, curious about anger, calm about fear, etc. we have a higher level state about another state. In this meta-cognitive experience, our thoughts-and-feelings reflect back onto itself and its products.

We never just think. As soon as we think or feel—we then experience thoughts and feelings *about* that first thought, then other thoughts-and-feelings about that thought, and so on. We call this self-reflective consciousness. In meta-states we layer states onto states to create higher levels of awareness.

Primary states are primary emotions like fear, anger, joy, relaxed, tense, pleasure, pain, etc. and involve thoughts directed outward to the things "out there." *Meta-*

states are higher level structures like fear of fear, anger at fear, shame about being embarrassed, esteem of self, etc. *Meta-States* as a model describes the higher *frames-of-references* that we set and use that create more stable structures (beliefs, values, understandings, etc.)

Wild and wonderful things result when we access and apply one state to other states, we develop frames of mind that we can keep with us. In these complex states, our self-reflexive consciousness relates (not to the world), but to ourselves, to our thoughts, feelings,, or to some abstract conceptual state. in thinking-and-feeling about previous state, the state in a higher position is *meta* (above, beyond) the second and so operates as a higher *logical type or logical level*.

A special kind of internal logic arises from this layering of states. When we *transcend* from one state (say, anger or joy) to another state (say, calmness or respect) we set the second state as a frame over the first and *include* it inside it. This gives us "calm anger," respectful joy, joyful learning, etc. It makes the first state a member of the class of the second.

It's not logical in a linear way, yet it is *psycho–logical*. And that's the difference. On the inside, when we put a state like anger or fear inside another state (calmness, respect, gentleness, courage, etc.), we change the internal logic of our nervous system and person. This is what we mean when we talk about "logical levels." When we put one state in a "logical" relationship to another state so that one is at a higher *level* then the higher one is *about* the other. This *about-relationship* establishes the "logic."

There are no such "things" as logical levels. They do not exist "out there." They exist only in the mind as how we represent categories and levels of distinctions. With this logical typing or leveling, the effect of each level is to *organize and control the information on the level below it.* In logical levels each level is progressively more psychologically encompassing and impactful.

Neuro-Semantics®
Via our states and meta-states we can and do translate the *meanings* in our minds (our semantics) into *feelings* in our bodies (neurology). This creates our neuro-semantic states. When something *means* something to us—we *feel* it in our bodies. The meanings show up in what we call "emotions." The meanings take the form of values, ideas, beliefs, understandings, paradigms, mental models, frames, etc.

Neuro-Semantics is a model of how we make meaning through evaluating experiences, events, words, etc. It's a model of how we then live in the World or Matrix of meaning that we construct and inherit. Neuro-Semantics describes the frames of reference we use as we move through life and the frames of meaning that we construct. It creates the Matrix of Frames in which we live and from which we operate.

The first model of Neuro-Semantics is the *Meta-States model* that enables us to think about the levels of states or mind. The second model of Neuro-Semantics is the *Mind-Lines model* for conversational reframing. The third model of is the *Frame Games mind* for diagnosing, understanding, and working with states and behaviors as "games" driven and modulated by "frames." The fourth model of Neuro-Semantics is the *Matrix Model* that specifies seven matrices as a diagnostic and modeling tool.

Appendix B

From Pleasuring to De-Pleasuring
The De-Pleasuring Pattern

In Chapter Twelve you explored the processes of pleasuring and then meta-pleasuring. We use this in Meta-States to add more and more pleasure to life. Yet as with anything, this can be over-done and create other kinds of problems. This is especially true when you find yourself getting too much enjoyment from the wrong things. What then?

Actually this happens frequently in life. Problems may arise in some areas of our life from having over-loaded a sensory pleasure with too much enjoyment. Food can come to mean *too much* to us. So can shopping, spending money impulsively, status, pleasing others, drinking, working, etc. At this point, our *neuro-semantics* (i.e., the meanings incorporated into our very neurology) get out of balance.

What's the problem? What happens when you endow something like smoking, drinking, over-eating, or any other pleasure with *too much meaning?* Then you use those behaviors to trigger your happiness even when you have to pay the price in various forms of unhappiness, misery and poor health in the long run. This is not a wise choice.

To transform things, reverse the Pleasure Pattern to reduce the pleasure that *you* have added and layered in your way of framing. You can decrease the pleasure by finding out where and how you have over-loaded too much meaning to the experience. This is one of the key processes we use in our book and trainings on *Games Slim and Fit People Play*.

Are there any pleasures that you have given too much pleasure to that you wish you did **not** give so much pleasure?

1) First identify the pleasure that you now want to de-pleasure (i.e., smoking, over-eating, drinking, taking the path of least resistance, arguing, yelling, giving vent to your anger, wallowing in self-pity, etc.).

2) Next, use the pleasure pattern to identify the meta-state levels of meaning and pleasure that govern and organize it. Explore, as you did before, the positive meaning of value and significance that you give to the pleasure. Sketch out your levels of valuing and pleasuring. Do this until you have the full structure. When you do, then step back to again appreciate the full gestalt.

3) As you do, simply notice all of the meanings, beliefs and states that give too much pleasure and drive to the pleasure that has become over-loaded and harmful. Now you know! Now you know why this pleasure has gained such power over you so that you act in ways against your higher judgment. Now also you know what to do to de-pleasure it.

4) *Identify the critical meanings.* Are you willing to deframe these meanings? Are you fully aware that *you* are the one who attached these meanings?

5) *De-pleasure* what you have pleasured. Cover one set of meta-level meanings and ask,

> "If I took away this line of meanings about the pleasure, how much would that reduce my enjoyment of it?"

Continue to do this until you get a sense of which meanings you need to eliminate to reduce the power of this pleasure.

> How many of the meanings do I need to take away before it starts to exist as just whatever it *is* at the primary level—eating for health and nutrition rather than for comfort, to de-stress anger, to overcome loneliness, etc.?

6) *Future pace the de-pleasure* by imagining yourself fully engaged in the primary pleasure again, for example, eating. When fully and honestly there, hear yourself say,

> "This is *just* food. It nourishes my body—it's a nice pleasure for the moment, but I refuse to over-load it with any more meaning than this. It *just* provides fuel. I refuse to over-load it and give to too much pleasure. I will fully enjoy it for what it is—food, fuel for my metabolism, and energy for my vitality. If I love it too much—I see globs of ugly fat growing at my mid-section" (attach whatever *dis*pleasure that works for you!).

7) *Access and apply.* Access your highest meta-pleasure states fully and allow yourself to step into those highest meaning and pleasures. When you are completely there, experience it fully as you *realize* that you can do so without needing to engage in that behavior anymore. You have many other ways to get to this pleasure and you can connect this feeling with many other things ... as you now allow your creative part to identify these other behaviors that you can do that will allow you to experience this meta-level meaning in everyday life.

Appendix C

FRAME GAME QUESTIONS

- *The Name* and *the Description* of the Game:
    - What is the game, how does it work?
    - Does the game enhance or limit?
- *The Rules* of the Game:
    - How is the game set up, structured, who plays the game, when, etc.?
- *The Cues* of the Game:
    - What are the questions that elicit the game, the terms that reveal the game? What triggers recruit us to playing the game?
- *The Payoff* of the Game:
    - What are the benefits, values, and outcomes of the game?
- Viewing my activities, actions, and interactions with others, my roles, persona, etc., *what games* do I play?
- What games does my loved one or intimates play? Name some of the games.
- What games do I *intend* to play? What games would I *like* to play? What games do I actually play?
- Which games do I consider fun and enjoyable?
- Which games brings out my best?
- Which games do I find sick, stupid, and worthless?
- Which games do I play unwillingly?
- Which games do I get suckered into playing even when I know better?
- What games are currently *playing* you with your loved one?
- Do you consciously choose to play these games?
- Do these games support you and your loved one to move in the direction you want?
- What game or games would you prefer to be playing?
- What cues and triggers hook you into the games?
- What frames drive these games?
- What do you believe about these games?
- What historical or conceptual references do you use to generate the frame to play the game?

Frame Games Worksheet — 1
Diagnosing a Toxic Game

1. *What's the Game?* Describe the "Game" being played out in terms of states meta-states, gestalt states. *What's the script of the game?* What sub-games or sub-frames are part of it all?

_____

_____

_____

2. *Cues & Clues:* What are some of the cues (linguistic, physical, environmental, etc.) that indicate the presence of a game? How do you know? What cues you to it?

_____

_____

_____

3. *Players:* Who plays the game? With whom? Who else has games going on? What's the larger social system of the game? (Use another Worksheet 1 for each additional person).

_____

4. *Hooks (triggers, baits):* What hooks you into the game? How does the game hook others to play?

_____

_____

_____

5. *Emotional Intensity of the Game:* How intense (0 to 10)? Are there any somatic responses or symptoms?

_____

6. *Rules of the Game:* How is the game set up? How do you play? (Commands, Taboos)

_____

7. *Quality Control: Do you like this Game?* Just how sick is this game? Ready to transform it?

_____

8. *Agenda of the Game:* What's the intention, motivation, or payoff of the Game? What's the payoff?

9. Name the Frame Game:

_____

10. Style: What is your Frame of Mind?   Style of thinking? Meta-Program or attitude?

      _ Matching / Mismatching   _ Reactive/ Thoughtful
      _ Fast/ Slow   _ Rigid / Flexible
      _ Aggressive/ Passive/Assertive _ Self / Other
      _ Options/ Procedures   _ Global / Specific

11. Leverage points: Where is the leverage in this game to stop it, change it, transform it?

_____

_____

_____

13. Preferred Frame Game: What game would you rather play?

_____

Frame Games Worksheet — 2
Design Engineering a New Frame Game

1. **Desired** *Game:*

_____

2. *Target:* Name the person/s you want to influence (it will undoubtedly include yourself, it may even exclusively be yourself):

_____

3. *Emotional Agenda/Motivation:* What concerns, him or her most? Values? What's really important to this person? What would hook X into this game? Vested interests?

_____

_____

_____

4. *Larger Systems:* What's the larger social system of the game? Who else is involved?

5. *Objective and Outcome:* What do I want in this? What do I want for the other/s in this?

_____

_____

6. *Description:* How will the new Game be played? What frames will work best? Describe.

_____

_____

7. *Leverage points:* Where is the leverage to change or stop the game? What frames will best leverage this person?

_____

_____

8. *Process:* How can I set up these frames? How can I implement my persuasion process?

_____

_____

9. *Check-list Stages:* Will you need to interrupt, shift, loosen, and/or transform the

frames? Which patterns or techniques would provide the most leverage?

_____

_____

10. Patterns for Installation: Which frame game (patterns) could you use to install the new frame games in yourself?

_____

_____

_____

_____

11. *Frames:* What frames of mind do you need in order to play the new game?

_____

_____

BIBLIOGRAPHY

Andreas, Steve; Andreas, Connirae. (1988). *Change your mind and keep the change.* Moab, UT: Real People Press.

Bryant, Andrew; Lewis, Michelle Lia. (2004). *The street guide to flirting.* Sydney, Allen & Unwin.

Cameron-Bandler, Leslie. (1985). *Solutions: Practical and effective antidotes for sexual and relational problems.* FuturePace Inc.

Bandler, Richard; Grinder, John. (1976). *Changing with families.*

Branden, Nathaniel (1980). *Romantic love.* NY: Bantam books.

Bushong, Carolyn N. (1997). *Seven dumbest Relationship Mistakes smart people make.* New York: Villard.

Carter-Scott, Cherie (1999). *If Love is a Game; these are the Rules.* Ten Rules for Finding Love and Creating Long-lasting Authentic Relationships. New York: Broadway books.

Chapman, Gary. (1992). *The five love languages: How to express heartfelt commitment to your mate.* Chicago: Northfield Publishing.

Covey, Stephen. (1987). *Seven habits of highly effective people.*

Gottman, John M. (2001). *The Relationship Cure: A five-step guide for building better connections with family, friends, and lovers.* New York: Crown Publishers.

Ferguson, David and Teresa; Thurman, Chris and Holly. (1993). *The pursuit of intimacy.* Nashville: Thomas Nelson Publishers.

Johnson, Robert A. (1983). *WE: Understanding the psychology of romantic love.* NY: Harper and Row.

Lewis, C.S. (1960). *The Four Loves.* New York: Harcourt Brace Jovanovick.

Mace, David. (1975). *Encounter: Love, Marriage and Family.*

Powell, John. S.J. (1969). *Why am I afraid to tell you who I am?* Niles, IL: Argus Communications.

Powell, John. S.J. (1974). *The secret of staying in love.* Niles, IL.: Argus Communications.

Prior, Robin; O'Connor, Joseph. (2000). *NLP and Relationships: Simple Strategies to make your relationships work.* London: Thorsons

Strauss, Richard; Strauss, Mary. *When two walk together.*

Zerof, Herbert. (1978). *Finding intimacy: The art of happiness in living together.* NY: Winston Press.

L. Michael Hall, Ph.D.
ISNS — International Society of Neuro-Semantics®
P.O. Box 8
Clifton, Colorado 81520—0008   USA
(970) 523-7877

www.neurosemantics.com

Dr. Hall is executive director of the *International Society of Neuro-Semantics* (ISNS) having co-founded it with his business partner, Dr. Bob Bodenhamer in 1996.   Prior to finding NLP in 1986, and studying with NLP co-founder Richard Bandler, Michael was a licensed psychotherapist in the state of Colorado with graduate degrees in Business, Literature, and Clinical Counseling.   He did his doctoral studies in Cognitive Behavioral Psychology and included NLP in his dissertation at Union Institute University in Cincinnati, Ohio.

Upon the discovery of Meta-States in 1994 during a modeling project on resilience, Meta-States won recognition as "the most significant contribution to NLP in 1995" by the   International NLP Trainers Association.   From there Michael began developing pattern after pattern using meta-states.   That, in turn, led him and associates to apply meta-states to facets of NLP itself and finding all kinds of new rich treasures.   It was translated to time-lines, "sub-modalities," the sleight of mouth patterns, meta-programs and more.   From this came two dozen practical training applications in sales, persuasion, defusing hotheads, leadership, coaching, relationships, wealth creation, etc.

Today Dr. Hall continues to model excellence as expressions of self-actualization. He is also an entrepreneur in several businesses (real estate, publishing, etc.).   He lives in the Colorado Rocky Mountains and trains internationally.   As a prolific writer and researcher, he has written more than 40 books.

Books:
 1) *Meta-States: Mastering the higher levels of your mind* (2000).
 2) *Dragon Slaying: Dragons to Princes* (2000).
 3) *The Spirit of NLP: Mastering NLP.* (1999).
 4) *Languaging: The Linguistics of Psychotherapy* (1996).
 5) *Becoming More Ferocious as a Presenter* (1996).
 6) *Patterns For "Renewing the Mind"* (w. Bodenhamer) (1997).
 7) *Time-Lining: Advance Time-Line Processes* (w. Bodenhamer) (1997).
 8) *NLP: Going Meta—Advance Modeling Using Meta-Levels* (1997/2001).
 9) *Figuring Out People: Design Engineering With Meta-Programs* (w. Bodenhamer) (1999).
 10) *A Sourcebook of Magic* (1997/2003).

11) Mind-Lines: Lines For Changing Minds (w. Bodenharmer) (2001).
12) The Secrets of Magic: Communication Excellence for the 21ˢᵗ. Century (1998).
13) Meta-State Magic (2002).
14) *Structure of Excellence: Unmasking "Sub-modalities"* (w Bodenhamer, 1999).
15) *Instant Relaxation* (1999, Lederer & Hall).
16) *The Structure of Personality:* Modeling "Personality Using NLP and Neuro-Semantics (Hall , Bodenhamer, Bolstad, Harmblett, 2001).
17) *The Secrets of Personal Mastery* (2000).
18 Frame Games: Persuasion Elegance (2000).
19) *Games Fit and Slim People Play* (2001).
20) *Games for Mastering Fear* (2001, with Bodenhamer).
21) *Games Business Experts Play* (2001).
22) *The Matrix Model* (2002/ 2003).
23) User's Manual of the Brain: Practitioner course, Volume I (1999).
24) User's Manual of the Brain: Master Practitioner Course, Volume II (2002).

25) *MovieMind* (2002).
26) *The Bateson Report* (2002).
27) *Make it So!* (2002).
28) *Sourcebook of Magic, Volume II, Neuro-Semantic Patterns* (2003).
29) *Games Great Lovers Play* (2003).

30) *Propulsion Systems* (2003).
31) *Coaching Conversation, Meta-Coaching, Volume II* (with Duval, 2004).
32) *Coaching Change, Meta-Coaching, Volume I* (with Duval, 2004).
33) *Winning the Inner Game* (2006, formerly *Frame Games*, 1999).
34) *Unleashed: How to Unleash Potentials for Peak Performances* (2007).
35) *Achieving Peak Performance* (2009).
36) *Self-Actualization Psychology* (2008).
37) *Unleashing Leadership* (2009).
38) *Inside-Out Wealth* (2010)
39) *The Crucible and the fires of Transformation* (2010).